COMPLETE HOCKEY INSTRUCTION

Skills and Strategies for Coaches and Players

DAVE CHAMBERS

CB

CONTEMPORARY BOOKS

A TRIBUNE NEW MEDIA/EDUCATION COMPANY

Library of Congress Cataloging-in-Publication Data

Chambers, Dave, 1940–
        Complete hockey instruction : skills and strategies for coaches
and players / Dave Chambers.
                p.   cm.
        Originally published: Toronto : Key Porter Books, c1989.
        Includes bibliographical references.
        ISBN 0-8092-3511-0 (paper)
        1. Hockey—Coaching.   I. Title.
GV848.25.C43   1994
796.962'07'7—dc20

94-12471
CIP

I wish to express my thanks to Noroc Sport Services, Inc., and *Hockey Coaching Journal* for their guidance in the preparation and typing of this manuscript as well as my special thanks to Robert Thom, production manager of *Hockey Coaching Journal*, for the preparation of the diagrams in the book.

Special appreciation is extended to the many coaches I have played for and been associated with, who contributed greatly to my knowledge of ice hockey.

Photographs by Doug MacLellan/Hockey Hall of Fame

Contemporary Books, Inc., edition 1994

10   9   8   7   6   5   4   3   2

CONTENTS

PREFACE

Hockey is one of the most exciting and fast-moving sports in the world. The game is composed of many intricate skills that can be mastered only by a highly skilled athlete. The European influence has had an impact on the game in such areas as conditioning and offensive tactics. The game now is a blend of the best from both North America and Europe. Hockey in the United States has never been more popular, as evidenced by the ever increasing numbers of minor league hockey players and the popularity of the National Hockey League, which has expanded to parts of the country such as Florida, California, and Texas.

Coaching has changed greatly in the past two decades. Coaching training and coaching certification now include areas such as technical, tactical, physical conditioning, and psychological preparation. The physical training is now periodized, and almost all hockey players engage in a year-round program.

This book is an accumulation of materials from my 30 years of coaching at the university, junior, international, and National Hockey League levels. I have accumulated this knowledge from observing other coaches, from my former coaches and coaches I have worked with, and through clinic attendance, reading, and my own innovations and experiences.

I have attempted to include all aspects of the technical areas of coaching hockey so this book will be useful for both coaches and players. In-line skating hockey is also becoming quite popular, and most of the skills, drills, and theory in this book apply, although that game is not played on ice but on the concrete floor of an ice arena.

Throughout this instruction book we have used male pronouns exclusively to refer to both coaches and players of hockey. The fact is, most are men. That is not to say that women and girls are not increasingly involved in hockey competition at every level. On the contrary, more and more women and girls are entering the sport as coaches and players, and the game is better for it.

I hope that this book will add to your knowledge of the great game of ice hockey.

LEGEND

PUCK(S)		TIGHT/180-DEGREE TURN		PASS	
PYLON(S)		360-DEGREE TURN		DROP PASS	
FORWARD SKATING		PIVOT		SHOT	
FORWARD STICKHANDLE		STOP	= OR ‖	KNEE DROP	— OR │
BACKWARD SKATING		KERIOAKAS		SCREEN/PIC	
BACKWARD STICKHANDLE		STEPOVERS	‖‖‖‖‖‖‖‖‖‖	BODY CHECK	
RIGHT WINGER	RW	OPPOSITION RW	RW	PLAYER	X
LEFT WINGER	LW	OPPOSITION LW	LW	OPPOSITION PLAYER	X
CENTER	C	OPPOSITION C	C	DEFENSEMAN	D
RIGHT DEFENSEMAN	RD	OPPOSITION RD	RD	OPPOSITION D	D
LEFT DEFENSEMAN	LD	OPPOSITION LD	LD	GOALTENDER	G

1. PHILOSOPHY OF COACHING

Coaching is a very complex and demanding job. It requires many technical and personal skills and a sound coaching philosophy. Rewards of coaching include competition and the development of athletes' physical, mental, emotional, and social skills.

The philosopher Will Durant once said, "Science gives us knowledge, but only philosophy can give us wisdom." It is therefore very important for every coach to have a well-thought-out philosophy of coaching that will guide the coach in decision making and in the direction he and his team will take. The coach must develop a philosophy of competition, winning and losing, the value of athletics, criticism, and interacting with and motivating athletes. A sound philosophy determines aims and objectives and is the basis of all decision making.

Coaching is a great challenge and not for the faint of heart. It requires long hours and intense interaction with people who are in competition with themselves and others. It runs the gamut of emotions involving success and failure, joy and despair. It involves wanting and trying to win and learning how to accept defeat. It also involves the opportunity of participating, having fun, and learning to work with others toward a common goal.

Walter Gillet probably summarized the job of a coach best in "What Is a Coach?"

> A coach is a politician, a judge, a public speaker, a teacher, a trainer, a financier, a laborer, a psychologist, a psychiatrist, and a chaplain. He must be an optimist and yet at times appear to be a pessimist, seem humble and yet be very proud, strong but at times weak, confident yet not overconfident, enthusiastic but not too enthusiastic.
>
> He must have the hide of an elephant, the fierceness of a lion, the pep of a young pup, the guts of an ox, the stamina of an antelope, the wisdom of an owl, the cunning of a fox, and the heart of a kitten.
>
> He must be willing to give freely of his time, his money, his energy, his youth, his family life, and his health. In return he must expect little if any financial reward, little comfort on earth, little praise but plenty of criticism.
>
> However, a good coach is respected and is a leader in his community, is loved by his team, and makes lasting friends wherever he goes.
>
> He has the satisfaction of seeing young people develop and improve in ability. He learns the thrill of victory and how to accept defeat with grace. His associations with athletes help keep him young in mind and spirit, and he too must grow and improve in ability with his team.
>
> In his heart he knows that, in spite of the inconvenience, the criticism, and the demands on his time, he loves his work, for he is the coach.

QUALITIES OF A GOOD COACH

Successful coaches do not seem to have any specific type of personality. They are as individual as the general population, but they do have specific leadership qualities. Many good coaches are outgoing and extroverted, while others are quiet and somewhat withdrawn. Some coaches are autocratic and hard-nosed, while others are democratic and accommodating. Here are some common characteristics of good coaches:

KNOWLEDGE OF THE SPORT
To be effective, the coach must have a sound knowledge of the sport. An athlete can learn a great deal from various coaches. However, in most cases, participation alone does not ensure a complete knowledge of the sport. A good coach will continually read, observe, and use any other methods to further his knowledge of the sport. Most good coaches attend at least one coaching clinic per year and take any coaching certification that is available.

ORGANIZATION SKILLS
One common characteristic of all good coaches is that they are highly organized in all areas of team operation. A well-organized team both on and off the ice gives the athletes confidence and pride in the team and the coach. An organized coach will generally be respected by the athletes for the time and effort spent to achieve a highly efficient organization. Today's coach should have a yearly, monthly, weekly, and daily plan for the organization of his team. The physical, technical, tactical, and psychological preparation of the athletes should be organized and directed in a year-round training plan.

KNOWLEDGE OF TRAINING AND CONDITIONING METHODS
A coach should have an up-to-date knowledge of various training and conditioning methods. This knowledge can be applied in the day-to-day training of a team or individuals, and the coach should also be able to advise athletes regarding off-season training programs. The coach should have the ability to develop a plan for improving and/or maintaining his athletes' conditioning levels throughout the year.

EFFECTIVELY RUN PRACTICES
One of the most important aspects of coaching is the ability to run effective, well-organized practice sessions. Most coaches believe the key to the success of teams and/or individual athletes is in the training or practice sessions. If the coach has the ability to run organized, active practices stressing the techniques used in competition, he has accomplished a great deal.

EVALUATION OF ATHLETES
A good coach should be able to evaluate the ability of the athletes. This is an ongoing process for the coach, but it is most important in the initial selection of a team. Good coaches have an ability to subjectively evaluate athletes based on previous observations of athletes and techniques in their sport. However, most good coaches also rely on other factors such as specific drills, reports by other observers, skill tests, potential, physical attributes, personality traits, and so on, to make their final selection of athletes.

STRATEGY
The ability to prepare a team for an opponent is an important attribute of a coach. The skill is developed through experience, learning, and the ability to analyze an opponent's strengths and weaknesses. As well as preparing a team for a contest, the coach should be able to improvise and adjust strategy during games.

EFFECTIVE USE OF PERSONNEL
In team sports a good coach has the ability to effectively use certain athletes at certain times. The coach must have a good understanding of what athletes can do in certain situations and must be able to react quickly and effectively in games to select the right players for critical situations such as face-offs and being behind by a goal or ahead by a goal.

COMMUNICATION
A good coach is an effective communicator with the athletes. Good communication leads to mutual understanding. Problem areas should be dealt with before coach and player become further polarized. Effective communication between coach and athlete is essential for a good coach-athlete relationship, and an athlete should feel that the coach is approachable.

ABILITY TO UNDERSTAND AND HANDLE THE ATHLETE
The ability to communicate is also related to the ability to handle and understand people. For the coach to be an effective communicator, he must understand the athlete and be able to relate to him. A lack of understanding of the athlete's motives and problems is one of the major reasons for the breakdown in the coach-athlete relationship.

FAIRNESS
It is important that the coach give fair treatment to the athletes on a team. Athletes can turn quickly on a coach if they feel he has been unfair in his treatment of the team or favors certain individuals over others.

MOTIVATION
Athletes should be self-motivated. A coach must also be able to motivate them in order to be effective. Not all coaches have this ability, but it appears to be a common quality of all outstanding coaches.

DEDICATION, ENTHUSIASM, MATURITY, RECTITUDE
Good coaches are dedicated to coaching and this has a positive effect on the athletes. A lack of dedication can seriously affect the athletes' view of the coach and can be extremely detrimental, as the coach may even be viewed as lazy.

Enthusiasm is an important quality in a coach. As most training seasons are long, it is important that the coach show enthusiasm throughout the year to help motivate the athletes.

The coach should act in a mature manner. Immature behavior such as harassing officials can affect the athletes. They could imitate this behavior or lose respect for the coach.

The ethical conduct of the coach on and off the ice is important. The coach is a role model whom the athletes may or may not admire. The coach should realize the importance of this position and be aware of the effect that he has on the more impressionable, younger athletes.

KNOWLEDGE OF HOW THE BODY WORKS (EXERCISE PHYSIOLOGY)

The coach should have a basic knowledge of exercise physiology in order to understand how the body works. This basic knowledge will allow the coach to understand the science behind various training techniques, such as work-rest ratios during training and games. A coach should also be able to interpret scientific articles on various training methods and conduct or interpret various fitness testing items.

KNOWLEDGE OF GROWTH AND DEVELOPMENT PRINCIPLES

In many cases, coaches are working with growing and developing younger players. It is important that the coach have a knowledge of both the physical and emotional stages that younger players go through. In some cases, growth spurts may affect athletes' coordination and create certain emotional problems for younger players. This, in turn, may affect their athletic performance.

ABILITY TO TEACH

The coach is in many ways a teacher, and as such he must have an understanding of basic learning principles and teaching techniques. A good coach needs the ability to teach a progression of fundamental skills as well as team play. Voice, appearance, teaching formation, planning, and progression are as important to the coach as they are to the classroom teacher.

CONCERN FOR THE ATHLETE

An individual concern for each athlete is very important for a coach. The athlete must feel that the coach cares about him and that he is important to the team. On a team, the athlete who is not playing as much as the others may need more attention from the coach than the ones who play more often. Athletes do not like to feel that they're pawns and that the coach has no concern for them other than as athletes. The coach should also show concern for the athletes after they have moved on, and some coaches receive a great deal of satisfaction by keeping in touch with athletes after they have stopped participating for their team or organization.

KNOWLEDGE OF THE RULES

An effective coach should have a thorough knowledge of the playing rules. This knowledge should be passed on to the players and is important in both practice and game situations.

DISCIPLINE

Most good teams have a basic discipline code in which guidelines for behavior are set. Team rules are best set up when the athletes have input and agree with the coach on rules such as punctuality for practices and games and general conduct on and off the playing surface. It is usually up to the coach to enforce team rules, but in general rules should not be too numerous, nor should they be so inflexible as not to allow for extenuating circumstances.

MEDIA

A coach should have a good relationship with the media, as publicity can greatly affect the support the team receives. It is important to be available and cordial no matter what the circumstances when dealing with the media. Regular reporting of game results and informing the media of team information can help the coach develop a good relationship with them.

HUMOR

Not all situations in sports are serious. A good coach should have a sense of humor. Athletes will feel more relaxed if the coach is able to see humor in some situations. A coach who is serious on all occasions may put added pressure on the athletes and may not be able to relate to them. It is also important that the coach not take himself too seriously and start to believe that he is the only reason for the success of an athlete or a team.

ABILITY TO RECRUIT AND BUILD A PROGRAM

Most good coaches have the ability to relate and sell both themselves and their program to a prospective athlete. If recruiting athletes is part of a successful program, the coach should have a recruiting plan in which he is able to identify and relate information about himself and the program to the potential athlete.

It is important to realize that each coach has his own personality. Coaches should attempt to study and emulate the good coaching techniques of successful coaches rather than their personalities. Be yourself, but do attempt to make yourself better by working hard at improving your coaching techniques.

2. EVALUATION OF TALENT

Evaluating talent and selecting the team are two of the more difficult tasks in coaching. Who the better and poorer players are is usually quite evident, but selecting from the middle group of talent is where evaluation criteria are extremely important.

Evaluation of hockey players can be categorized in four areas: physical, technical, tactical, and mental.

PHYSICAL, TECHNICAL, AND TACTICAL ATTRIBUTES

The physical attributes include size, strength, cardiovascular endurance, quickness, and agility. Size is an important aspect in hockey, but quickness and agility are also extremely important. Don't rule out a small player if that player has strength and quickness.

The technical skills include skating, passing, puck handling, shooting, and checking. All these skills are important. The checking skill can be taught to all players, provided they have the basic skating skills.

The tactical skills lie in a player's ability to read the play and react, to understand team systems, and to adjust to different situations. Hockey sense and intelligence are important factors that some players seem to have more of than others. The great hockey players have hockey sense and that great ability to read and react to different situations.

MENTAL ATTRIBUTES

The mental attributes include work habits, general attitude and character, leadership, coachability, mental toughness, self-confidence, team orientation, motivation, and intensity. The mental attributes are sometimes more difficult to determine in a short period of time, and it is probably wise to get as much background information on a player as possible before the selection process begins.

Psychological profiling can be a useful tool in the coach's assessment of the mental attributes of athletes. Profiles with names such as TAIS (Test of Attentional and Interpersonal Style) and SportProFile are two such tests commonly used by a number of sports organizations. The TAIS measures factors such as leadership capabilities, impulsive behavior, extroversion, performance anxiety, desire to win, and ability to organize and plan. The SportProFile assesses competitiveness, motivation, self confidence, effort, team organization, leadership, self management, the handling of pressure, and mental toughness. Information on the SportProFile can be obtained by writing to SportProFile, c/o Self Management Resources Corporation, 155 Rexdale Boulevard, Suite 304, Toronto, Ontario, Canada M9W 528.

A brief description of these attributes is outlined as follows:

WORK HABITS
A player with good work habits works hard during practices and games.

GENERAL ATTITUDE AND CHARACTER
Does the player mix well with his teammates, and is he enthusiastic? Can he handle adversity with a positive attitude? Character signs to watch for are moodiness and negativity.

LEADERSHIP
Not every player can be a leader, but leadership skills are evident in successful players in varying degrees. Some players are quiet and lead by example, while other players are more vocal. Good teams have more than one leader, and the leaders cooperate with each other and the coach.

COACHABILITY
Does the player accept the coach's direction, and is he willing to learn and improve? Most top players are very coachable, as they wish to improve their skills and need the feedback and direction of the coach.

MENTAL TOUGHNESS
Does the player react well under pressure and adversity? Is the player able to be positive and under control when situations are not going well?

SELF-CONFIDENCE
Does the player have confidence in his own ability? Can the player keep his confidence when he is not playing, or does he lose confidence when things are not going well?

TEAM ORIENTATION
Does the player put the team first and himself second? Will he sacrifice for the team, or is he selfish? Can the player accept his role on a team, especially if he does not get as much ice time as other players?

MOTIVATION
A highly motivated player wants to make the team, to improve, and to be a success.

INTENSITY
A player with intensity plays hard on the ice and in practice.

SAMPLE FORMS

A Background Information Sheet like the one on page 12 may be used to record each player's experience and personal information.

During training camps it is important to have a standard evaluation form. The coach should meet with the evaluators before the training camp to discuss what he is looking for in players, and then the evaluators should meet after each practice or scrimmage to discuss and compare their observations. Evaluation at training camp usually comes from observing scrimmage games, regular practice drills, and special evaluation drills.

In the regular practice drills and scrimmage games the evaluators should be looking for a subjective evaluation of the physical, technical, tactical, and mental skills previously mentioned. Forms like Subjective Evaluation Form 1 on page 13 and Subjective Evaluation Form 2 on page 14 can aid in the evaluation process.

An overall ranking form like the Scrimmage Evaluation Form on page 15 may be helpful in evaluation when observing game scrimmages and practice drills.

EVALUATION DRILLS
Evaluation drills can be of assistance when the coaches have the final decisions to make. The following are some sample drills that can be used to assess defensemen, forwards, and goaltenders.

EVALUATION DRILLS FOR DEFENSEMEN
1. Agility
The front player in each line skates from the goal line to the blue line, chop-steps halfway across the blue line, skates backward to the middle of the circle, pivots to the outside, and skates to the corner. There, he makes a sharp turn and returns to the front of the net.

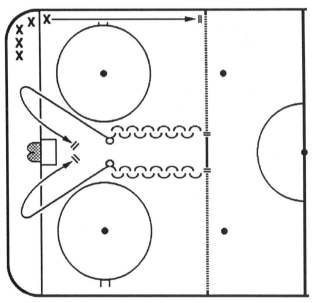

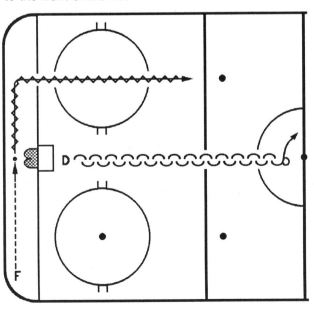

2. Backward Skating
F starts from the corner and skates behind the net, where he picks up the puck. He then skates down the boards outside the face-off marker. As soon as F touches the puck, D starts skating backward without turning until he reaches the centerline. He then turns and tries to ride F out to the boards; F attempts to cut in and score.

Note that D starts this drill halfway between the top of the goal crease and an imaginary line drawn between the face-off markers.

BACKGROUND INFORMATION SHEET

PERSONAL INFORMATION

Name: _____   Position: _____

_____

_____   Telephone: _____

_____   Doctor's Telephone No.: _____

Next Year's School: _____   Grade: _____

Age: _____ Height: _____ Weight: _____   Date of Birth: _____

Skate Preference: _____   Skate Size: _____

PLAYING EXPERIENCE

List teams and stats for last five years.

Year	Team	League	Goals	Assists	Points

List championship teams.

Year	Team	League	Championship

List academic (e.g., scholarship) or athletic (e.g., MVP) awards won in the past four years.

Year	Award

SUBJECTIVE EVALUATION FORM 1

Skating (agility, speed, acceleration, pivots) Can the player skate at this level? Does he have a definite liability in his skating?	
Puck Control Skills (passing, receiving, stickhandling) Can he handle the puck in a crowd? Can he handle the puck under pressure? Are his hands good or bad? Can he handle the puck at top speed?	
Defensive Play Does he show a desire to check? Is he active away from the puck? Does he show defensive anticipation, taking away options from the puck carrier? Would you use him as penalty killer? Would you use him in critical situations (e.g., one-goal lead late in the game)?	
Offensive Play Does he display imagination and variation in moves? Can he beat the defender with speed and/or finesse? Would you consider him a "threat" man, one that you (as an opposition coach) would worry about? Would you give him special attention?	
Overall Comments Would you want him on your team? Do you rate him in the top 10 percent or top 1 percent? Do you consider him dependable? Does he have the skills and intelligence to play at a more competitive level in a few years?	

SUBJECTIVE EVALUATION FORM 2

The criteria below have been identified as parameters by which players may be evaluated at a camp. Each player is to be ranked on these criteria on a scale of 1 to 5.

1	2	3	4	5
Very Poor	Poor	Good	Very Good	Excellent

Name _____

	Rank
Hockey Sense Does he play with a sense of anticipation? Does he make the high-percentage play both offensively and defensively? Does he display an understanding of important concepts (e.g., headmanning, support, angling)? Does he understand the concept of picking or blocking out players? Does he play well away from the puck?	
Positional Play Does he play with discipline in his own end? Is he capable of moving to open ice at the right time when attacking? Can he adjust his positioning to the movement of others?	Rank
Determination Does he show second effort when required, or does he quit? Does he work hard both offensively and defensively? (Is he "tough" on the puck and is he persistent when checking?)	Rank
Maturity Is he coachable? (Will he accept suggestions?) Does he have a good attitude toward referees? (Can he accept a bad call?) Does he have a good attitude toward opponents? (Does he retaliate or is he cool?)	Rank
Techniques Does he have any weak skill areas? Does he have skating agility? (Is speed a prime concern?) Are his strongest skill areas significant?	Rank

SCRIMMAGE EVALUATION FORM

To aid in the analysis and selection process, we are asking you as an evaluator to observe the ice sessions and assist us in the evaluation process.

These are the rosters for both the red and white teams for our scrimmages. Please indicate in the boxes your evaluation of each player using these ratings.

| 2 for outstanding, exceptional performance |
| 1 for good, average performance |
| 0 for below average performance |

Rank all players from the best to the poorest.

Red Team		White Team	
1.		1.	
2.		2.	
3.		3.	
4.		4.	
5.		5.	
6.		6.	
7.		7.	
8.		8.	
9.		9.	
10.		10.	
11.		11.	
12.		12.	
13.		13.	
14.		14.	
15.		15.	
16.		16.	
17.		17.	
18.		18.	
19.		19.	
20.		20.	
21.		21.	
22.		22.	
23.		23.	
24.		24.	
25.		25.	

Goal
1.
2.
3.
4.
Defense
1.
2.
3.
4.
5.
6.
7.
8.
9.
10.
Center
1.
2.
3.
4.
5.
Left Wing
1.
2.
3.
4.
5.
Right Wing
1.
2.
3.
4.
5.

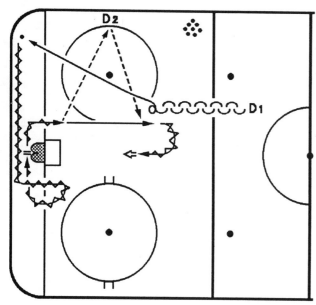

3. Agility, Skating, and Shooting

The coach shoots the puck into the corner. D1 skates backward, turns at the face-off marker, and skates to the corner to pick up the puck, executing a head-and-shoulders fake. He skates behind the net and toward the face-off circle, where he does a tight turn and returns behind the net. He stops, then starts again and passes to D2 near the boards. D1 skates out in front for the return pass from D2, does another tight turn, and shoots on goal. D1 then skates to D2's place on the boards, and D2 goes to the blue line to repeat the drill.

4. Shooting

The defenseman passes the puck from the corner to the near blue line to the middle of the ice for a low shot on goal. The defenseman in front deflects the puck at the goalie or acts as a screen. The defensemen rotate clockwise in this drill.

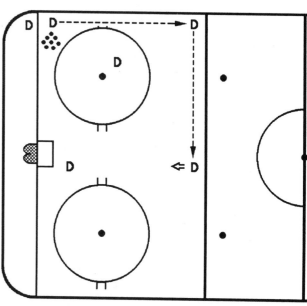

EVALUATION DRILLS FOR FORWARDS

1. Skating Speed

The players skate for speed at five distances: centerline and back, far blue line and back, far boards (one length), down and back (two lengths), and down and back twice (four lengths).

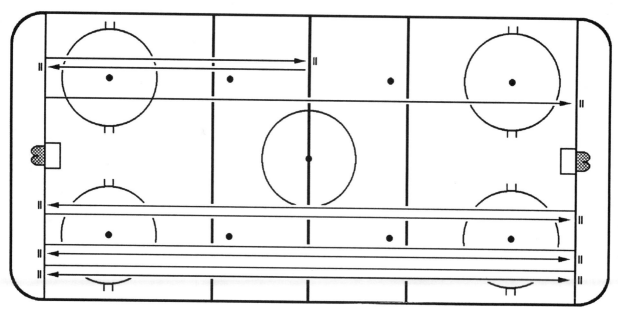

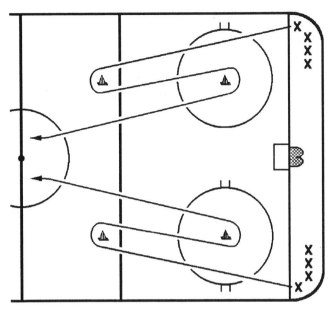

2. Race for the Puck

The forwards start in opposite corners, skate around the pylons, race for the puck, and shoot on the goaltender at the far end. The coach at the far blue line places a puck at the center of that blue line for which the players have to race.

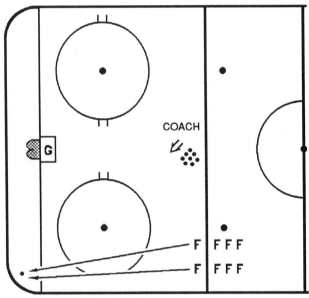

3. One-on-One

The coach shoots the puck into the corner, and the two players race for the puck and attempt to score. The play continues until the coach blows the whistle, a goal is scored, or the goalie freezes the puck.

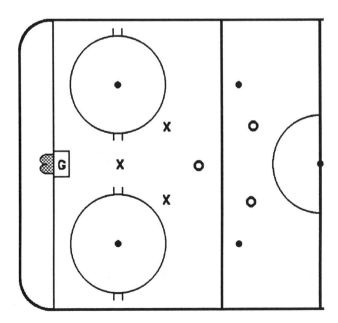

4. Three-on-Three

The forwards play three-on-three on the entire ice surface or in the two halves. Rotate the players and have them change every minute. The players change on the move with a whistle, and the team with the puck on the change passes back to its own goalie.

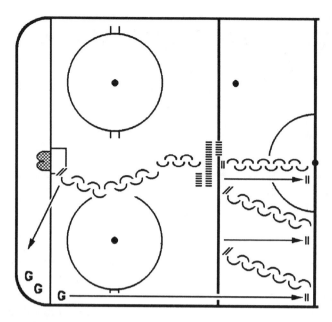

EVALUATION DRILLS FOR GOALIES
1. Agility Skating
Players start from the goal line, skate in the goaltender's stance to the blue line, skate full stride to the red line and stop, skate sideways and backward to the blue line, skate forward in the goaltender's stance to the red line, skate sideways and backward to the blue line, skate full stride to the red line, and skate backward to the blue line; then they shuffle three steps left, six steps right, three steps back to the middle, backward to the top of the circles, backward and sideways to the right and then to the left, and end up in the crease.

2. Reaction, Agility and Stopping, Shots and Rebounds
The forward and rebounder start from the first line. The shooter shoots from the top of the far circle, and the rebounder drives for the net. The forward from the second line skates in and shoots from in close. The rebounder follows and drives for the net. The forward from the third line shoots from the near face-off dot, and the rebounder drives for the net.

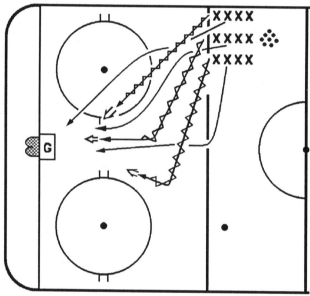

3. Side-to-Side Movement
The forward from one side skates in behind the goal line and passes the puck behind the net to the other forward coming from the other side of the ice. The pass is returned and passed out to the incoming third forward, who shoots a quick shot from the slot.

3. ORGANIZATION AND IMPLEMENTATION OF TEAM PRACTICE

One of the most important aspects of coaching is the organization and running of effective practices. Practices should be developed with the points outlined here in mind:

ORGANIZATION

Practices should be organized down to the last detail. Drills should show a natural progression through the practice from individual skills to team skills. The practice should have a smooth transition from drill to drill with constant movement and very little standing around.

DRILLS

Drills should be meaningful and related to the game of hockey. They should be used to develop individual and team skills and in most cases be at game intensity. New drills can be explained, diagrammed, and demonstrated before commencing. Drills should be repeated a number of times during the season for improvement, and it is the coach's responsibility to give the athletes feedback on errors.

The coach should make sure the drills are done correctly. Repetition and patience are important in the perfection of skills. Drills should also be competitive and at the intensity and duration that would occur in a game wherever possible. The coach should also make sure the length of time spent on a drill is neither too short nor too long. It is important that the drills be interesting and that the coach have a number of drills to accomplish such skills as one-on-one and two-on-one. Using the same drills over and over can become monotonous, so the coach should attempt to keep drills and practices interesting. The coach should also guard against giving the athletes too many drills, especially if they are not meaningful.

WARM-UP AND COOL-DOWN

It is important that the athletes be fully stretched and warmed up before the intense part of the practice begins. Stretching exercises should be performed in the dressing room or in an exercise room in the arena if possible.

At the end of each practice the few remaining minutes should consist of stretching and slowing the intensity of work. The practice can end as it began, with basically the same stretching and flexing.

OTHER DETAILS

It is important that water be available to the athletes during practice. Individual plastic squirt bottles are best. The coach should schedule two or three water breaks during the practice.

The number of pucks available should be checked before each practice. The standard number for a team of 20 players is usually 40 pucks.

It is important that the practices are interesting and fun. There should be good discipline and order. The coach should talk to the players in a semicircle formation so that no player is behind the coach when he is speaking. Establish a signal, such as a short double whistle, at which the team assembles in front of the coach for practice directions.

It is sometimes a good idea to have a light, short skate between drills, especially if the drill was not of high intensity.

USE OF ASSISTANT COACHES

It is important that the assistant coaches are used effectively during practices. The assistant coaches should be active in giving feedback to the players and should have specific duties to support the coach. There are many occasions when the ice can be divided for specific defense and forward drills. A good practice has constant activity and high intensity with drills at both ends of the ice. The assistant coach should be constantly evaluating talent and should meet with the head coach after each practice to evaluate and plan the next practice.

Often assistant coaches direct the warm-up and conditioning part of the practices, and in some situations the head coach may have the assistant coach run certain drills.

It is important that the assistant coach feel like part of the practice's organization and implementation and that all coaches have agreed on systems of play and teaching techniques. The designing and implementation of conditioning programs is also another area in which assistant coaches play an active role.

ON-ICE STRETCHING DRILL

If time permits, stretching drills, such as PNF, can be used for flexibility training (see chapter 20, "Conditioning").

The regular skating warm-up can consist of leg and groin stretches, leg slow kick to outstretched hands, knee to chest, trunk twisting with the stick on the shoulders, toe touching by raising the arms with the stick in both hands over the shoulders and then touching the toes, and wrist rotation holding the stick in one hand and then the other. This type of stretching is usually followed by fast and slow skating, either on the whistle or sprinting between the blue lines. Agility training can be added to this skating by having players turn backward between the blue lines, turn 360 degrees, or go down on one or both knees at the blue and red lines. Carrying a puck can be added to this warm-up, with the players starting by kicking the puck with the skates.

Drill

This skating warm-up can be used with or without pucks. Players form two lines. Pairs of players skate together forward and backward down the ice. Turning at lines can be added. The players then skate down the ice and back, passing the puck.

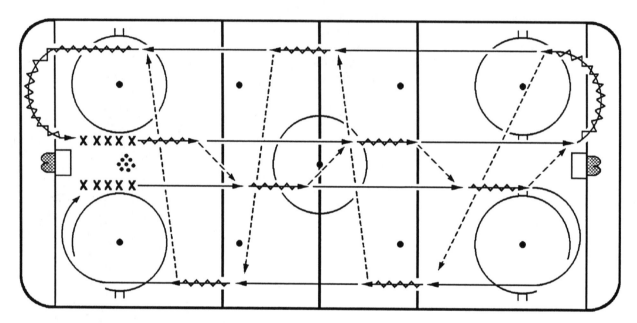

TYPICAL PRACTICE (90 MINUTES)

1. Dressing Room Stretch (45 minutes)

2. Pre-Practice Drill Explanation (10 minutes)

3. On-Ice (15 minutes)
(a) Stretching Exercises (5 minutes)
(b) Skating Warm-Up (5 minutes)
(c) Goalie Warm-Up (5 minutes)

It is important that all hockey players be able to take a body check, recover quickly, and get back into the play.

4. Shooting Drill (5 minutes)

Three lines shoot one drill from the following.

(a) Wrist Shots

A player from each line skates in and shoots from the top of the circles starting at the right, then center, then left. Players should alternate lines and use wrist shots only.

(b) Shooting from Three Spots

One player from each line skates toward the goalie simultaneously. The player on one side shoots from just inside the blue line, the player in the middle shoots from the high slot, and the player on the far side pulls the goalie. The three players can start skating in on the goalie on the command of the coach. The players can change lines, and the order can be switched for shooting or pulling the goalie.

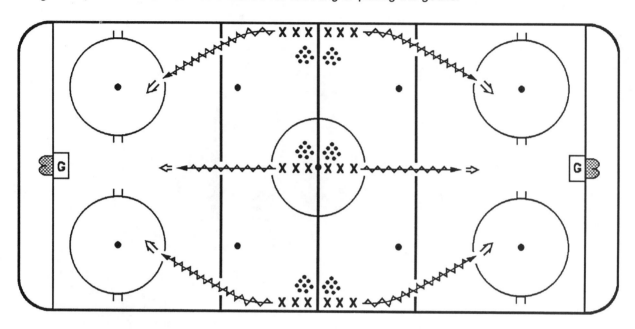

(c) Rapid Shoot

The players skate in one line coming in from the right, the center, and the left. The players are a few feet apart and shoot wrist shots in rapid succession.

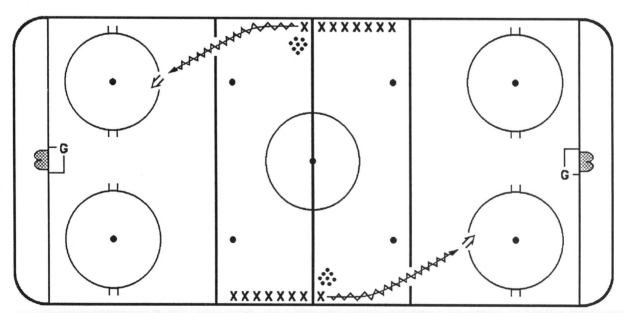

5. One-on-None Drill (5 minutes)
Players shoot one drill from the following.

(a) One-on-None Carousel and Variation
Players loop inside the blue line and receive a pass from the opposite line. The player passing the puck then goes over the far blue line, skates in, and shoots on the goalie from the end on which he started.

Variation: The player receives a pass, turns backward between the red and the blue lines, and then turns forward, skates, and shoots on the net.

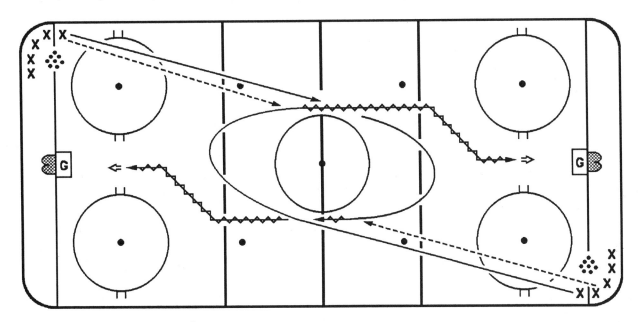

(b) Neutral Zone One-on-None
The player skates from the corner to the center red line and passes the puck to the near defenseman. The near defenseman passes the puck to his defense partner, who then passes the puck back to the forward, who has skated in front of the defenseman. The forward skates back to the end he came out of, shoots on the goalie, and then returns to the same line he started from.

Variation: The forward skates behind the defenseman, skates up the middle of the ice, and receives a pass from the other defense partner.

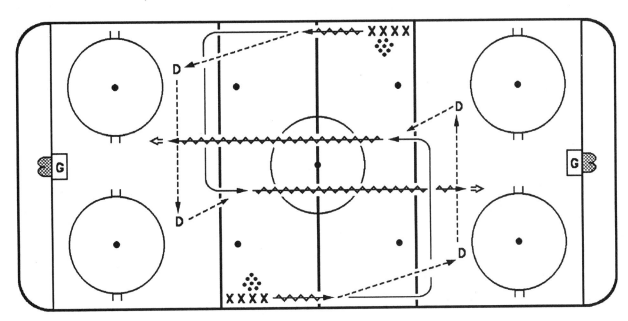

(c) Rebound Drill

Two players start the drill. The first player goes in on the net and shoots. The second player trails the first and goes for the rebound (if there is one), turns off, and receives a pass from the first player in the other line. He then skates the length of the ice and shoots. The player passing the puck then follows the shooter down the ice, goes to net for a rebound, takes a pass from the other line, and returns and shoots at the same end he started at.

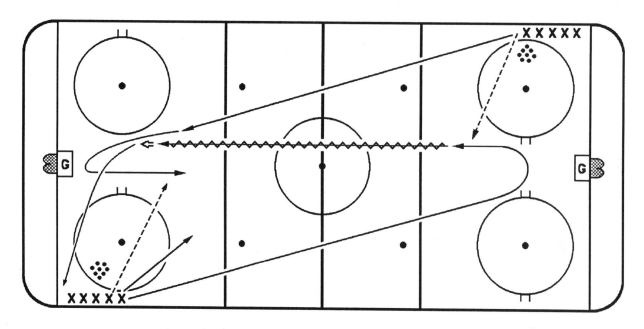

(d) Half-Ice Two-on-None

Two players skate down the ice passing the puck between them. Moving over the far blue line, the player on the board side shoots from just inside the blue line.

Moving in the opposite direction and after passing the far blue line, the player on the board side skates wide and passes the puck back to the trailing player in the high slot. The player who is shooting attempts to shoot the puck in one motion.

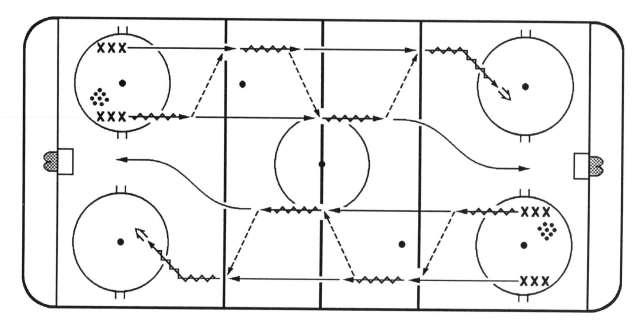

(e) One-on-None, Two-on-None, Pucks in the Middle Drill

The player skates to the middle of the ice, gets a puck, skates back to the same end, shoots, and returns to the same line he started in.

Variation: Two players skate from opposite corners of the same end, with one player picking up a puck at center and then returning to the same end two-on-none.

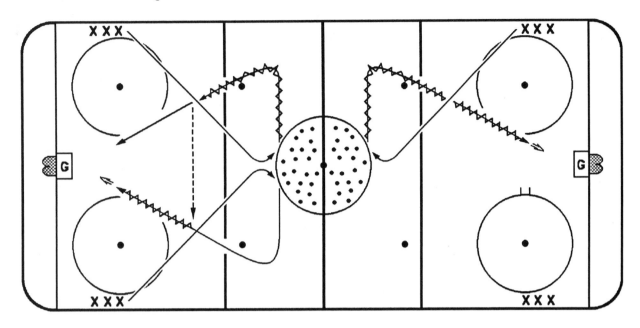

(f) Pucks in the Middle Variation

Add a defenseman on each blue line. The player, after picking the puck up at center ice, passes to the defenseman at the far blue line, receives a return pass, skates in, and shoots on the goalie at the end he started from.

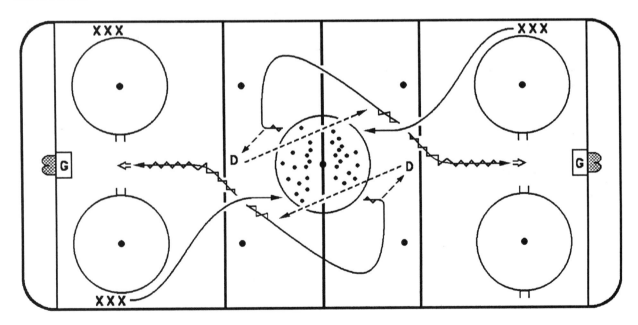

(g) Pucks in the Middle Variation

This drill can be done as a two-on-none as well having two players skate from opposite corners, one picking up a puck at center and passing to the defenseman, and both returning two-on-none to the ends they started from.

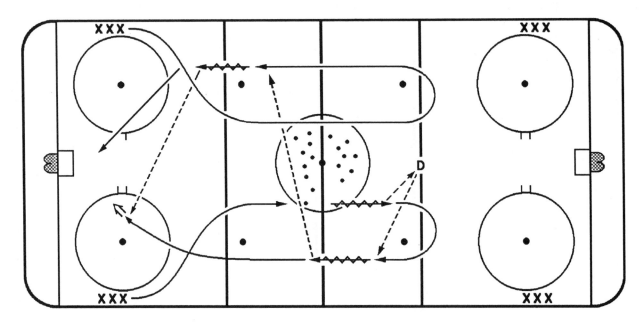

6. One-on-One (5 minutes)

Select one drill from the following.

(a) One-on-One

Pucks are at the blue lines.

The defenseman skates two strides in from the blue line, passes the puck to the forward, and skates backward to take the forward on a one-on-one. The defenseman returns to the same side of the rink, while the forward moves to the opposite corner after attempting to shoot the puck on net.

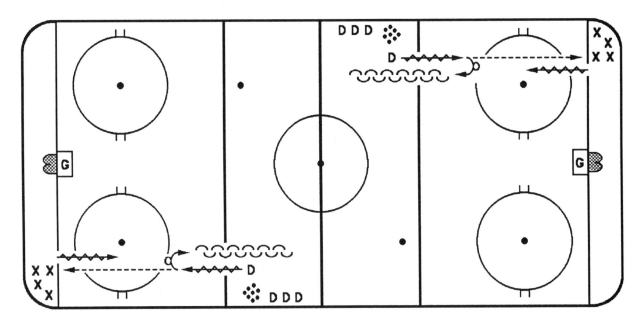

26

(b) One-on-One Flow

The defenseman skates around the center circle and turns backward. The forward skates inside the blue line and receives a pass from the defenseman who is standing at the far end. After the defenseman passes the puck, he and the forward beside him start another one-on-one by skating down the ice and taking a pass from the defenseman at the far end.

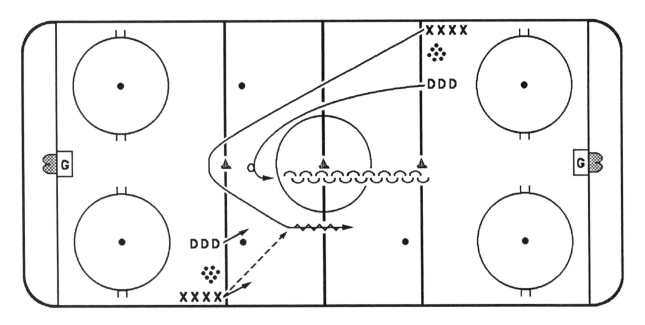

(c) One-on-One from the Middle of the Ice

The defenseman passes the puck to the forward at the face-off dot. The defenseman skates forward around a pylon, turns, skates backward, and takes the forward on a one-on-one. The defenseman returns to the same starting position while the forward moves to the opposite corner after completing the one-on-one.

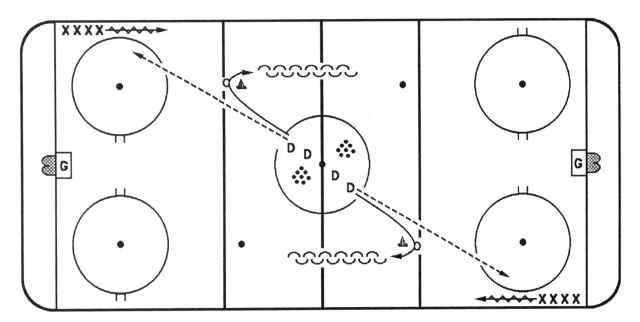

7. Two-on-One (5 minutes)
Select one drill from the following.

(a) Two-on-One
The defenseman starts the play by coming from behind the net, passing the puck to the forwards, continuing up ice to take part in the play, and then taking a two-on-one defensively from the opposite end.

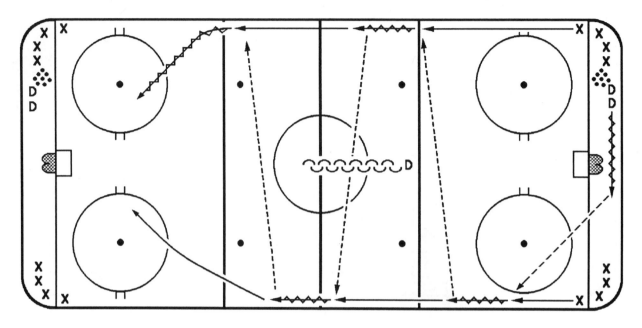

(b) Two-on-One Flow Drill
The two forwards skate inside the far blue line and take a pass from the defenseman at the far net. The defenseman skates forward around the center circle and takes the forwards on a two-on-one situation.

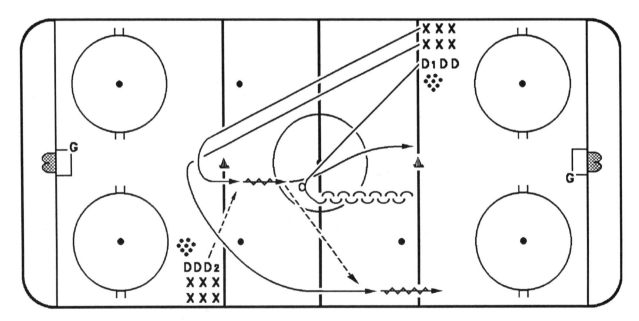

(c) Half-Ice Two-on-One

The defenseman passes to the forward. The forwards pass the puck between them, move outside the blue line, and swing back to the same end. The defenseman skates forward to the blue line and skates backward, taking the forwards on a two-on-one.

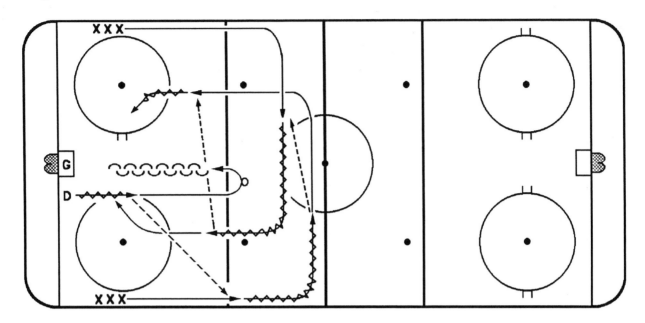

(d) Three-on-One

The defenseman starts the play and follows it up the ice to take a three-on-one in the opposite direction.

Variation: Players perform five-on-two breakouts in both directions (20 minutes).

The center shoots the puck in, and the three forwards and two defensemen break out against two defensemen using various breakout plays. If there is no direct play on the net in the offensive zone, have the forward with the puck pass it back to the defenseman at the blue line, who passes across to the other defenseman, who then shoots a low shot at the net. The forwards then drive to the net to deflect the puck or screen the goaltender. If the offensive play is broken up at the offensive blue line, the five attacking players can regroup in the neutral zone and attack again.

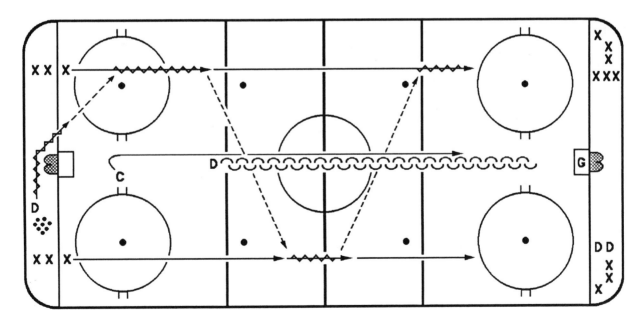

SCRIMMAGE PRACTICE (56 MINUTES)

1. Short Conditioning Skate (5 minutes)

Three groups skate over and back across the ice, working 10 seconds and resting 30 seconds with five repetitions.

2. Resurface the Ice (15 minutes)

Use this time for a dressing room talk and/or rest.

3. Controlled Scrimmage (20 minutes)

The coach should stop the scrimmage for major errors and, along with the assistant coaches, give feedback to the players. Having players change lines quickly (as in a game situation) adds to the intensity of the scrimmage.

4. Shooting Drills (5 minutes)

5. Conditioning Drills (8 minutes)

6. Cooldown and Short Talk (3 minutes)

The cooldown should consist of the same skating and flexibility exercises that started the practice and could end with bent-knee sit-ups and push-ups.

A short discussion by the coach before leaving the ice is appropriate here. Details for the next practice or game plus a comment on the practice is usual at this time.

OFFENSIVE PRACTICE (90 MINUTES)

Some practices can be designated as an offensive practice. In this type of practice the emphasis is on moving the puck quickly and accurately, driving for the net, and scoring goals. Even the scrimmage should emphasize goal scoring and offensive team play. This type of practice seems to be very enjoyable for the players. It is a good idea to have it early in the week or two or three days before the next game. The defensive practice should follow the offensive practice, and the power play–penalty killing practice should take place the day before the next game.

1. Stretching and Warm-Up (5 minutes)

2. Drive-for-the-Net Drill (6 minutes)

3. Neutral Zone Lead-Up Drills (8 minutes)

4. One-on-One and Two-on-One Flow Drills (8 minutes)

5. Neutral Zone Regroup Breakouts (15 minutes)

Emphasize driving for the net.

6. Resurface the Ice (15 minutes)

7. Offensive Scrimmage (15 minutes)

This scrimmage should emphasize moving the puck, shooting, driving for the net.

8. Shooting Drills (5 minutes)

9. Conditioning Drills (10 minutes)

10. Cooldown (3 minutes)

DEFENSIVE PRACTICE (81 MINUTES)

Defensive practice should emphasize checking and preventing goals. The aspects of forechecking, backchecking, and defensive zone coverage should be stressed throughout the practice, including the scrimmage.

1. Cross-Ice Agility and Cross-Ice One-on-One (5 minutes)

2. Give-and-Go with a Backchecker (5 minutes)

3. Two Groups (15 minutes)

Two groups perform drills emphasizing the defense taking the man in front of the net, taking the man coming from the corner, and forechecking.

4. Backchecking Drill (15 minutes)
Players perform breakouts, five-on-two, with one and two checkers, and then with one forechecker and one backchecker.

5. Defensive Zone Coverage (5 minutes)
Players drill on five-on-none defensive zone coverage and then on five-on-five defensive zone coverage.

6. Resurface the Ice (15 minutes)

7. Defensive Scrimmage (10 minutes)
Emphasis is on defensive zone coverage and preventing goals.

8. Conditioning (8 minutes)

9. Cooldown (3 minutes)

POWER PLAY PRACTICE (64 MINUTES)
The power play and penalty killing practices are usually not as fatiguing as the other types of practices and are ideal as day-before-the-game practices. The emphasis is on execution and quick shooting in the power play and positioning in penalty killing.

1. Warm-Up and Stretching (8 minutes)

2. Power Play Shooting Drills (8 minutes)
(a) Forwards
Playing the offside (right shots on the left side, left shots on the right side), the forward skates out of the corner and passes the puck across to the stationary forward who one-times the puck (shoots in one motion). The passer of the puck then receives a pass from the opposite side and shoots.

(b) Defense
The defenseman passes the puck from the corner to the near point. The defenseman moves across the blue line to the middle and shoots low. Another defenseman deflects the puck in front of the net. Rotate the skaters clockwise, working on one side of the ice and then moving to the other side.

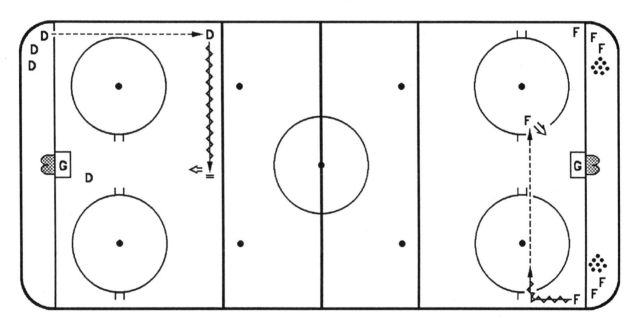

3. Offensive Zone (20 minutes)
(a) Defense Across the Blue Line
The defenseman moves across the blue line and passes to the forward, who comes off the boards. Work right-handed defensemen and forwards at one end and left-handed defensemen and forwards at the other end. The forwards shoot in one motion. A guide to this drill is to have the forwards skate on the face-off circle line before receiving the pass.

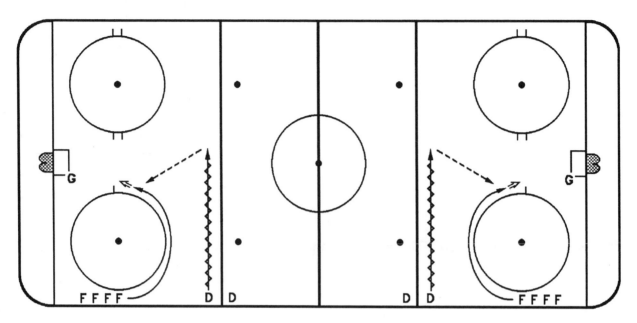

(b) Five-on-None
This offensive zone power play takes place at the blue line with five-on-none. Use numbers to work the various plays.

(1) The defenseman moves across the middle of the blue line and shoots.

(2) The defenseman passes to the forward coming off the boards. The forward shoots.

(3) The defenseman passes to the forward on the boards and then passes to the offside forward who shoots.

(4) The defenseman moves across the blue line and passes to the defense partner, who has moved to the top of the circle. The defenseman shoots the puck in one motion, if possible.

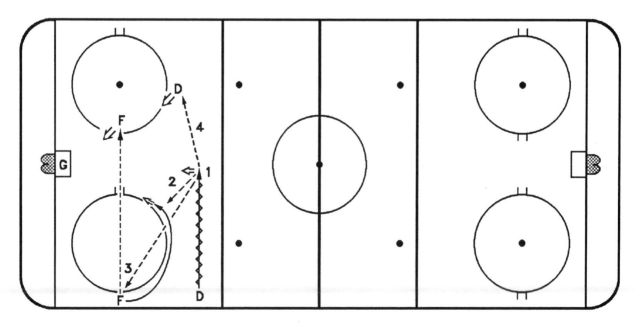

(c) Offensive Zone Power Play from the Corners

This is a give-and-go drill. Going around the net, the offside forward picks (blocks out) the defenseman. The forward moves to the near side, and the other near side forward picks the defenseman. The forward moving out passes the puck across to the offside forward, who then shoots.

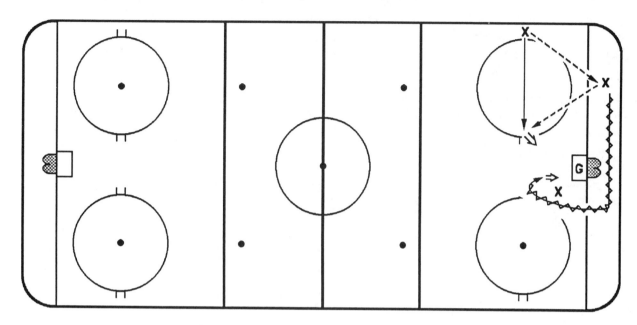

The forward (right-hand shot) moves out in front of the net and shoots or passes across to the offside forward, who then shoots.

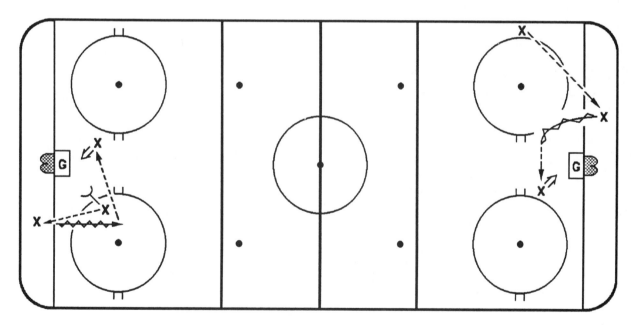

4. Power Play Breakouts (10 minutes)
(a) Five-on-None and Five-on-Two
This drill can be done from one end or can be done from both directions, using the full length of the ice, as a breakout drill.

(b) One Man Short and Two Men Short Five-on-Four
Penalty killers work first without sticks, then with sticks turned blade end up, then with the sticks as usual.

(c) Five-on-Three
Same as (b) above, but the penalty killers are working three versus five. Work at both ends of the rink.

5. Power Play Scrimmage (15 minutes)
Work first five-on-three to allow the power play unit to have some success. Then work five-on-four. The puck can be shot into the power play defensive zone to start the power play with the power play breakout.

6. Cooldown (3 minutes)

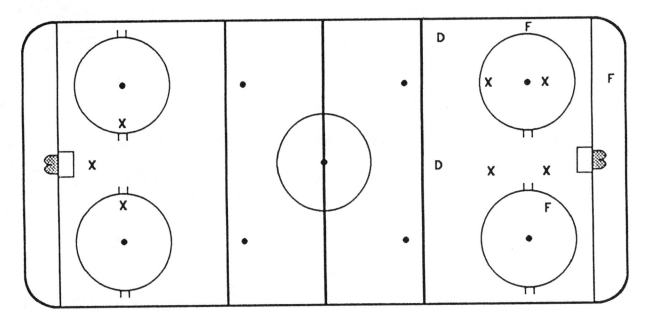

4. BASIC HOCKEY GUIDELINES

There are some basic rules that both the coach and the player must follow in order to become successful. The coach will teach his players these rules both on and off the ice so that they are clearly understood.

DEFENSIVE ZONE

- Think defense first and offense only when in full control of the puck.
- Keep your head up and take the man first and then the puck. Take the offensive man out after he has passed the puck to eliminate a return pass.
- Only one man moves to cover the point. If two men move to the point, the second man should drop back on the board side. Keep the head up when moving to the point and don't let the defenseman move around you.
- Cover the slot at all times. Move to a man coming from behind the net only when he is a direct threat to score.
- One defenseman should always be in front of the net and control any player in the low slot area. The defenseman should face up ice and be aware of players in front of the net. To watch the play in the corner, the defenseman should turn his head but keep his body squared up ice. The defenseman should not turn his back from the slot area unless a player is coming from behind the net and is a direct threat to score.
- When the defenseman has the puck just inside the blue line and is being pressured, he should dump the puck out over the blue line on the board side.
- When experiencing difficulty in moving the puck out under pressure, freeze or ice the puck to get a face-off.
- Never pass the puck rink-wide or through the center in your own end.
- Never pass the puck up the middle in your own zone unless you are absolutely sure. Pass to the winger on the boards or a defenseman in the corner if in doubt.
- Never pass the puck without looking in your own zone. The man must be there.
- Don't shoot the puck around the boards unless a man is in position or the puck has been shot in directly and the far side offensive defenseman is not in a position to pinch in.
- Never go backward in your own zone unless you're on a power play.
- Never allow your team to be outnumbered in the defensive zone (e.g., forwards up too high).

NEUTRAL ZONE

OFFENSE
- If men are covered, dump the puck in or turn back and pass to the defense, and then regroup and attack again.
- Never try to stickhandle past the opposition when teammates are with you.
- The forwards without the puck should move to open ice with the stick on the ice, preparing to take a pass.
- Never go offside; straddle the blue line or cut in front of or behind the puck carrier.

DEFENSE
- Backcheck by picking up the offside forward. Take the man to the net if he stays outside the defenseman. If the player cuts to the middle in front of the defense, stay in the lane. The backchecker should be on the inside of the offensive man and should be slightly ahead of the man. Make contact with the man.
- If two forwards are back, pick up the lanes or one lane and the middle of the ice. The defense can force the play at the defensive blue line.
- If the backchecker is trailing the play, pick up the high slot area.
- Some teams have the first backchecker chase the puck carrier in the neutral zone.

OFFENSIVE ZONE

- One man always drives for the net.
- Drive for the rebounds. You must want to score. Release the puck quickly.
- One man should always be in the slot with the stick on the ice, ready to score or in a position to screen the goalie.
- Shoot the puck when in the scoring area (slot). Extra passes can end up in missed opportunities.
- The defenseman must shoot the puck quickly from the point. If the puck is mishandled or too much time is taken, the puck should be passed or shot back into the corner.
- Never pass the puck blindly from behind the net. If you do not see a man and have to release the puck, shoot the puck at the goaltender's skates.

PENALTY SITUATIONS

- Force the play in the opponent's zone but keep skating.
- Pick up the lane in the neutral zone whether an offensive player is there or not.
- Never go by the opponent's point man in the defensive zone.
- Cover the slot for cross passes.
- Force the play in the defensive zone until the offensive team sets up. Some teams continue to force the play.
- The man in the penalty box replaces the missing forward position, whether right winger, center, or left winger, no matter what position he usually plays.

POWER PLAY

- On a delayed penalty, the center on the next line replaces the goaltender. Some coaches designate a certain player to replace the goalie. If the puck is in your zone, the player goes to the center line; in the offensive zone the player goes to the front of the net.
- Have several methods of moving the puck out of your own end.
- Use four men in the neutral zone to move the puck over the offensive blue line.
- Move the puck to the point in the offensive zone.
- Move the puck quickly. If there is no man to pass to, the player should move. Don't stand still with the puck. Moving the puck quickly allows a man to move to the opening.

5. SKATING

It is very important for each of your players to have a good pair of well-fitting skates. Growing children should not wear a skate more than one half-size larger than necessary. Most hockey shops now have specialists who will fit skates properly.

When tying their skates, skaters should be sure the middle eyelets are pulled tightly together around the ankle. The top eyelets do not need to be pulled too closely together. The laces should not be tied around the skate (leg), as this could cause a lack of blood circulation to the feet.

Skates should be sharpened regularly to allow quick stops and turns. The sharpness of the skates can be tested by executing quick stops or tight turns. Off the ice, scraping a fingernail on the edge of the skate blade or placing a coin on the bottom of the blade to see how much hollow there is in the blade will tell you if the skate blade is still sharp.

SKATING TECHNIQUES

FORWARD STARTING
Front Start
- The body weight is over the drive leg.
- The drive leg is rotated outward at an angle of 90 degrees to the direction of the motion.
- The feet are a shoulders' width apart.
- The body leans forward, and the center of gravity shifts forward.
- The initial strides are short and quick without gliding, and the feet are lifted off the ice slightly.
- As the number of strides increases, the push is to the side rather than to the back.

Crossover Start
- The skates are slightly closer together than in the front start.
- The skates are parallel and perpendicular to the direction of motion.
- The lean of the body and the head and shoulders are toward the direction of motion.
- After the crossover, the outside skate is placed at an angle of 90 degrees to direction of motion.

FORWARD SKATING
A solid, well-balanced stance is important in skating.

- The feet should be a shoulders' width apart.
- The foot of the drive leg (back leg) is turned outward for a lateral thrust (to the side, not to the back).
- The drive leg is fully extended at the hip, knee, and ankle joint.
- The knee of the drive leg is flexed beyond the toe of the skate.
- The trunk and glide leg should form an approximate 90-degree angle.
- The drive leg should be recovered close to the ice in a circular motion, passing under the center of gravity.

DRIVE LEG

GLIDE LEG

The skater should allow for a natural arm swing but not overswing the arms to cause overshift, which will interfere with the forward motion. The skater should try to develop a smooth action stride with maximum thrust from the drive leg. Excess motions are a waste of energy and may cause a reduction in the forward speed.

FORWARD STOPPING
Two-Foot Stop
- The knees are bent, and the skates turn to a 90-degree angle to the direction of motion by the rotation of the hips.
- The skates are staggered six to eight inches apart. The inside skate is slightly beyond the outside skate (to arch).
- The weight should be distributed as evenly as possible on both skates.
- The stop is executed on the outside edge of the inside skate and the inside edge of the outside skate.

One-Foot Stop
The front leg stop is similar to the two-foot stop except all the weight is on the front leg (inside edge). The back leg is off the ice, ready to initiate the next stride.

The back leg stop is rarely used, as it puts the player in a vulnerable position to be hit (off balance). The weight is on the outside edge of the back leg.

FORWARD CROSSOVER
Players use the forward crossover to accelerate while changing direction.

- The head, shoulders, and arms are rotated in the direction of movement.
- The body leans toward the inside, with the trunk bent forward and the knees bent.
- The weight transfers from the inside to the outside leg.
- The outside leg drives with an extension of the hip, knee, and ankle.
- Following the extension of the outside leg (inside edge), the outside leg crosses over the inside leg (outside edge).

BACKWARD SKATING
- The knees are bent and a shoulders' width apart.
- The toe of the drive leg is rotated inward to a 90-degree angle to the direction of the motion.
- The drive leg extends in the sequence of hip, knee, and ankle (inside edge) in a semicircular motion.
- The extension is not full, which allows for a quick recovery.
- The glide leg is flexed to allow for a longer push by the drive leg.
- During the extension of the drive leg, the weight is transferred to the glide leg, which is ready to become the drive leg.

BACKWARD STOPPING
One-Foot Stop
- The back skate rotates outward in a semicircle before stopping at a 90-degree angle to the desired direction.
- The weight of the body is on the rear leg and the front part of the skate.
- The knee of the back leg is flexed, ready to extend for movement in the opposite direction.

Two-Foot Stop
- Both skates are rotated outward at 180 degrees with heels close together.
- Both legs are flexed, with pressure on the front part of the blades (inside edges).

BACKWARD TURNING
Two-Skate Quick Turn
- Both skates turn in the desired direction.
- The skate on the side of the turn is slightly ahead.
- The head, shoulder, and arms are turned in the desired direction.
- The knees are bent, and the weight is on the back of the blades (outside edge of the front skate, inside edge of the back skate).

Forward to Backward
- The weight is placed on the glide leg opposite the intended pivot side (right skate if turn is to the left).

- At the end of the stride, the player straightens up and rotates the left skate outward at 180 degrees, bringing it to the other side of right glide skate.
- The head and shoulders rotate to the left, and the right skate rotates 180 degrees and is then parallel to the left skate.

Backward to Forward Heel-to-Heel Pivot (Mohawk Turn)
- The skates are brought close together.
- The weight of the body is brought over the glide leg.
- The head, shoulders, and arms are turned in the desired direction.
- The pivot skate is raised slightly off the ice, rotated in the desired direction, and placed back on the ice.
- The glide leg pushes and transfers the weight to the pivoting leg, allowing for rapid acceleration with short strides.

Backward to Forward Crossover
- The skates are brought close together with the arms close to the body.
- The body weight shifts over the glide leg.
- The other leg crosses over with the blade (inside edge) at a 90-degree angle to the desired direction.
- The crossover is short and close to the ice.

SKATING AND TURNING DRILLS
Note that these drills can be done with players skating backward or forward.

1. Figure Eight
Have players skate around the rink, going behind the nets and moving in both directions.

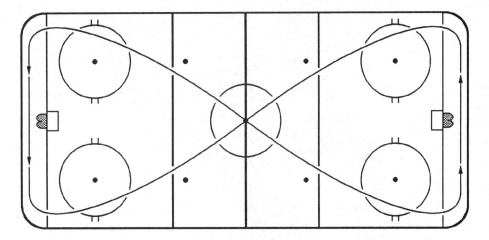

2. Small Figure Eight

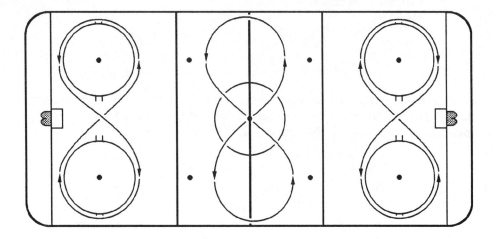

A solid, balanced stance is important in skating. The foot of this skater's drive leg turns outward for maximum thrust, and his body leans forward, placing the weight over the glide leg.

3. Circle Skate
Players skate in circles in five groups, changing direction forward and backward.

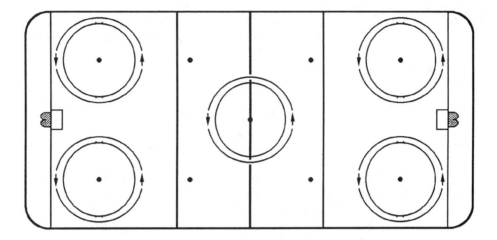

4. Skate the Circles—Two Groups

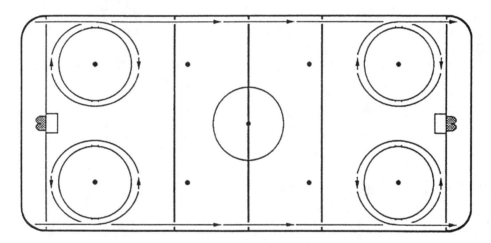

5. Skate the Circles—One Group

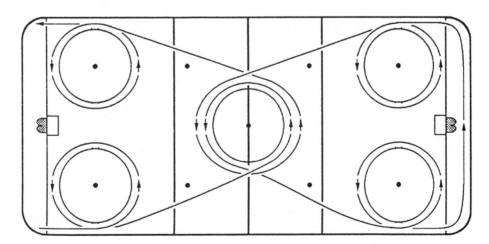

6. Weaving Through Markers

(A) With the pylons in a zigzag position, players skate forward through the markers and then skate backward through the markers.

(B) Players skate forward clockwise around the markers, then backward clockwise around the markers, then forward counterclockwise around the markers, and then backward counterclockwise around the markers.

(C) Players deke around each pylon using a sharp turn both right and left.

(D) Players skate forward then backward through the markers in a straight line.

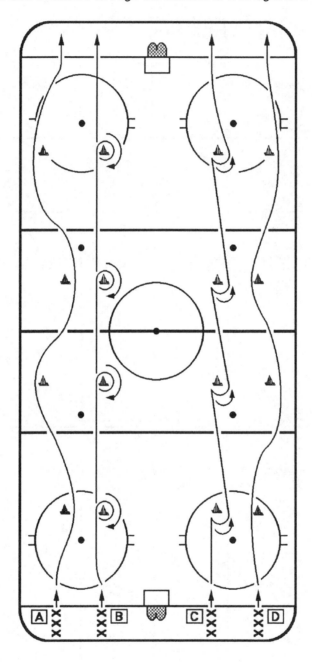

7. Zigzag Drill

All players skate forward stopping at each point (1 through 7) up the ice. The second player leaves when the first reaches the blue line. All players stay at one end when they complete the drill, then reverse directions.

Variation: All players skate forward to points 1, 3, 5, and 7 and backward to points 2, 4, and 6.

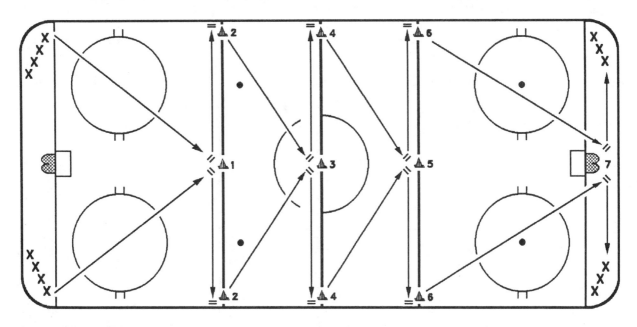

8. Overback Drill

Players skate forward across the blue line, stop, skate backward to the top of the face-off circle, pivot toward the other group, skate to the corner, stop, and then move into the back of the line.

Note that you must have groups 1 and 4 and 2 and 3 switch sides halfway through the drill to be sure the players work on stopping and turning both ways.

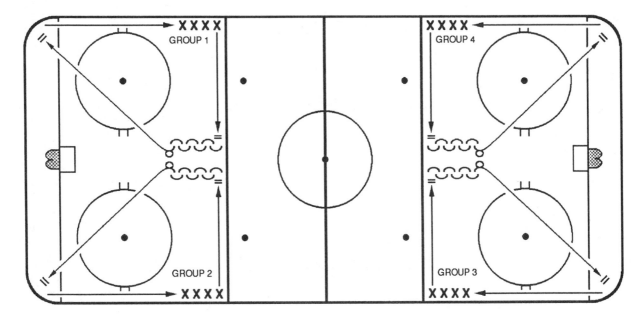

9. Skating Agility

Three forwards and two defensemen skate down the ice. The wingers cut at the far blue line and skate directly to the net and back to the blue line twice. The center skates to the crease and moves laterally side to side twice. The defensemen skate to the far blue line and cross-step to the pylons three times. After this skate, the players skate the length of the ice to the starting position.

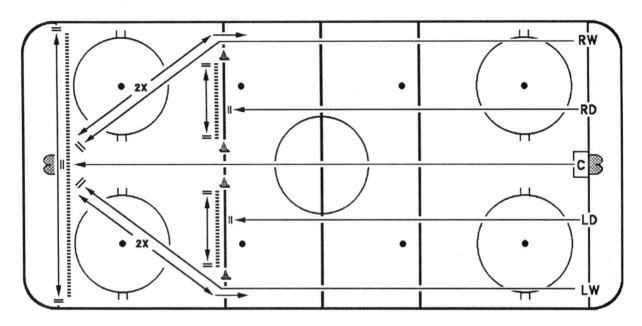

10. Forward and Backward

Players skate forward; on the whistle, they skate backward. Have them turn the opposite way each time in order to practice the movement in both directions.

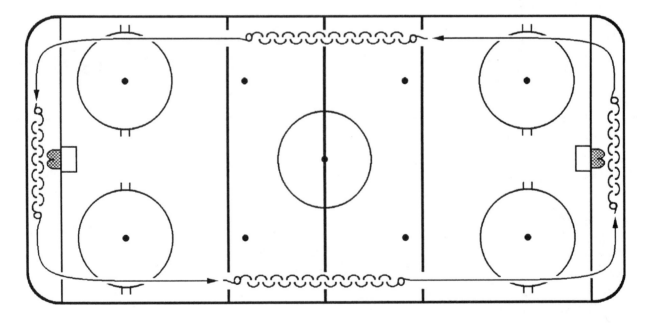

11. Skating Agility Variation
This drill is done the same as 9, except the players skate around the outside of the rink and change directions at the blue lines.

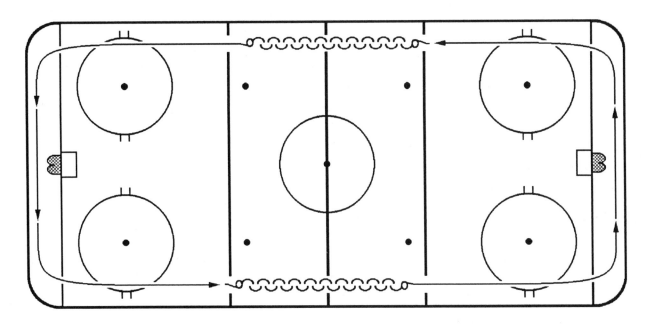

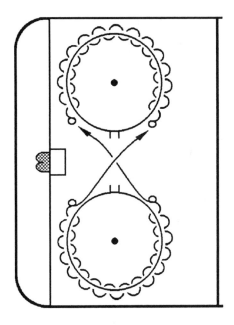

12. Circles
Players skate backward around the circles and forward between the circles.

13. Between the Blue Lines (not shown)
Players skate forward straight up and down the rink, skating backward between the blue lines.

14. Turns Between the Blue Lines (not shown)
Players skate around the rink doing 360-degree turns, as many as they can, between the blue lines.

AGILITY DRILLS

1. Wave Drill

On the coach's hand signals, players move forward, backward, and sideways, keeping their heads up and staying up on toes.

2. Shadow Drill (not shown)

Players work with partners. One player skates forward, the other backward. The offensive player moves and the defensive player must react to the offensive player.

3. Lateral Drill

Players skate backward, moving laterally side to side across the ice.

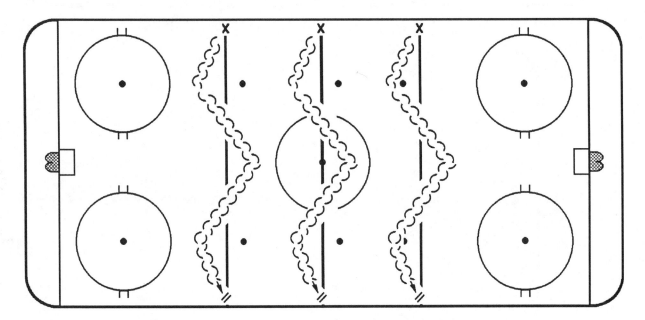

4. Knee Drops (not shown)

Players skate around the rink, and at the red and blue lines they drop down on both knees and quickly recover. Then they skate around the rink, and at the red and blue lines they drop down on one knee and recover (alternate knee each time).

6. PASSING AND RECEIVING

STICKHANDLING AND PUCK CONTROL

CHOOSING A STICK

It is very important that each of your players chooses a stick that feels right and is correct for his skating and puckhandling styles. The thickness of the shaft varies from manufacturer to manufacturer. Be sure each player picks one that allows him to close his hands completely around it.

LENGTH OF STICK

The length of the stick varies with the individual. In general, the stick should reach the player's chin in shoes and the player's collarbone on skates. The style of skating is also a very important consideration in choosing a stick, as some players skate with the upper body in a more upright position than others.

LIE OF STICK

Lies of sticks normally range from four to seven, with five and six being the most common. The player's skating style is important. More upper body lean means a lower lie stick is appropriate and less upper body lean means a higher lie stick. A test for the proper lie of a stick is to have players stand at a normal stance with the stick on the ice in front of them. If the heel of the blade is off the ice, a higher lie should be used. If the toe of the blade is off the ice, a lower lie should be used. When a player is skating, check if the heel or toe of the stick is off the ice. If so, the stick has the incorrect lie.

WEIGHT OF THE STICK

The stick should feel comfortable to the player, as each individual has a different preference. As a general rule, the stick should be stiff but not whippy. Bigger, stronger players often need longer, heavier sticks.

CURVED STICK

Young boys should not use a curved stick. Some stick manufacturers have reintroduced the straight blade stick. When all passing, stickhandling, and shooting fundamentals have been mastered, older boys should be allowed to experiment with a curved blade. The curve is measured by the distance of a perpendicular line measured from a straight line drawn from any point of the heel to the end of the blade.

The rules for most leagues state that the curve should be no greater than half an inch. All instructors and coaches should be alert to pick out boys who are having difficulty with passing, stickhandling, or shooting. A curved stick may be one of the reasons for these problems. Backhand passing and shooting are the skills most affected by the curved stick.

TAPING THE KNOB OF THE STICK

Taping the knob depends on the grip and feel desired by the player. If his upper hand is on or over the end of the stick, the knob is usually smaller. If his upper hand does not reach the end but rests against the knob, larger amounts of tape are usually used. White tape (as opposed to black friction tape) should be used on the knob to prevent the glove palm from deteriorating.

TAPING THE BLADE OF THE STICK

Taping the blade is usually a matter of choice. Some players now use little or no tape on the blade. Generally, the stick is taped from heel to toe without large amounts of overlap. The use of talcum powder or the rubbing the blade of the stick on the bottom of a shoe is sometimes used to take the stickiness off the tape. White tape is easier to apply, adheres better, and is now preferred by many players.

PASSING AND RECEIVING

PASSING

The puck is cradled with the blade of the stick slightly over the puck. The puck should be in the center of the blade or slightly to the heel of it. The weight shift moves from the back foot to the front foot with a sweeping motion of the stick blade on the ice. Instruct your player to push with the lower hand and pull with the upper one. The puck should be released with the blade at a 90-degree angle to the direction the puck is traveling. Remind your player to lead the man and make passes quickly.

RECEIVING

To be in position to receive a pass, the player keeps the stick blade on the ice or just slightly off. The hands are tight on the stick but arms remain loose. The player should give with the blade of the stick and tilt it toward the puck. The blade of the stick is turned to the direction the puck should go.

TYPES OF PASSING

FOREHAND SWEEP

The stick blade is on the ice, and the puck remains in contact with it until it is released. Body weight transfers from back to front leg and the follow-through is low.

BACKHAND SWEEP

The same fundamentals used in the backhand sweep are used in the forehand sweep, except the puck is moved on the backhand side. The puck begins well on the backhand side and the weight shifts from the back foot to the front foot. The backhand sweep is a more difficult pass and requires a low follow-through.

SNAP PASS

The snap pass is similar to the forehand sweep. The stick is brought back slightly from contact with the puck in a sweeping motion and snapped. It is a quick, hard pass.

FLIP PASS (SAUCER PASS)

The flip pass is used to pass over an opponent's stick. The puck spins off the stick from the heel to the toe. The puck should be approximately four to six inches off the ice and land flat in a spinning motion. It must land before the receiver's stick. Players should lead the receiver more than usual, as the pass is slower.

DROP PASS

To make a drop pass, the offensive player skates in front of the defensive player and drops the puck to his trailing teammate. The puck is dropped from the forehand or backhand position but is not passed back, as this allows the trailer to skate into the puck.

BACK PASS

This pass differs from the drop pass because the puck is passed back to a teammate. The puck can be passed back from the forehand or backhand side. The trailing teammate is usually 10 to 15 feet behind.

BOARD PASS

The board pass is used by defensemen behind the net or by any player attempting to pass by a defensive man with a teammate slipping behind. The pass should be low and not too hard, so the rebound will be easy to handle. As the puck rebounds, the angle of incidence equals the angle of reflection.

BANK PASS

This pass is used by a forward driving down the boards in the offensive zone. The forward bounces the puck back off the boards to a trailing player or passes off the boards to another defenseman behind the net (a defense reverse). The pass is executed by bouncing the puck off the boards backward to be picked up by a trailing player. The puck is kept on the ice and is at a sharp angle without being passed too hard.

ONE TOUCH PASS

The player redirects a pass without stopping or cradling the puck.

TYPES OF RECEIVING

OFF SKATES

The weight is put on the nonreceiving skate. The blade of the receiving skate is turned with the toe pointing slightly in. The puck is deflected up to the blade of the stick.

IN THE AIR

The player should attempt to knock down a low pass in the air with the blade of his stick in a downward slapping motion. He should attempt to bunt down a pass high in the air with his glove or body.

TOO FAR AHEAD

The arms are extended completely and the stick is extended in one hand. A player may go down on one knee and extend the stick flat on the ice if the puck is coming from behind at an angle.

OFF THE BOARDS

If no defensive man is in the area, the player should start skating and pick up the puck while moving. Otherwise, he must stop and/or deflect the puck with the back skate onto the blade of the stick.

PASSING DRILLS

1. Stationary

In a stationary position, players pass a puck with a partner across the ice. They lengthen the distance of the passes in stages. Players pass over a stick for flip passes.

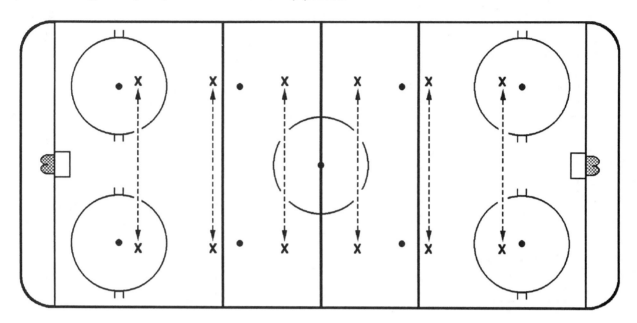

2. Circles

Players pass in circles, across and around. This drill is the same as 1 except the passing player follows the pass and replaces the receiver in his line.

3. Interceptor (not shown)

Players pass in a circle with one man in the center attempting to intercept the passes.

4. Pepper Passing

Players keep the puck moving as quickly as possible.

5. Pairs

Players pass in pairs around the ice using both forehand and backhand passes.
  Variation: Players pass in pairs around the ice deliberately aiming passes at the skates.

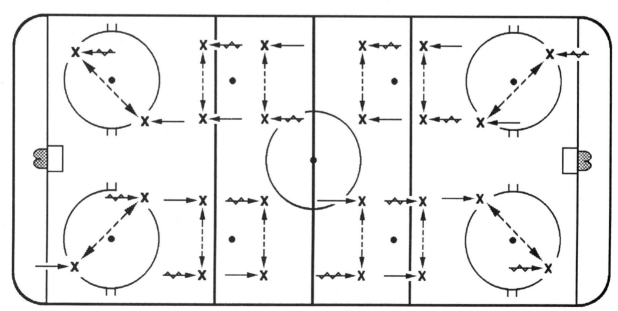

6. Two Pairs Passing

Players pass in pairs down the ice. They stop at the far end and return in the opposite direction when the drill is completed. Forehand passes then progress to backhand passes.

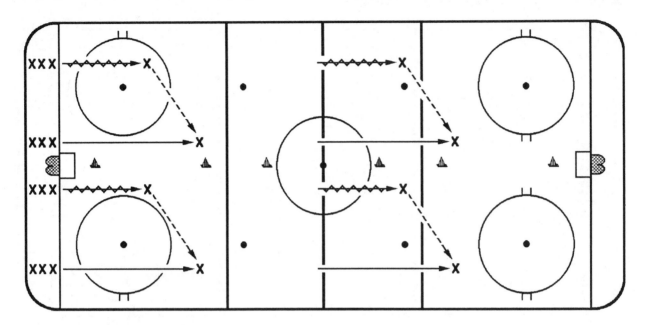

7. Two Pairs Passing Variation

This drill is the same as 6 except the pylons are put in a line between the two passing players.

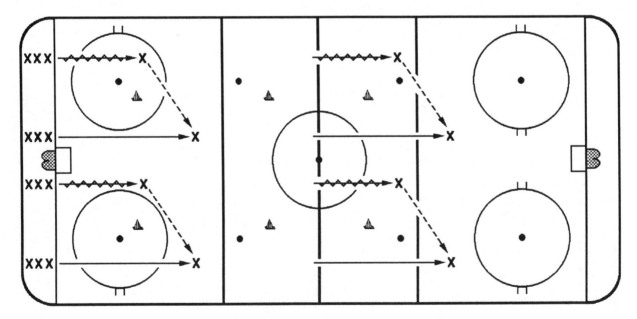

8. Give-and-Go

The player with the puck passes to a stationary man who returns the pass.

Variation: Two players start at the X2 position. After X2 returns the pass to X1, he joins the back of the X1 line. X2, who shot on goal, returns to the X2 position.

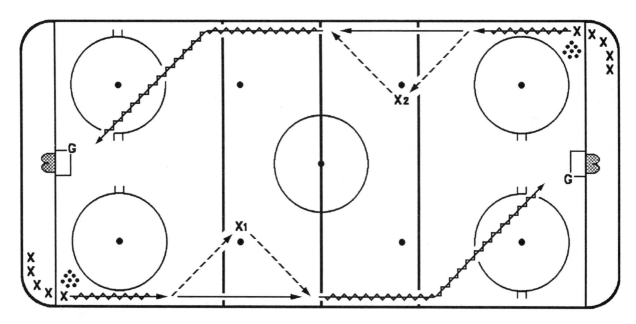

9. Two-on-None

This two-on-none passing drill works in both directions.

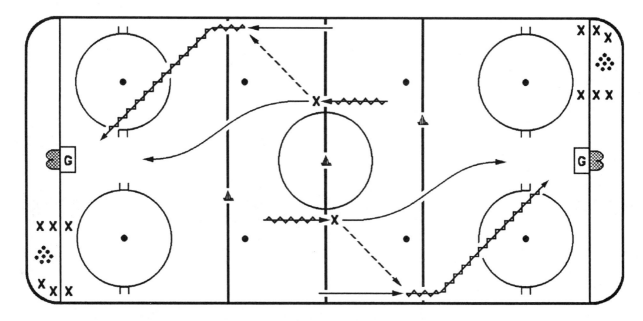

10. Wide Ice

This two-on-none drill works in both directions. This is a variation of 8 in which only one group must wait until the two-on-none is finished from the other direction. Passes are longer and more accuracy is required than in 8.

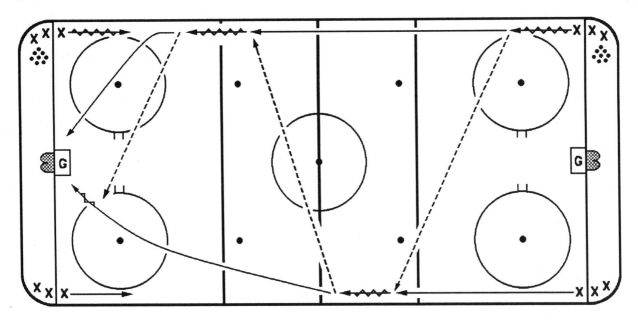

11. Defense Behind the Net

This drill is the same as 10 except a defenseman starts the two-on-one from behind the net and passes to the forward. The defensemen operate out of both ends. The defenseman who starts the play goes to the blue line, stops, and skates backward to the goal line.

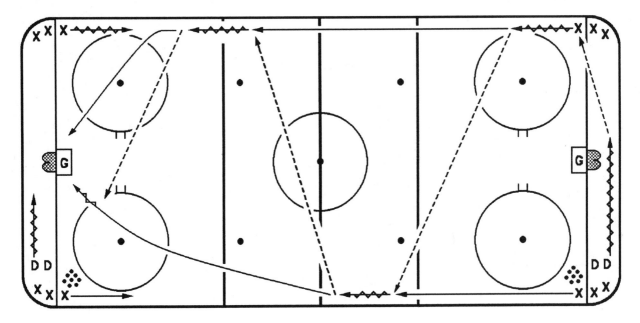

12. Three-on-None in Both Directions

Groups of three, passing one puck between them, spread out after passing center ice.

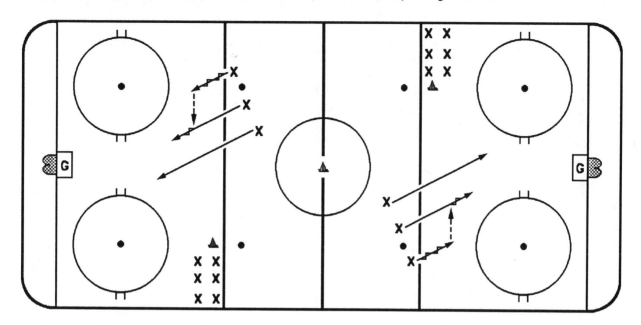

13. Passing Off the Boards

The player skates the length of the ice passing off the boards and receiving his own pass back.

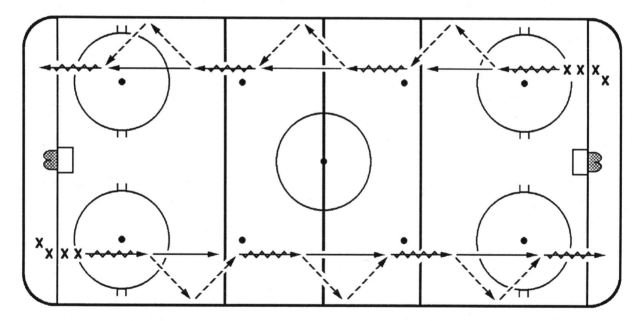

14. Pairs

In this drill players pass off the boards working in pairs. Two players alternate passing off boards and receiving the pass.

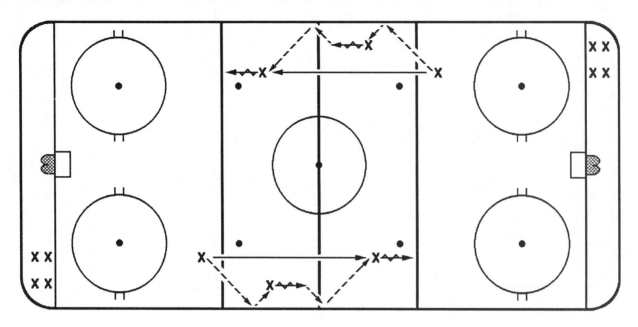

15. Keep Away

Skaters play keep away using the three zones of the rink, with three to four players on a team.

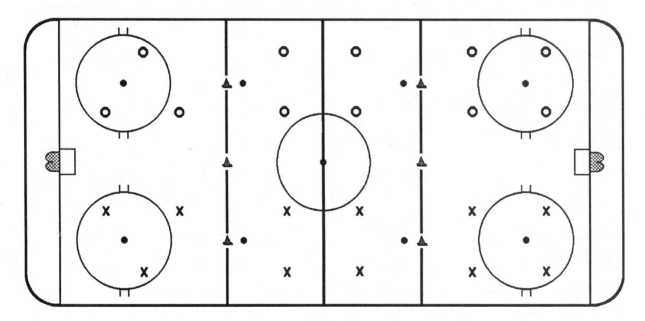

Additionally, all two-on-one, three-on-one, and three-on-two team play drills involve passing and receiving.

7. SHOOTING

Accuracy and getting the shot away quickly are key factors in goal scoring. The speed and power of the shot depend on the strength, mechanics, and coordination of the shooting movement. Note the following shooting principles.

- The puck should be placed in the middle to the heel of the blade. Any deviation from this position will result in a loss of power and accuracy.
- The base of support (i.e., the relationship of the puck and the skates) is very important in obtaining maximum velocity in shooting. Shooting should be performed at the base of support between the two skates. The puck should be released at a 90-degree angle to the intended direction.
- The lower arm provides the pushing action while the upper arm provides the pulling motion. Upper body rotation is very important in shooting. Strength in the arms, shoulders, and wrists is essential in shooting.
- Getting the shot away quickly is important, and therefore a player should be able to shoot the puck off either foot.
- The follow-through should be toward the net and the shooter should be ready for any rebound and maintain balance to receive a possible body check.
- In shooting, the force exerted on the stick is downward and forward, throwing the puck forward.

TYPES OF SHOOTING

FOREHAND
- The lower hand is a comfortable distance from the upper hand (usually 12 to 18 inches apart).
- The puck is brought back to the side and opposite or slightly behind the rear skate.
- The body is at a 45-degree angle to the direction of the puck.
- The puck is in the middle to the heel of the blade of the stick, which is slightly cupped.
- The lower wrist is extended and the upper wrist is flexed.
- The puck comes forward in a sweeping motion.
- The weight shifts from the rear foot to the front foot, and the puck is released from the front skate at a 90-degree angle to its intended direction.
- The arms extend, the upper body rotates quickly, the lower wrist flexes, and the upper wrist extends.
- The turning of the stick blade follow-through determines the height of the shot. If the blade is turned over the puck, the shot is low. If the blade is turned under the puck, the shot is high.
- Balance should be maintained at all times to receive a possible body check.

BACKHAND
The backhand shot is often neglected because players tend to use the curved stick. The shot is valuable coming off a shift to the backhand side and cutting toward the net. The shooting principles for the backhand shot are similar to those for the forehand shot, and the follow-through is important.

- The puck is drawn to the backhand side and the lower wrist is in a reversed or flexed position.
- The weight shift is from back to front foot.
- The upper body rotates quickly, and the lower wrist extends.

SNAP
The snap shot is a valuable shot, as it is quick and accurate from 30 feet away.

- The stick blade is at a 90-degree angle to the desired direction of the puck, and the puck is cupped in the middle of the stick blade.
- The stick is drawn back about one inch from the puck.
- The wrists are extended and flexed when the stick blade hits the puck. The follow-through is short.

SLAP
The slap shot should be developed after the forehand and snap shots have been mastered. The slap shot is valuable because the puck can be shot at a greater speed from a greater distance. Accuracy and quickness of release are sacrificed for velocity.

- The body is parallel to the desired direction of the puck and the puck is close to the heel of the skate.
- The lower hand is shifted down the shaft of the stick until fully extended.
- The stick is drawn backward to shoulder height with the lower arm rigid and the eyes focused on the puck.
- On the downswing, the weight shifts from the back leg to the front leg.
- The stick contacts the ice just before it hits the puck, usually one-half to one inch from the puck. The puck is struck at the middle of the blade.
- The wrist moves from extension to flexion, and pressure is exerted downward on the ice as contact is made with the puck.

FLIP

The flip shot is used to get the puck up in the air quickly when clearing the puck from the defensive zone, lifting the puck over a fallen goaltender, or flipping the puck into the offensive end.

- The lower hand is moved further down the blade than usual.
- The blade of the stick is open, the puck is lifted in a scooping motion, and the follow-through is high.
- The flip shot can be executed with a forehand or backhand motion.

TIP-INS

Many goals are scored by a player changing the direction of a shot using the blade of the stick. It is important to get in a good scoring position for a tip-in, in order to prevent the opposition defenseman from tying the player up. The forward should attempt to block the goaltender's vision by moving in front of the goal crease.

- The player should keep his feet in an open stance to avoid being knocked down by opponents. He should angle the blade of the stick down to deflect the puck downward and angle the blade of the stick upward to deflect the puck upward.
- The player must keep a tight grip on the stick for all deflections and maintain a low balance stance.

SHOOTING OFF EITHER FOOT

Players should be able to shoot the puck off either foot in order to get the shot off quickly. The shot is used to execute a quick shot. All good goal scorers are able to shoot the puck off either foot as in many cases there is no time to relocate the footing when receiving the puck in a shooting position.

- The weight is on the foot nearest the puck.
- The speed of the shot comes from the arm, wrist, and shoulder action, with little or no body rotation.
- The follow-through is short, as the player is not in a stable position and is vulnerable to a body check.

Accuracy and quickness in getting the shot away are key factors in goal scoring. All good goal scorers are able to shoot the puck off either foot in order to shoot as quickly as possible.

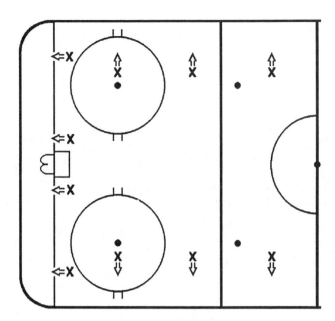

SHOOTING DRILLS
1. Against the Boards Stationary
Combination drills may be executed combining many types of shooting drills using the entire ice surface whenever possible. Have players rotate from group to group. Be innovative. Shoot against the boards in a stationary position. Have them shoot ten high shots, ten low shots, then alternate high and low shots. Mark the low and high spots on the boards and have the players shoot for the marks. Use half-ice or full ice.

2. Moving from the Middle
Players shoot against the boards from a moving position, working from the center of the ice. Use half-ice or full ice.

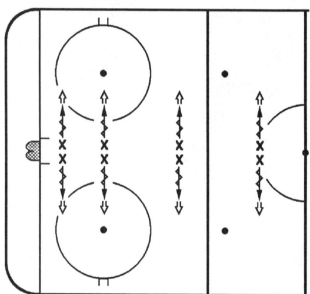

3. Moving Across the Ice
Players shoot against boards starting from one side and moving to the other side. For large numbers, divide players into two groups. Use half-ice or full ice.

4. Skating the Length of the Ice

Divide the players into two groups. Players skate the length of the ice and shoot on the goaltender from the slot area. The shot area can be marked by pylons on the ice. Have players switch sides halfway through the drill. The drill can be varied with the give-and-go drill.

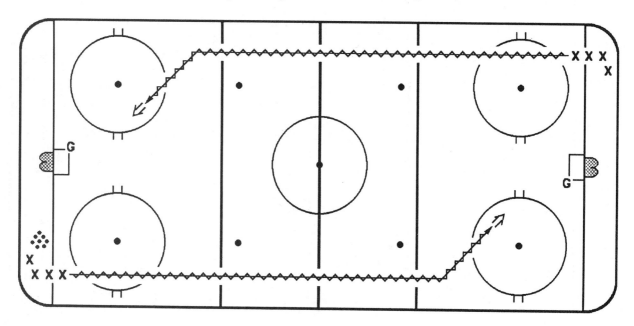

5. Around the Pylons

This drill is the same as 4 except players cut around pylons and shoot. This drill can be varied with the give-and-go drill.

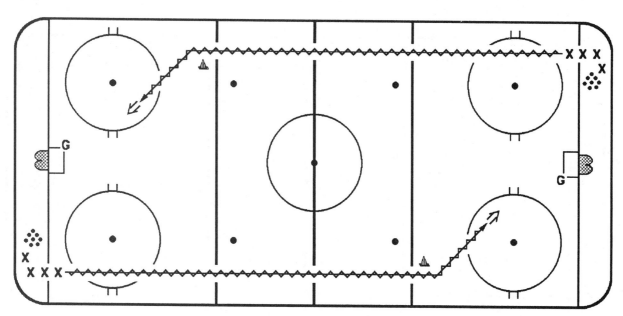

6. One-Way Shooting

Divide the players in half in two corners at the same end of the rink. Have players alternate shooting from the right and left side. This drill can be useful if only one goaltender is available for practice. Players should shoot from both sides. The drill can be varied using pylons and the give-and-go drill.

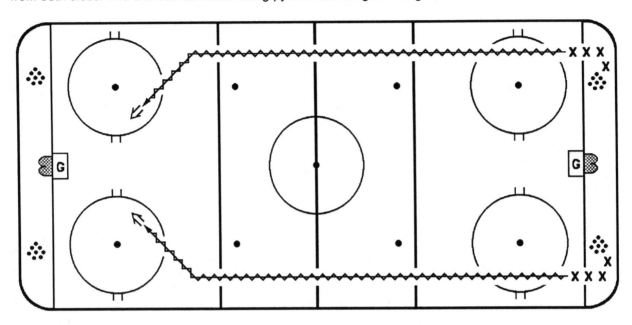

7. Cross-Ice Pass and Shoot

Players start at the same time from opposite corners, each carrying a puck. Between the blue lines, each player passes the puck to another player, continues, and shoots after receiving the pass. The players move to the opposite corner after shooting.

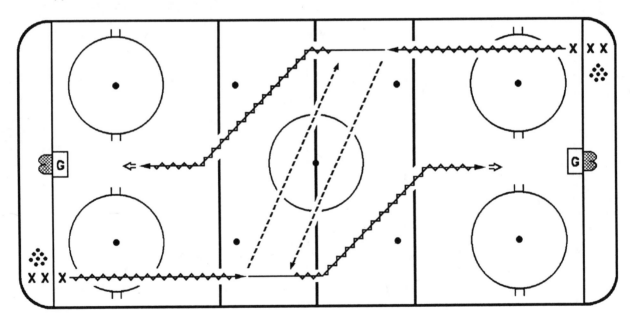

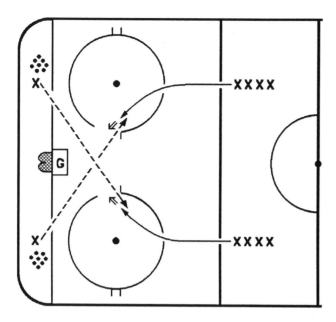

8. Pass Out Shooting

A player in each corner passes the puck alternately to the players skating in on goal. Players should follow the puck after shooting and go for a second shot if a rebound comes out.

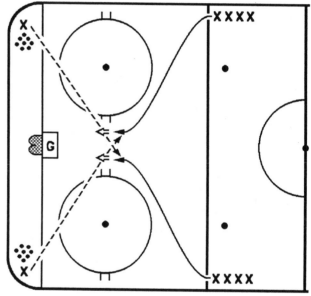

9. Pass Out Shooting Variation

In this variation on 8, after shooting the puck, the player goes to the corner the pass came from. The player passing the puck then goes to the end of the line on the same side of the rink.

10. Pass Out Shooting Variation

This drill is a variation of 8 in which the pass comes from the same side instead of from the opposite side. The player goes to the corner from which he received the pass.

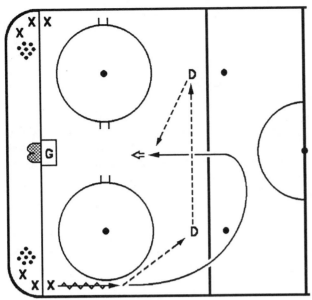

11. Defenseman to Defenseman

A player skates from the corner and passes to the nearest defenseman. The defenseman passes the puck to the other defenseman, and then back to the forward. The forward then goes in, shoots to the goaltender, and moves to the other corner. The next forward up moves from the other corner. The defensemen stay in the same positions for this drill.

12. Defenseman to Defenseman Variation

The pass goes from X1 to X2 and then to X3, who goes to the line in the corner after a shot on goal while X2 goes to the position of X1. X1 goes to the shooting line. This drill differs from 11 because all players rotate, playing all positions.

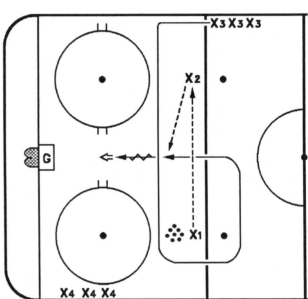

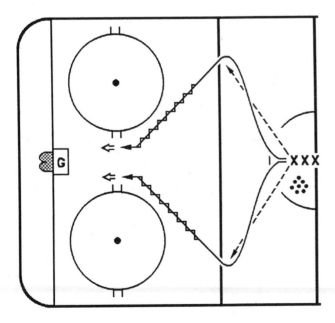

13. From Center Ice

A player receives a pass from the center, cuts in, and shoots from the wing. The puck is returned to the center. The next player swings to the opposite side and receives a pass from the next player in line.

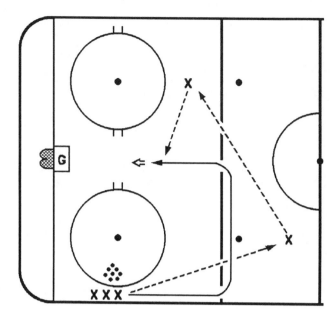

14. Pass, Return Pass, and Shoot
The player skates from the corner and passes the puck to one stationary man, who passes to the other stationary man, and then a return pass is made to the forward.

15. Race for the Puck and Shoot
Players must start at the same time. They round the pylons, and the first player then shoots on net while the other player tries to check him.

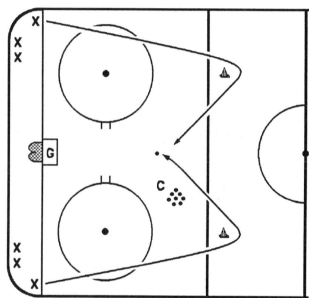

16. Pass Out Variation
After the player has taken the first shot, he stops in the high slot, receives a second pass out from the opposite corner, and then shoots again.

Variation: X moves while trying to take a second shot.

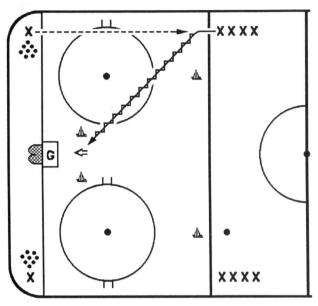

17. Backhand Drill

This drill is the same as 16 except the pass comes early from the corner, and the player cuts around a pylon and shoots from his backhand side from the slot area.

18. Rebound Drill

This is another variation of 16. A player from the opposite line trails the shooter and picks up and shoots any rebound. Alternate the shooter and the rebounder each time.

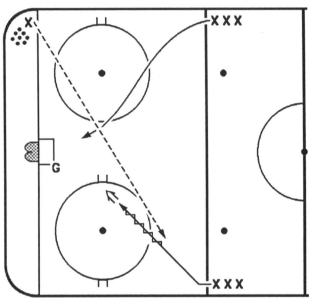

19. Along the Ice Drill

This is another variation of 16. In this drill the goaltender is without a stick and all shots are along the ice.

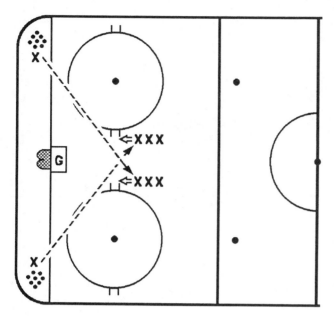

20. Stationary Pass Out Drill

Players are stationary in the slot and shoot as soon as the puck is passed out. Alternate their pass outs.

Variation: Players pass from one corner and shoot, then pass from the other corner and shoot.

21. Pass Across Drills

Drills 7 through 11 can be performed with passes coming across instead of from the corner.

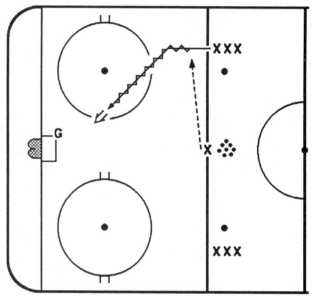

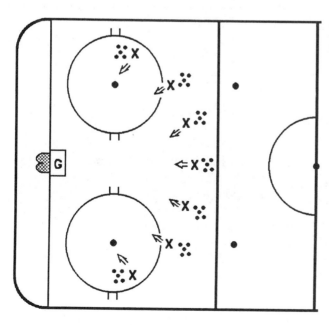

22. Semicircle Drill

The players are stationary in a semicircle starting from the blue line. The players shoot in rapid succession. After each player has shot one puck, he retrieves it and moves in five feet, using wrist shots only.

Variation: Players shoot alternately rather than in succession (left side, right side, next left, and so on).

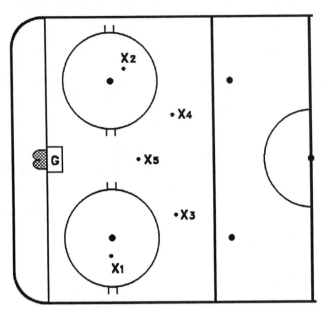

23. Shoot by Numbers

Each player has a puck, and shots are from different angles. The players shoot by numbers in order. The goaltender should know the order as well. Move players into different positions to create new angles.

24. To the Slot

Pucks are passed from different angles with the last shot chased by a checker. Rotate positions.

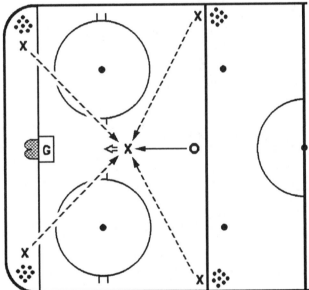

25. Three-Line Shooting Drill

The players form three lines and move with a puck simultaneously. One winger shoots from the blue line, the center shoots from the high slot straight out from the goal, and the other winger shoots from an angle at the bottom of the circle. The players alternate lines. Halfway through the drill, the long shots come from the opposite side.

26. Moving Slot Drill

The center skates to the center line and passes to the winger. The winger moves down the boards and passes the puck back to the center (after he passes the pylon), who then shoots from the slot area, one-timing it (shooting without stopping). The forwards alternate positions of the center and wing. Work with the center and one winger alternating from one side to the other.

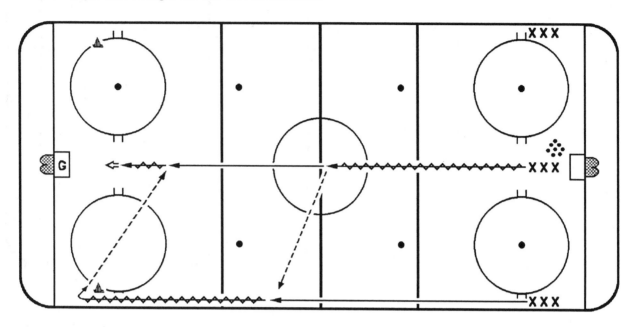

27. Chase the Rabbit

In this drill on shooting under pressure, the puck carrier says "go," skates the length of the ice outside the pylon, and shoots with the checker starting two steps behind him and on the inside of the pylon.

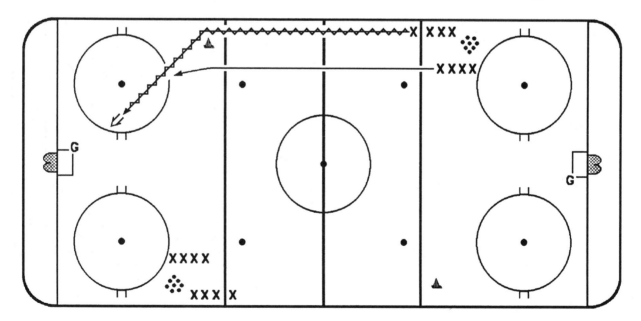

28. Shooting Under Pressure

In this variation of 27, the shooter receives a pass from center ice.

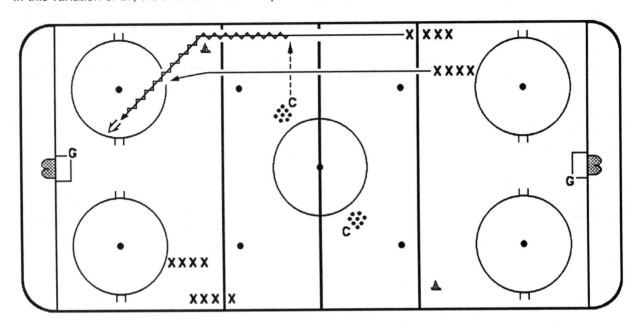

29. Shoot and Chase

The player skates the length of the ice, shoots, and then chases the player coming from the side as he skates the length of the ice and shoots. Players work both sides of the ice.

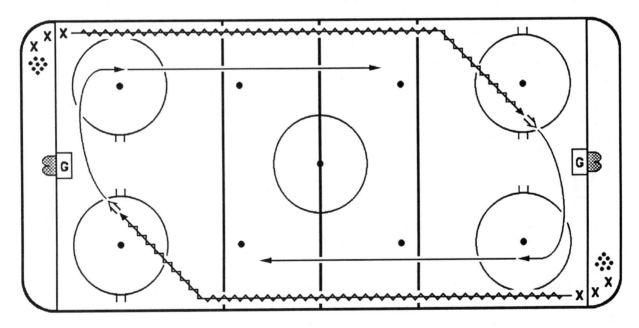

30. Shooting Under Pressure Variation

The player skates from the corner with the puck, cuts around the pylon, and shoots. As soon as the puck carrier hits the far blue line, the checker from the opposite side cuts across and attempts to stop the player from shooting.

Variation: A pass is made from the neutral zone to the player coming up the ice.

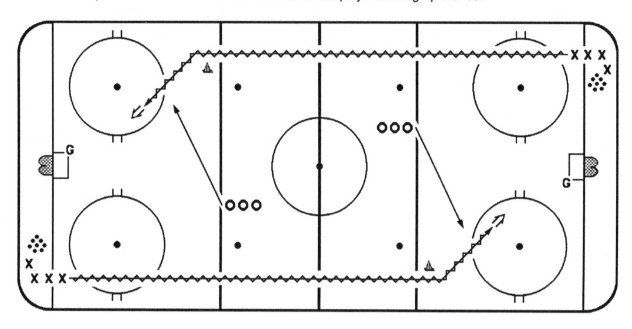

31. Continuous Shooting Drill

The player skates down one side, cuts around the pylon, shoots, goes for the rebound, turns, receives a pass going in the opposite direction, skates down the center of the ice, and shoots. The shooter works the drill from both directions.

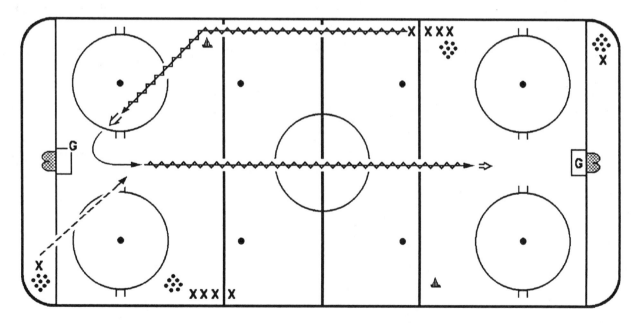

32. Group Shooting Drill

The first player in group 1 skates diagonally across the ice, receives a pass from the first player in group 2, skates around the pylon, and shoots on goal. Group 1 player moves to group 4, and group 2 player moves to group 3. The type of shot can be predetermined. Players work the drill from both directions.

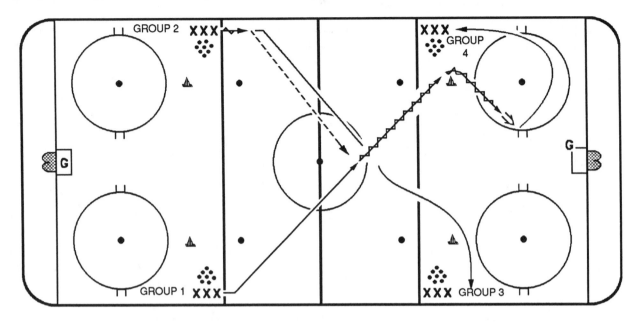

33. Horseshoe Drill

The player passes the puck to a player who has come from the other side of the rink and skated around the center circle. The player receiving the puck goes in for the shot. After passing the puck, the player skates around the circle and receives a pass from the other side. The players return to the same side they started on.

   Variation: Have two men starting together for a two-on-none. Then progress to three men starting at the same time to create a three-on-none.

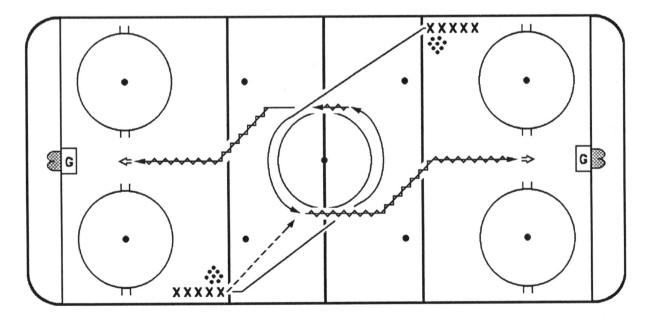

34. Horseshoe Variation

The puck is passed from corner to corner and then passed to the player skating around the center circle from the other end. The player receiving the pass then goes in and shoots. The players rotate, following the puck. After shooting, the player returns to the corner where he started.

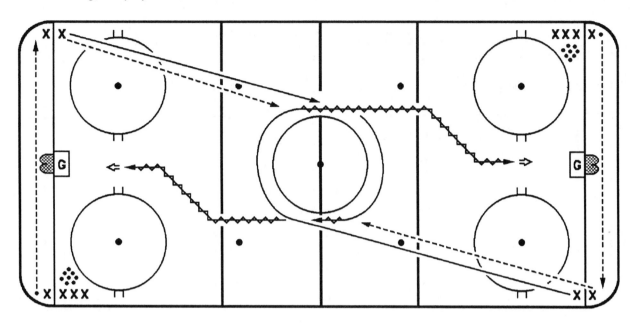

35. Horseshoe Variation

This is a variation of 33. After taking the pass, the player skates backward to the blue line, turns, skates forward, and shoots at the net.

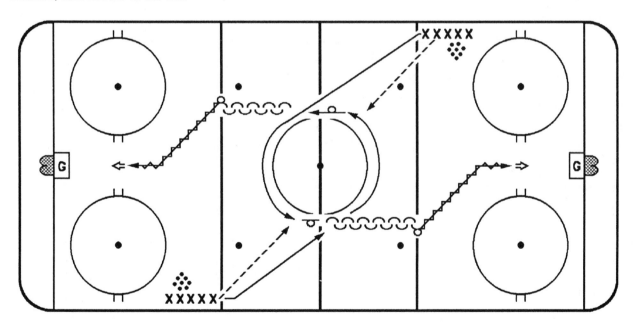

36. Horseshoe Variation

In this variation of 33, the puck is passed from the forward to the defenseman, then from defenseman to defenseman, and back to the forward, who then goes in and shoots on the goal. The forward returns to the same line he started in.

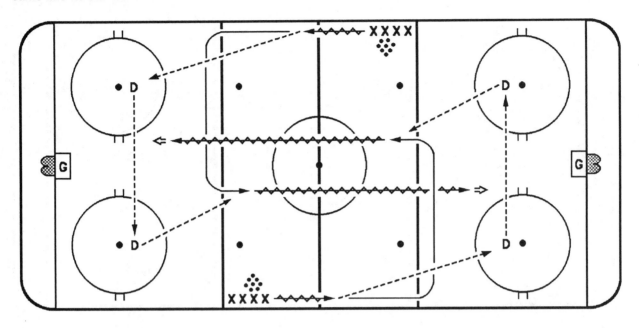

37. Shoot and Pass

The player skates in on the net, takes a pass from the preceding player, picks up a puck in the corner, and passes the puck across to the next shooter. A pylon may be added for the player to skate around before shooting.

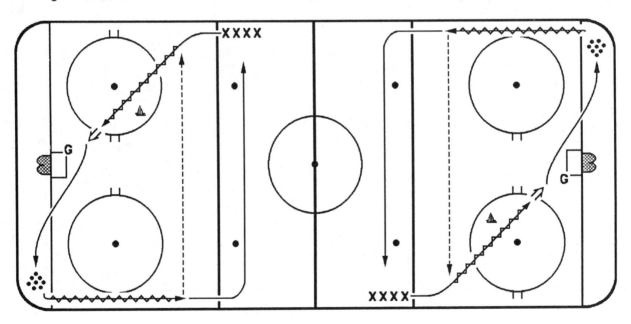

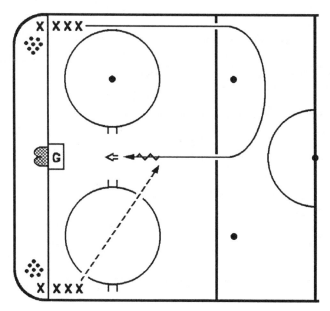

38. Out of the Corners

The player shooting the puck comes out of one corner, cuts in the middle of the ice at the blue line, receives a pass from the opposite corner, and proceeds to shoot on the goaltender. The player passing the puck then becomes the next shooter and receives a pass from a player in the opposite corner.

39. Tip-In Drill

Tip-ins should be executed from a stationary and moving position and from the short or long side. The drill can be run faster by having the defensemen shooting directly from the blue line without receiving a pass out. All shots should be on the ice or low.

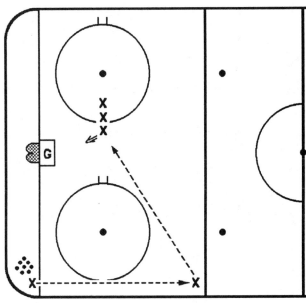

40. Tip-In Variation

Player passes the puck from the far side and moves for the tip-in.

41. Tip-In Drills for Young Players
Much time can be wasted with young players when they attempt to tip in pucks shot inaccurately from the blue line. A variation for tip-in drills can be worked in pairs with one player shooting the puck at the boards and the other player tipping the puck to the boards at certain spots. The shooter should be 15 feet away from the tipper. They should change positions every few shots and tip from both sides.

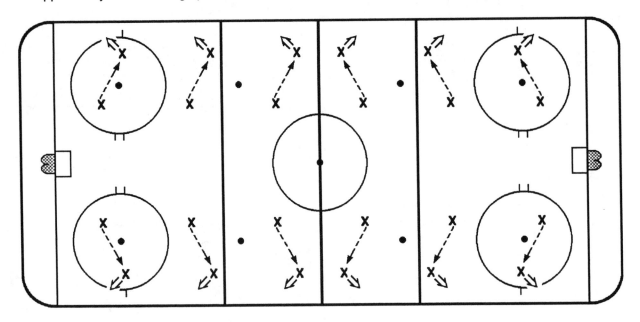

42. Flip Shot Drill from Defensive End
Players skate around the net and flip the shot high in the air down the ice. They should try not to let the puck go over the goal line. This drill may be executed from the backhand and forehand side.

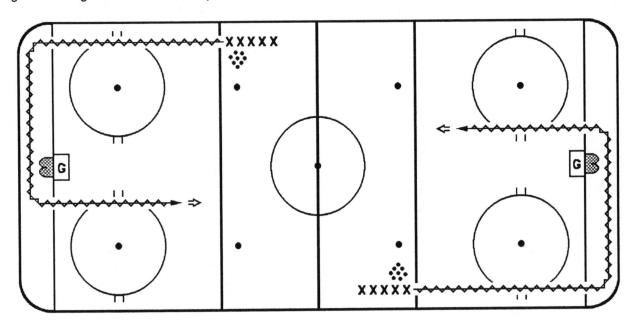

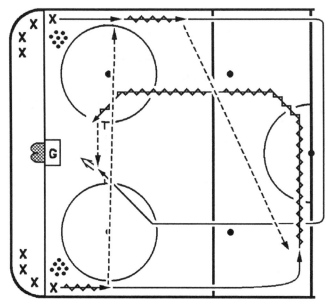

43. Two-on-None from the Corners
Players skate from two corners, pass the puck diagonally across, turn, and work a two-on-none. The players return to the opposite corners.

44. Two-on-None Behind the Net
The puck is passed to the player at the blue line. The forward goes behind the net and receives a return pass for the two-on-none.

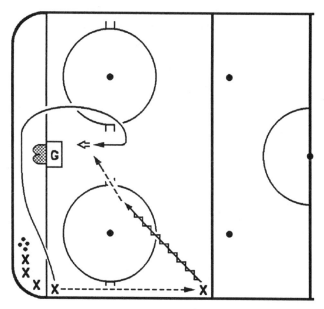

45. Defenseman Breaks to the Net
The defenseman passes the puck to the forward. The forward then skates around the pylon and passes to the breaking defenseman for a shot on goal.

46. Flip Shot Drill for Shooting in the Offensive End

Players skate to center ice and flip the shot into the offensive end toward the goal or in the corner.

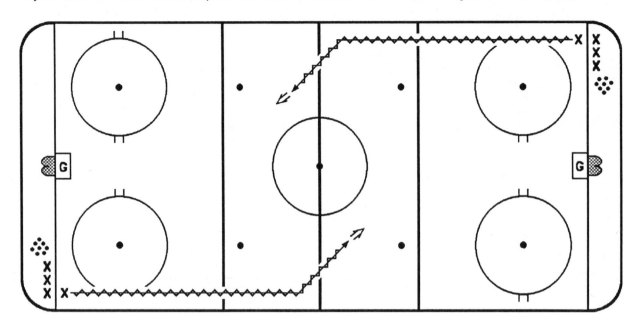

47. Horseshoe Rebound Drill

The first player shoots and goes to the corner. The second player follows for a rebound and then turns and takes a pass. He skates to the other end and shoots. The person giving the pass follows the shooter for the rebound, turns and takes a pass, and skates to the other end and shoots.

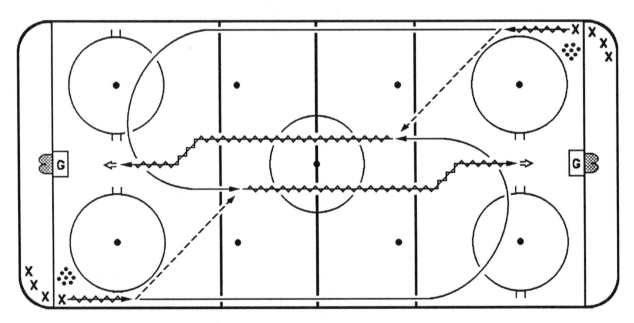

8. STICKHANDLING AND PUCK CONTROL

Stickhandling is important for a one-on-one, for maneuvering at close quarters, or when playing close in on a goaltender. The puck is passed whenever possible, and stickhandling should not be used in open ice or on a breakaway. Players should remember the following points whenever practicing stickhandling and puck control:

- Keep your head up. Your peripheral vision allows you to keep the puck in view.
- Cup the puck in the center of the blade, cushioning it while you stickhandle. Be sure to roll your wrists.
- Slide the blade of the stick along the ice but do not bang it. There should be little or no noise created by the stick's hitting the ice.
- Try not to shift your lower hand down, as it will tip off the opposition that you are about to change to a shooting position.

BASIC STICKHANDLING TECHNIQUES

SIDE-TO-SIDE STICKHANDLING
Stickhandling should be done with the puck in front of the body. The puck should be moved from side to side, from forehand to backhand. The skater's weight is over the top of the puck. That is, if the puck is off to his right, then his body weight should be to the right. The same goes for the other side.

BACK-TO-FRONT STICKHANDLING
This is the same as side-to-side stickhandling except that the puck is moved off to the side of the body.

BACKWARD STICKHANDLING
This is the same as side-to-side and back-to-front stickhandling except the skater is skating backward. The puck must be drawn toward the body in the side-to-side action, or the player will lose control of it. This is an essential skill for the defensemen. The head must be kept up.

STICKHANDLING WHILE CUTTING IN
The player should keep his feet moving when turning and try to eliminate gliding.

DRILLS FOR STATIONARY AND MOVING STICKHANDLING
1. Stationary Stickhandling
Direct the team into three lines, each ten feet apart. Have the players watch the coach's hand. If his arm is straight up, they stickhandle in front. If his arm is to one side, they stickhandle to that side.

2. Stickhandling While Moving
Divide the players into three lines, each ten feet apart. Have them stickhandle down the ice at half speed. This is a puck control drill, and skating speed is not essential.

3. Stickhandling While Stationary and Moving
Players start stickhandling while stationary, and then they move on the instructor's command at half speed. They stop on command and continue stickhandling in a stationary position. Then they repeat these movements for the length of the ice.

4. Stickhandling Around the Rink
Players skate around the rink in one direction outside the pylons. They change direction halfway through the drill.

5. Stickhandle and Breakaway
Players stickhandle to the red line and then push the puck to the goal line, eliminating stickhandling in open ice.

6. Stickhandling in Both Directions
Two groups skate in opposite directions. The players must keep their heads up to avoid collisions.

7. Stickhandling in All Directions
All the players have pucks and stickhandle in all directions. You may divide them into three groups, divide the ice into three areas, and have each group keep the puck in a separate area.

8. Backward Stickhandling
Players perform drills 1 through 7 while stickhandling backward.

9. Forward-Backward Stickhandling
Players skate forward while stickhandling and then stop and stickhandle while stationary. Then they skate backward while stickhandling. Use a whistle or a verbal command to signal them to change direction. This drill can be done in lines across the ice or while the whole group is skating around the ice.

10. Forward-Backward Stickhandling
Players stickhandle forward to the red line, backward to the blue line, forward to the far blue line, backward to the red line, and forward to the end of the rink.

11. Stickhandling Changing Direction
Set pylons in a straight line, with four pylons in each of four lines. Players skate through the pylons, first without and then with the pucks.

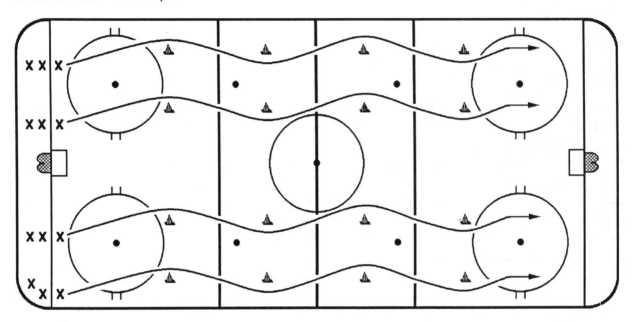

12. Stickhandling Changing Direction Variation
In this variation of 11, the player stickhandles forward to the first pylon and then stickhandles backward to the second pylon, and so on. Have each player execute the drill without a puck first.

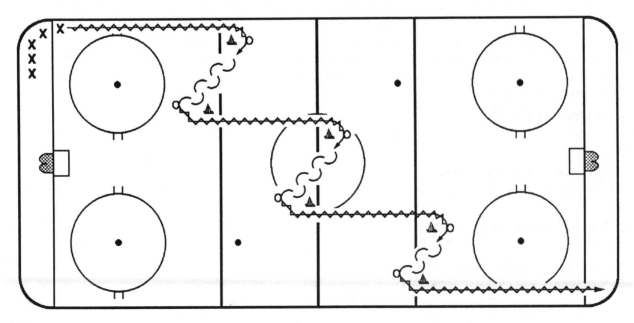

STICKHANDLING AROUND A PLAYER

It is important that a player knows when to stickhandle and when to pass to beat a player. Many plays are broken up by the defending team when a player attempts to stickhandle around another player instead of passing.

Generally, a player should attempt to stickhandle around a man when he does not have a teammate in a position for a pass, when the player is in close quarters and a pass cannot be made, or in a one-on-one situation with no trailing teammate. A cardinal sin in hockey is for a player to attempt to stickhandle around an opposition player in his own end of the rink or if he is the last man. He must ascertain the defender's speed and direction and whether he is sweeping his stick, looking down at the puck, off balance, or reaching slowly, as all of these positions can be taken advantage of. Discourage players from using the same move all the time (e.g., going to backhand side). Encourage them to analyze the situation and make an appropriate move. A discussion of moves for this situation follows.

FOREHAND SHIFT

The puck is shifted to the forehand side. The arms are fully extended, and the puck is brought out slightly back and away from the defender. The body is used as much as possible to protect the puck. The head is kept up. Speed is important in this move. As the skill is learned, the player should set up the move with a slight move to the backhand and/or a head-and-shoulders fake to the backhand side. As an advanced skill, the player's lower hand can hold the stick while the upper hand is used to ward off the defender.

BACKHAND SHIFT

The puck is shifted to the backhand side. The arms are extended. The body can be used to protect the puck. The head is up. The move can be set up with a fake to the forehand side.

SLIP THROUGH

The puck is pushed forward between the defender's stick and skates or between the skates. The defender should have slowed down, the stickhandler's head should be down, and a large space should be between his legs or between his stick and skates.

SLIP ACROSS

In the slip across, as opposed to the slip through, the puck travels across the forward direction instead of straight ahead. The player sets this move up by shifting to one side to get the defender to shift weight on that side. The puck is slipped across between the defender's skates and the heel of the stick. The player shifts directions and picks up the puck on the other side of the defender.

DOUBLE SLIP ACROSS

This is an advanced skill. It works the same as the slip across except the puck is slipped across a second time and ends up on the same side as the original shift.

FAKE SHOT

This shot involves a shift to backhand or forehand. An initial slap or wrist shot motion is executed. A shoulder drop or lower hand side is beneficial. The puck is then shifted to the forehand or backhand side. This move is especially useful when the defender has slowed down or stopped in his defensive zone.

SPIN AROUND (DELAY)

The player stops quickly, close to the defender. The puck is kept away from the defender on the forehand side. The player spins 180 degrees with the puck on the backhand and accelerates forward quickly or passes.

PUCK OFF BOARDS

This is used to advantage when the player is moving out of his own end and a defender, usually a defenseman, is standing still. The puck should be shot off the boards at approximately 45 degrees and at only moderate speed (the puck will come off the boards at the same angle it hits the boards: angle of incidence equals angle of reflection). The player skates around the defender on the off-board side and picks up the puck.

CHANGE OF PACE

The player skates under control at three-quarter speed. Just as he reaches the defender, the player accelerates. This move is especially useful when a defenseman is skating backward slowly and there is room for the player to move on either side.

DRILLS FOR STICKHANDLING AROUND A DEFENDER (ONE-ON-ONE)
1. Across the Ice Against a Stationary Object
First have the player practice the stickhandling move against a pylon. Next have the player practice stickhandling against a stationary player without a stick and then against one with a stick.

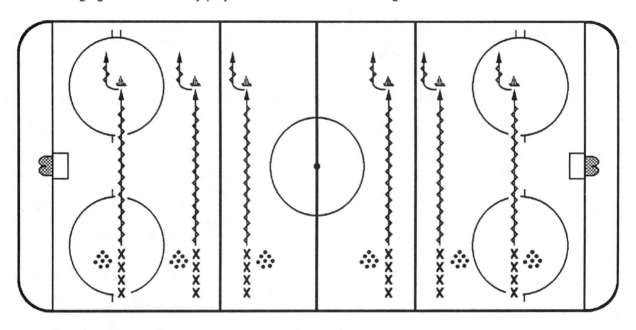

2. Across the Ice in Pairs
One player acts as an attacker and the other acts as a defender. They change positions coming back across the ice. Have them execute the drill at half speed and passively at first. This allows the player to beat the defender with a move. Then have them execute the drill at full speed. If you have a large number, divide pairs into two groups, and have one group move across the ice with the other group following.

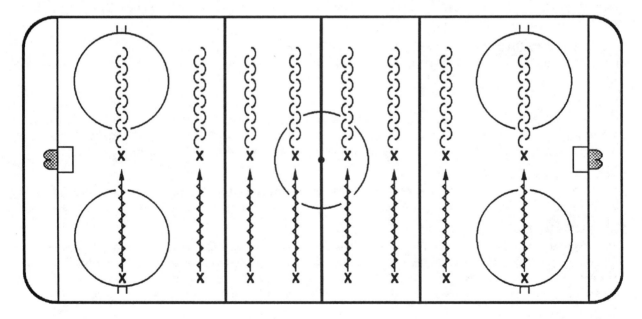

3. Both Directions

The defender is with the puck on the blue line. The offensive man is at the top of the face-off circle. The defender passes the puck to the offensive player, and the one-on-one begins. They change positions moving back in the opposite direction, with the forward acting as a defenseman and vice versa.

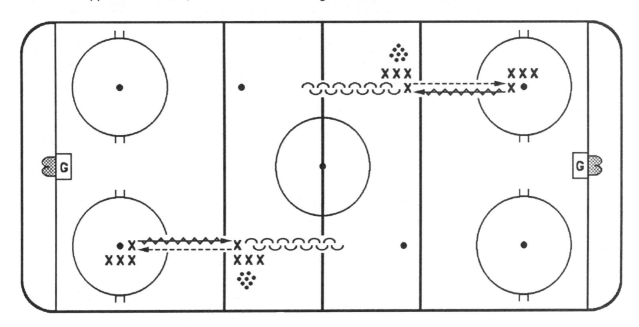

PUCK CONTROL USING THE SKATES

Controlling the puck with the skates is difficult and requires long hours of practice. Russians and other European players are highly skilled in this area and make use of soccer for carryover application of this skill. Soccer, ball hockey, lacrosse, etc., are all helpful for stickhandling and puck control. Kicking a ball on the ground is also helpful. The Europeans make great use of off-ice drills and games to develop these skills.

BETWEEN SKATES
The puck is passed from one skate to another, with the player always kicking the puck in a forward direction.

SKATE TO STICK
The puck is kicked ahead to the stick. This is practiced with both skates.

STICK TO SKATE TO STICK
The puck (in front of the body) is passed directly back to the skates and returned to the stick from the skates.

OVERSKATE THE PUCK
The player deliberately overskates the puck. He brings one skate behind the other and kicks the puck up to the other skate. This is practiced with both skates.

STICK TO BACK SKATE TO STICK
The puck is drawn back and to the side of the body and then passed back to the back skate. The puck is kicked up as in overskating the puck.

DRILLS FOR PUCK CONTROL USING SKATES
1. Slow Speed
Players skate around the ice at slow speed practicing various skills.

2. High Speed
Players skate around the ice at high speed practicing various skills.

3. Length of the Ice
Players skate the length of the ice practicing skills.

4. Skate Around the Pylons
Players skate around the pylons using only the skates to control the puck.

5. Three Groups

Divide players into three groups and divide the ice into three sections. Have three games in which the players do not use sticks. A team scores by holding the puck against the opposite side boards.

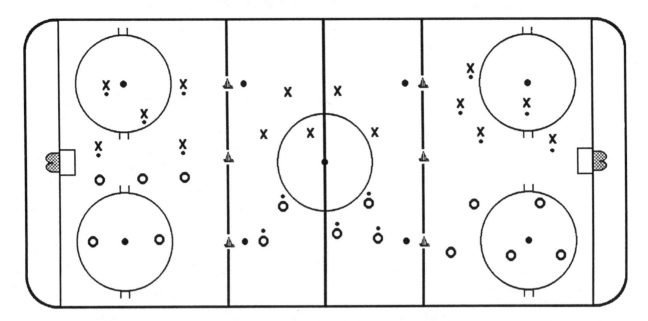

DEKING THE GOALTENDER

When a player breaks in alone on a goaltender, he must decide whether to deke the goaltender or shoot. When the goaltender is far out in the crease is an ideal time to deke the goaltender. Remind each player not to telegraph his moves by dropping his head or shoulder or slipping his lower hand down the shaft to indicate a shot. He must make his move quickly. Discuss the following types of dekes on the goaltender with players.

BACKHAND SHIFT
This was described previously. The puck is moved completely around the goaltender.

FOREHAND SHIFT
This was also described previously. The puck is moved completely around the goaltender.

HALF BACKHAND SHIFT
The puck is shifted to the backhand side and then slipped between the goaltender's legs.

HALF FOREHAND SHIFT
The puck is shifted to forehand side and then slipped between the goaltender's legs.

BACKHAND-FOREHAND SHIFT
The puck is moved to the player's backhand side and then quickly moved to his forehand side. This maneuver is effective when the goaltender moves with the first shift.

FOREHAND-BACKHAND SHIFT
This deke is the opposite of the backhand-forehand shift.

BACKHAND DRAG
The player approaches the goaltender on his backhand side at a sharp angle. The player starts to cut across the front of the net. The puck is dragged behind with the player's top hand only on the stick. The puck is slipped in on the short side by the post.

FAKE SHOT AND SHIFT
The player fakes the shot to one side by dipping his shoulder. The player should shift to the other side when the goaltender makes a move.

DEKING DRILL
Breakaway Drill
Line up players in three lines and have them break in on the goaltender. Have the players switch lines as they come back.

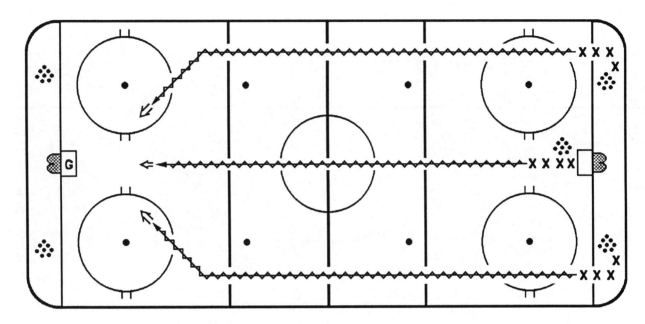

In all body checking it is important that the head be kept up.
Agility and balance are essential to effective checking.

9. CHECKING

Checking is a very important aspect of hockey, and in many cases it is neglected in practice sessions. Play-off hockey puts stress on checking, but the checking skills should be used in every game.

STICK CHECKING

In all stick checking, the checker should watch the man, not the puck.

POKE CHECK

The poke check is often used in one-on-one situations or with forechecking forwards. The elbow of the arm holding the stick is bent and close to the side. The head is up and one hand is on the stick. This move must be used when the opponent is in close range. The arm holding the stick extends quickly. The body is kept in a stable position and there is no lunging at the opponent. The arm and blade of the stick do the checking. The stick is held in until the opponent is in close range.

STICK LIFT

The player approaches the puck carrier from behind and to the side of the puck. He lifts the opponent's stick at the shaft near the heel of the stick. He takes possession of the puck.

STICK PRESS

The stick is pressed down over the opponent's stick or lower arm. The approach is the same as the stick lift. Upper body strength is also important in this move.

SWEEP CHECK

The checker approaches the puck carrier from the front in a semicrouched position. The stick is swept in a flat position to knock the puck from the offensive player's stick. The head is kept up in anticipation of a body check that may result if the sweep check fails.

HOOK CHECK

The hook check should be used only when the puck carrier cannot be fully overtaken. The player approaches the puck carrier from behind with one hand on the stick. He goes down on the inside knee, extending the arm holding the stick after obtaining the puck. The weight is on the other skate so a quick pivot can be made. The blade of the stick is turned flat on the ice toward the puck, and the puck is hooked back. He regains balance, gets up off his knee, and resumes skating stride.

DIVING POKE CHECK

This check is used as a last resort, when the offensive player is in a breakaway situation. The player skates as close behind the player as possible. He keeps inside of the puck carrier and approaches from an angle. The player leaves his feet in a diving motion when the offensive player reaches 30 to 40 feet from the net. He extends his arms and puts the stick flat on the ice. He aims the stick and his body at or ahead of the offensive player's stick and attempts to knock the puck away. The player should not knock the opponent's feet away, as this could cause a tripping penalty and/or penalty shot.

BODY CHECKING

It is important in all body checking that the head is up and the eyes are on the opponent's chest area, not on the puck. A player's getting the proper handle and speed when checking an opponent will allow him to take an opponent out of the play regardless of size. Agility and balance, including lateral and backward skating ability, are essential in good checking.

SHOULDER CHECK

A player should be able to use either shoulder. The point of the shoulder hits the opponent's chest. Knees are bent and extend on contact. The skates are turned outward and dig in a shoulders' width apart. The drive is off the back leg. One hand is on the stick with the other flexed to the side. The hand is close to the body to prevent injury. The push is up and through on contact. The head up, and the player should not commit too early. The player should watch for an opponent with his head down; this is a good time for the shoulder check.

RIDING THE MAN OUT OF THE PLAY

This check is used mainly along the boards. The checker stays between the offensive man and the goal and is even with or slightly ahead of the man. Body contact is made with the side of the upper body and hips. If possible, the inside arm is extended across the body of the offensive man. The players cuts the offensive man off and angles him toward the boards. He rides the man off and goes for the puck.

HIP CHECK

This check is used mainly by defensemen along the boards. When mastered, it is an effective mid-ice check. The check is started by the player's skating backward, usually with one hand on the stick. He pivots and pushes off the far side foot and moves into a low crouch position. He swings his hips at a 90-degree angle and drives sideways into the puck carrier. Timing is extremely important in this skill.

BACKCHECKING

Backchecking is an essential skill for all forwards. It assists the defensemen by allowing them to stay up and force the play. The backchecker should stay at least one stride ahead of the offensive man and within a stick's length away. The man, as well as the puck, should be watched using peripheral vision. The checker should not let the offensive player get ahead of him. As the man moves closer to the goal, the checker moves tight with the opponent's forward progress. He always stays in the lane; he should not chase a puck carrier into the center area and leave his check, as the defensemen will pick up the center area.

FORECHECKING

Forechecking (one-on-one) is an important defensive skill and can also become an offensive skill if possession of the puck is gained in a scoring position. The forechecker must always keep his head up and play the man, then go for the puck. The stick may be held in one hand in order to poke the puck away. The man should be angled toward the boards and his skating space cut off. The player should not approach the offensive man straight on or chase the man behind the net unless he is very close to him. Agility is important. A good forechecker can stop quickly, change direction, pivot, skate backward, sweep, and poke check effectively.

TAKING A CHECK

It is important that all hockey players be able to take a body check to prevent injury or to recover quickly to get back into the play. When an opponent is moving toward a player to body check, the player taking the check can tense his muscles and gain momentum by moving toward him. As momentum equals mass times velocity, the smaller the player, the more important speed is in head-on contact. It is important to spread the body check force over a large area against the boards. Consequently, the whole body should be against the boards, and the body should give on contact and spring off the boards from the check. A player should keep in a semicrouch position and should not use the hand or wrist to cushion a blow. He must learn to fall properly, quickly regain his feet, and start skating again.

CHECKING DRILLS

1. One-on-One Drill Moving Across the Ice

Players practice using the various types of stick and body checks. They work at half speed passively and then work at full speed, using the full length of the ice.

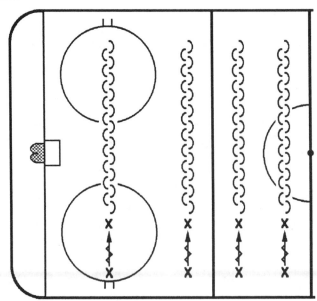

2. One-on-One Drill Using the Length of the Ice

This drill is the same as 1 except in this drill there is no more space in which to maneuver. Players switch from offense to defense.

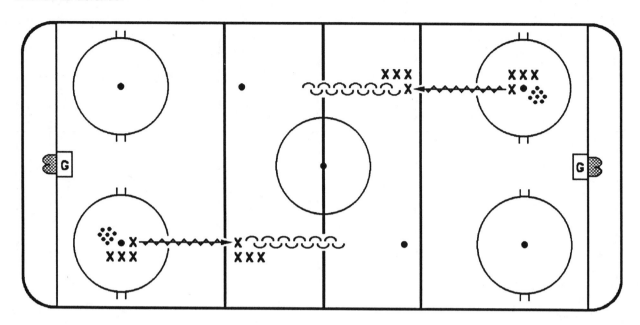

3. One-on-One Swing Drill

The forward skates to the far blue line, turns, and receives a pass from the opposite side. The defenseman skates forward around the center circle and turns backward. The forward goes one-on-one against that defenseman. The player who passes the puck then goes around the center circle and turns backward. The forward starting beside him skates inside the far blue line and takes a pass from the defenseman.

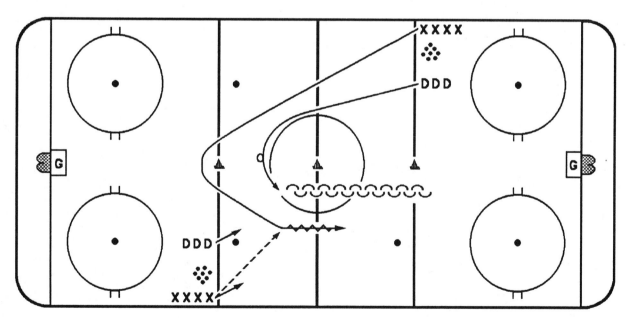

4. Checking the Player Stopped Behind the Net

The puck carrier carries the puck behind the net and stops. The checker stops in front of the net. The puck carrier then moves to either side, and the checker moves with him. The puck carriers then become the checkers, and the checkers become the puck carriers.

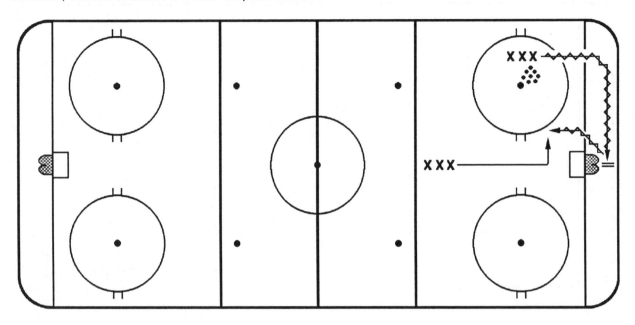

5. Checking the Player Moving Behind the Net

This drill is the same as 4 except in this drill the puck carrier does not stop behind the net but moves out the far side. The checker moves in at an angle and attempts to force the puck carrier to the corner.

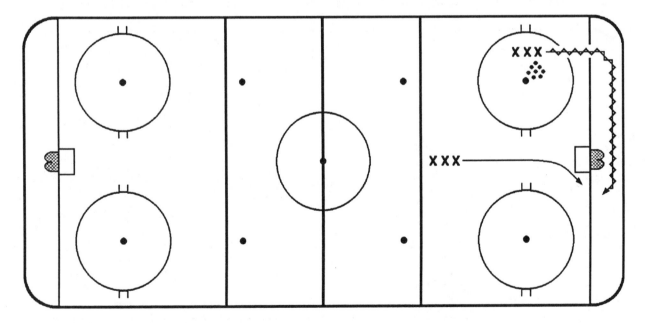

6. Backchecking

On a command, the player starts down the boards with the checker starting slightly behind. The player receives a pass from a center, cuts around the pylon, and moves in on the goaltender. The checker stays on the inside of the pylon and attempts to check the offensive player. The drill is worked in both directions.

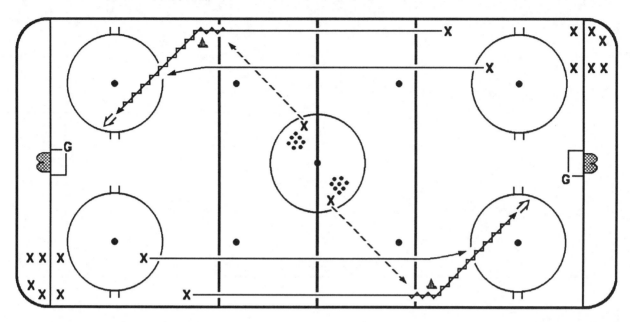

7. Chase the Rabbit

The puck carrier says "go," skates to the outside of the pylon the length of the ice, and shoots, with the checker starting two steps behind him and to the inside of the pylon.

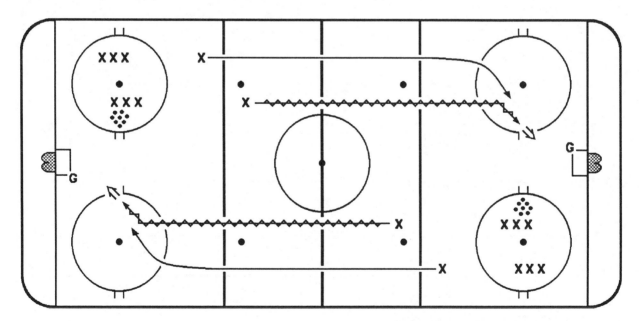

8. Body Checking
Players work in pairs around the boards taking and giving body checks.

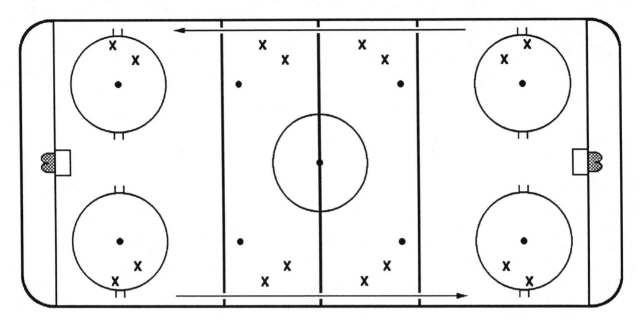

9. Falling Drill
Players practice falling front rolls, falling side rolls, falling to one knee, and recovering the skating stride. Have them do a different maneuver between each set of lines.

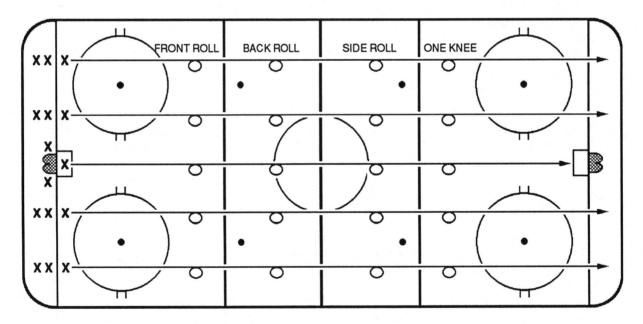

10. Diving Poke Check Drill (not shown)
Players practice leaving the feet and diving at an angle at a puck carrier in the clear who is cutting in from the boards.

10. OFFENSIVE TEAM PLAY

Offensive play begins when a team gains possession of the puck in its own end. Offensive play can be divided into three categories:

1. moving the puck out of the defensive zone (breakout)
2. moving through the neutral zone
3. playing in the offensive zone (attack)

MOVING THE PUCK OUT OF THE DEFENSIVE ZONE

The following drills demonstrate standard methods of moving the puck from the defensive zone when the puck is shot in by the opposition or when possession is gained by the defensive team, usually by the defensemen.

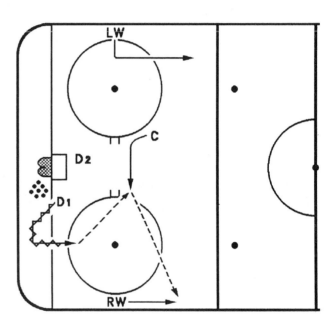

DEFENSIVE ZONE DRILLS
1. Quick Turn
The defenseman turns quickly with the puck. D1 can pass to the center or to the right wing or carry the puck himself. If D1 passes to the center, the center then makes a quick pass to the winger. The wingers move as soon as the defenseman turns with the puck and the center cuts across in position for a pass.

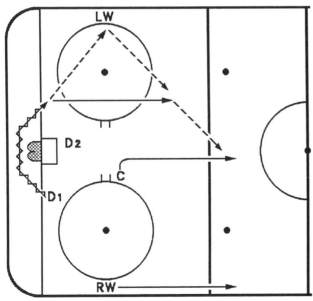

2. Behind the Net Without Stopping
The defenseman skates behind the net without stopping. D1 passes to the winger, who in turn passes the puck to the center, who has curled and is starting to break up ice.

91

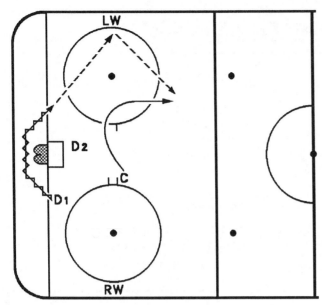

3. Give-and-Go

In this variation of 2, the defenseman skates behind the net without stopping. D1 passes to the winger, who returns the pass to the defenseman on a give-and-go. The center cuts straight up the middle of the ice. The winger takes the position of the defenseman after he returns the pass.

4. Pass to Winger

The defenseman stops behind the net. D1 passes to the winger. The winger passes to the center. D2 stations himself in front of the net.

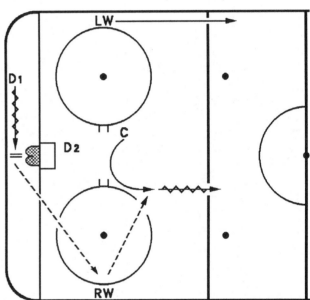

5. Pass to Center

This is a variation of 4 in which D1 passes to the center. The center passes to the winger. D2 is in front of the net.

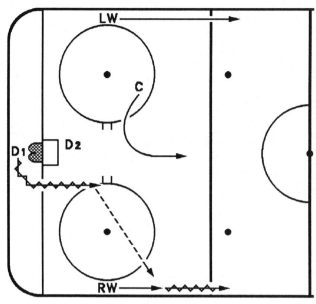

6. Defenseman Carries the Puck
This is another variation of 4, in which D1 carries the puck and passes it to the winger or the center. D2 trails the play.

7. Defenseman in the Corner
D2 moves to the corner when D1 is in full possession of the puck. The winger moves up the boards. D1 passes to D2. D2 passes to the center. The center passes to the wing.

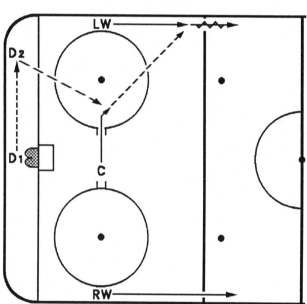

8. Defenseman in the Corner Variation
In this variation of 7, D1 passes to D2. D2 skates with the puck and then passes to the center or the winger.

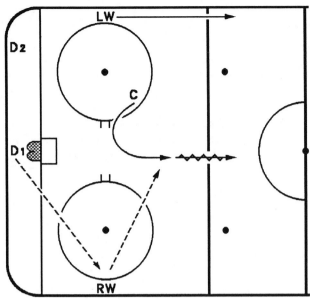

9. Pass to Offside Winger
In this variation of 7, D1 passes to the offside winger, who passes to the center.

10. Defenseman Carries the Puck
In this variation of 7, D1 carries the puck up the center of the ice and then passes to the winger.

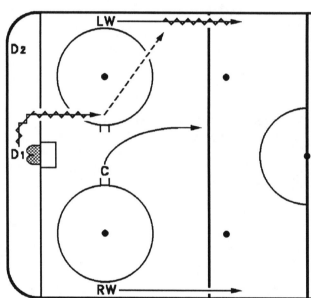

11. Defenseman Behind the Net
In this variation of 7, D1 passes to the winger on the side with the defenseman in the corner. The winger then passes to the center.

94

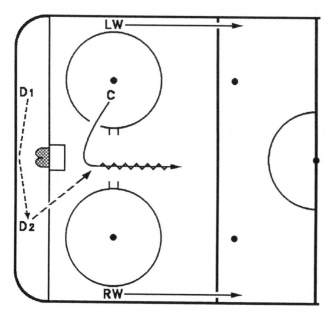

12. Off the Boards to the Center

D1 passes the puck off the boards to D2. D2 passes the puck to the center. The center passes the puck to the winger.

13. Off the Boards to the Winger

In this variation of 12, D1 passes the puck off the boards to D2. D2 passes the puck to the winger. The winger passes the puck to the center.

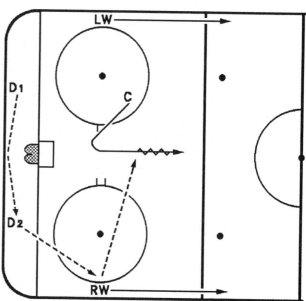

14. Carry and Pass

In this variation of 12, D1 passes the puck off the boards to D2. D2 skates with the puck and then passes to the center or winger.

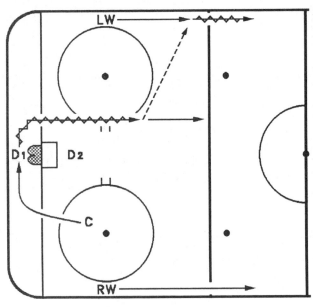

15. Center Behind the Net
D1 stops behind the net. The center comes behind the net and picks up the puck. The center moves up the middle of the ice and passes to the winger.

16. Pass Back
In this variation of 15, D1 stops behind the net. The center swings wide to the corner and drops the puck back to the defensemen. The winger on the puck side pulls off the boards. The center moves up the wing. D1 passes to the winger coming off the boards or passes to the center, or D1 carries the puck.

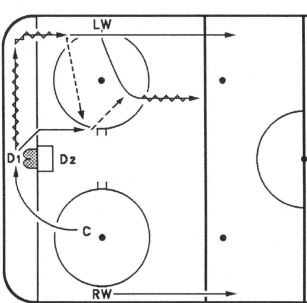

17. Leave the Puck
In this variation of 15, D1 stops behind the net. The center circles behind the net. D1 allows the center to go by but keeps the puck and passes it to either winger. The winger passes to the center.

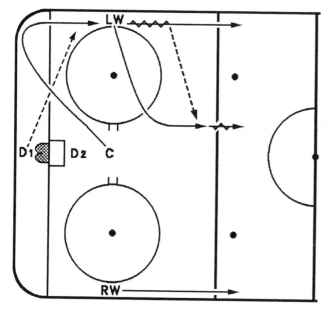

18. Center in the Corner

D1 stops behind the net. The center circles to the corner, and the winger on the puck side cuts across to the middle area of the ice. D1 passes to the center. The center passes to the winger in the middle area of the ice.

19. Winger in the Middle

In this variation of 18, D1 stops behind the net. The center circles to the corner, and the winger on the puck side pulls off the boards to the middle area of the ice. D1 passes to this winger.

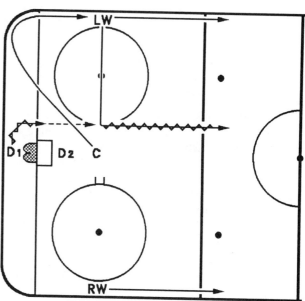

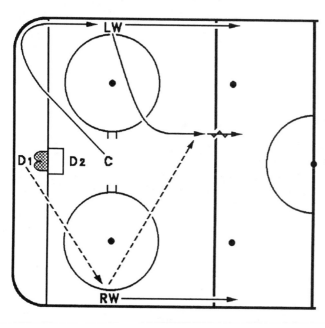

20. Pass to Offside Winger

In this variation of 18, D1 stops behind the net. The center circles to the corner, and the winger on the puck side pulls off the boards and moves to the middle area of the ice. D1 passes to the offside winger, who passes to the other winger.

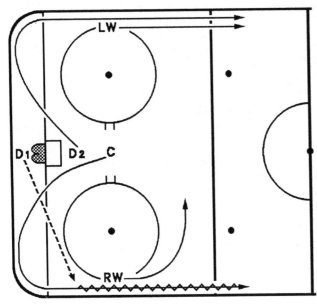

21. Double Swing

D1 stops behind the net. D2 moves to the corner. The center swings to the opposite corner. D1 passes to D2 or the center.

22. Around the Boards

The defenseman shoots the puck around the boards, and the winger picks the puck up on the move. This play is usually used from a face-off or when the puck has been shot directly in the corner and the defenseman is being chased.

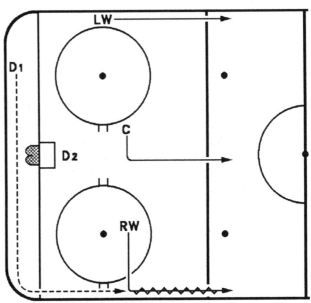

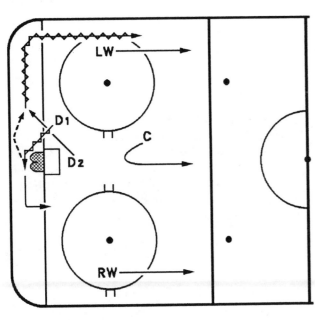

23. Defense Reverse

D1 carries the puck behind the net and is being chased by a forechecker. D1 drops the puck back to D2, who has moved from his position in front of the net. The defenseman in front of the net always calls the reverse.

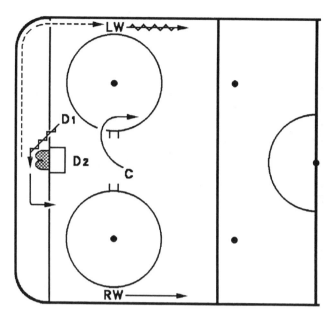

24. Reverse to the Winger

This drill is the same as 23 except the defenseman passes the puck back to the winger, who is stationed at the hash marks. The puck is passed on the ice along the boards. The winger should not be too high up on the boards. He can receive the pass moving or standing still.

25. Center Tight Turn

The center makes a tight turn at the goal line. The defenseman passes the puck to the center.

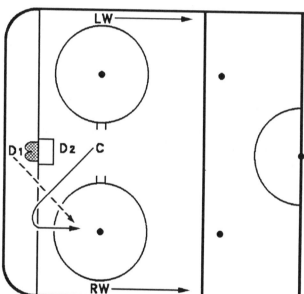

26. Center Tight Turn Variation

This drill is the same as 25 except, instead of passing puck to center, the defenseman moves out from behind the net and passes to the other defenseman. This pass must be made with caution.

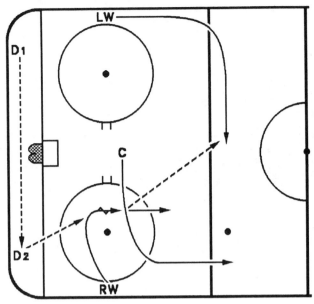

27. Center and Winger Cross
D1 passes to D2. The offside winger goes high and cuts across the middle outside the blue line.

DEFENSE ZONE DRILLS FOR MOVING OUT OF YOUR OWN END
1. Breakouts from a Shoot-In
Line the players up by position at the blue line. The puck is shot in by the center, and the first player in each line moves in to bring the puck out. The coach designates the method of bringing the puck out of the end.

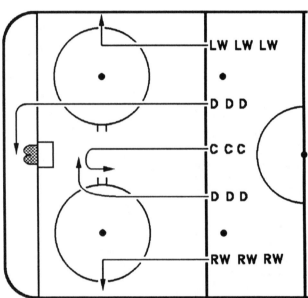

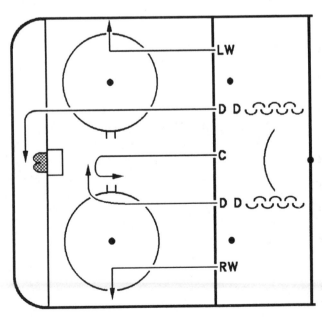

2. Five-on-Two
This drill is the same as 1 except the breakout progresses offensively the length of the ice as a five-on-two. When the offensive play is completed, another breakout starts from the opposite end with another offensive line. The defense pair who start the play follow it down the ice and then act defensively for the next five-on-two from the opposite end.

Variation on the offensive play: Have the forwards pass the puck back to the points if a direct play is not made on the net. The forwards should go to the front of the net to deflect or screen the shot coming from the point.

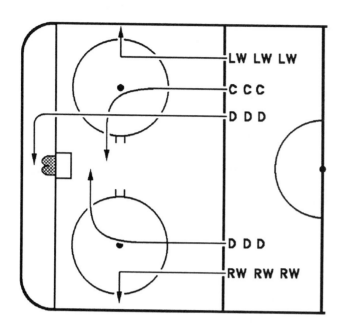

3. Centers on the Boards

The players line up in lines and defense pairs against the boards outside the blue line. The centers line up on the boards with either wing. Lines and defense pairs go in order and the puck is shot into the defensive zone by the coach. The coach states the method of bringing the puck out of the end.

4. One Forechecker

Players execute drills 1 and 3 with one forechecker moving on the puck.

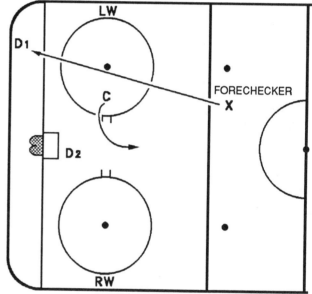

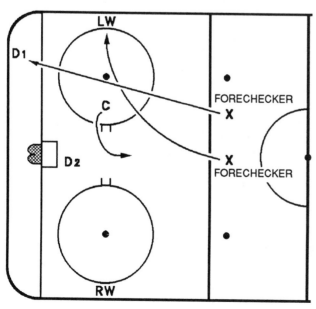

5. Two Forecheckers

Players execute 1 and 3 with two forecheckers moving into the zone.

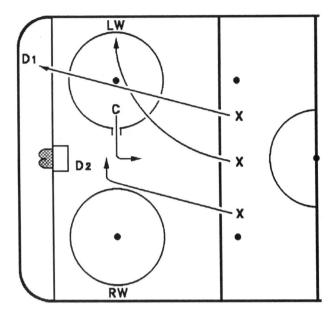

6. Three Forecheckers

Players execute 1 and 3 with a complete forward line forechecking.

7. Five-on-Five

Players work five-on-five drills with one team forechecking and the other team attempting to bring the puck out of their own end. Each team has a forward line and two defensemen. The puck is shot in by the forechecking team from the red line.

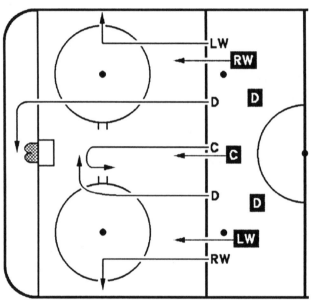

PLAY IN THE NEUTRAL ZONE

Neutral zone regroups have been used extensively by European teams to take full advantage of their wide ice surface. More recently, North American teams have adopted this system of play.

The Russians were probably the first to make use of the neutral zone by devising special plays for that area. Now, it's a major part of the game for all European teams and successful North American teams.

The neutral zone regroup is used offensively when a team is unable to penetrate the opposition's blue line. Instead of shooting the puck in, the offensive team keeps possession by turning back, passing the puck to the defense, and regrouping to attack the opposition's blue line again.

After passing back to their defense, the three forwards swing back up ice, going for open space, and gaining speed for another attack.

Players have to learn to switch with their linemates so they don't all end up in one part of the ice, leaving one or more lanes wide open. They have to find the right timing so that they swing and regroup as a unit and are ready for a quick, simultaneous attack from a good position.

It's an organized system rather than a chaotic, every-man-for-himself scramble across the ice. Once mastered, it can be used by almost any team, provided the defensemen are fairly adept at handling the puck and passing well.

These are the principles of the neutral zone regroup:

• The puck is passed back to the defense. The receiver then passes across to his defense partner. They should be positioned so that they are slightly staggered, with one deeper in the defensive zone than his partner.
• As the puck is passed back to the defense, the forwards move to open ice by swinging back toward the defense.
• The forwards must skate under control with their sticks on the ice, getting themselves into position for a pass. They should fill all three lanes of the ice.
• If a forward is not open for a pass and the defense cannot move the puck up immediately, the man in possession should make a return pass to his defense partner. The forwards must then swing back again to be in position to receive a pass.
• Assuming the defense receives the pass back at the defensive blue line, the three forwards should cover the following areas: near the defense, mid-ice, and past mid-ice.
• If no forward is open for a pass, the defensemen should move forward with the puck themselves.

The progressive drills that follow can be used to teach the neutral zone regroup. The objective is to initiate the player to the idea of swinging across the ice from his wing and regrouping with his linemates for an organized attack. This sounds simple enough but may not be a natural move for someone schooled in the straight-line, up-and-down-the-wings approach to hockey. Note that these are progressive teaching drills with no checking involved.

NEUTRAL ZONE DRILLS
1. Horseshoe
Players, including defensemen, line up along the boards. On the whistle, the first man in the line skates down the wing, swings inside the offensive blue line, receives a pass from the first player in the other line, and moves down to the other end for a shot on the goaltender. He then returns to the back of the line from which he started while the first player in the other line takes his turn.

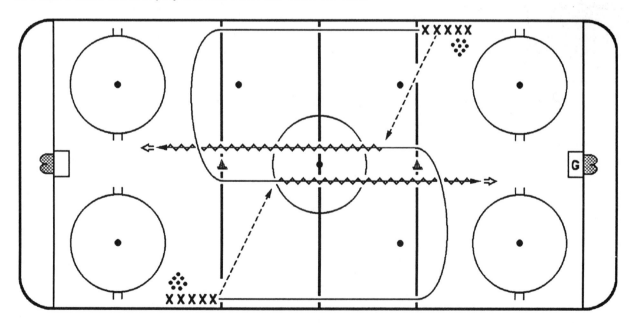

2. Horseshoe with Two Defensemen

The forward passes back to the defense and swings. In this variation of 1, two defensemen are included. They don't check but receive and give passes. They should be staggered with one deeper in the defensive zone than the other. The first forward skates across the blue line and passes the puck to the near defenseman, who then relays it across to his partner. The forward swings either in front or behind the first defenseman and up center ice to take a return pass from the other defenseman. He then goes up for a shot on goal. The drill continues, each side going in turn.

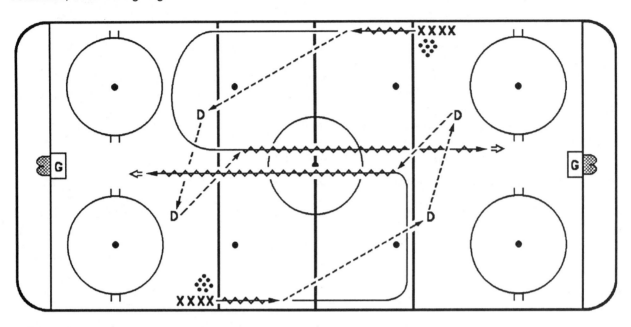

3. Two Forwards Swing from the Same Side

This drill teaches forwards to swing together so they don't interfere with each other. Each must look for open ice rather than bunching together. The first two men come down the wing and swing across, one in front of the defenseman, the other behind. The first forward passes the puck to the defenseman, who then relays it to his partner. The forward takes the return pass and goes up ice with his teammate for a shot on goal. If his teammate goes wide, he should go up the center; if the teammate chooses center, he should swing wide.

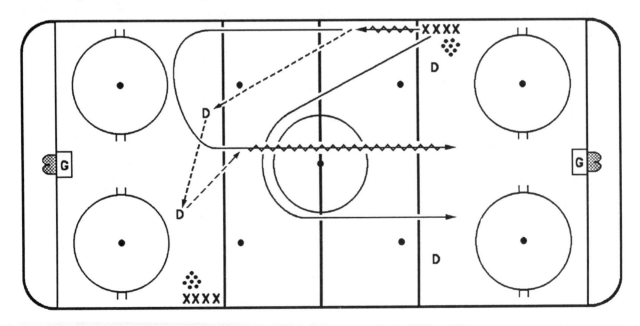

4. Two Forwards Swing from Opposite Sides

In this variation of 3, the two forwards swing from opposite sides of the rink. One swings near the defense or behind it, and the other swings in the center ice area. They alternate.

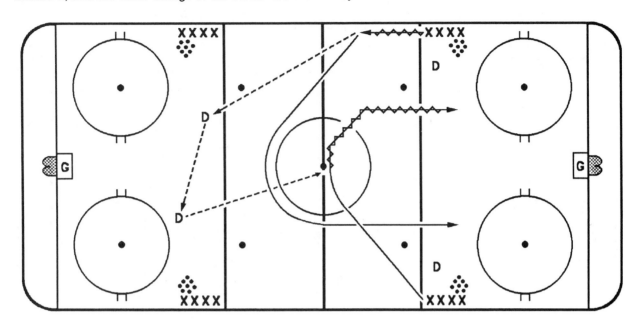

5. Three Forwards Swing

This drill combines 3 and 4 using three forwards, two from one side, one from the other. They should cover the areas near or behind the defense, the center line, and the far blue line alternately.

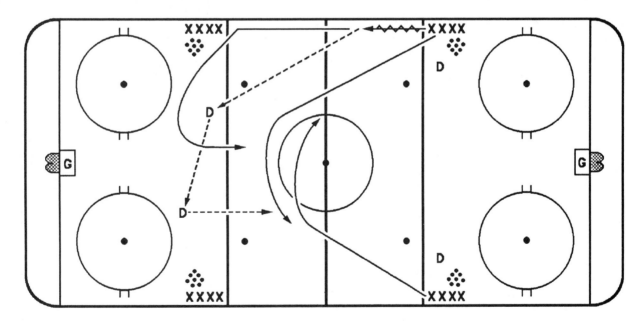

6. Two Regroups

In this drill, the goal is attacked twice. Three forwards start at the blue line, pass the puck to the defense, swing, and receive a return pass. They skate to the far blue line, pass the puck to the defense, regroup, receive a return pass, and attack the goal three-on-none. They then return to the starting point. Forwards should try to find open ice so they're not jamming the same area at the same time.

Remember that depth is a factor. Have players swing so that zones near the defense, mid-ice, and past mid-ice are covered.

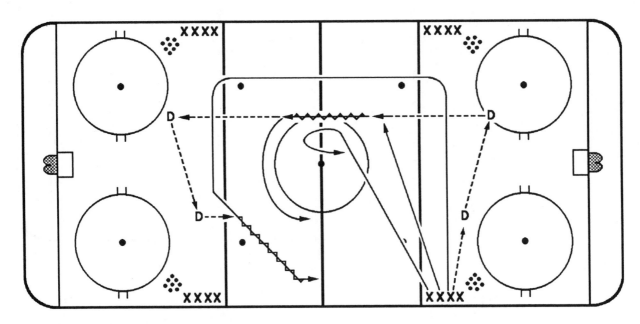

7. Breakout with Neutral Zone Regroups

In this drill there are five players (three forwards and two defensemen) working as a unit. The forwards dump the puck in from outside the blue line. The defense retrieves it, and they all break out, five on two, using whatever system the team has been practicing. The drill continues in 8, on opposite page.

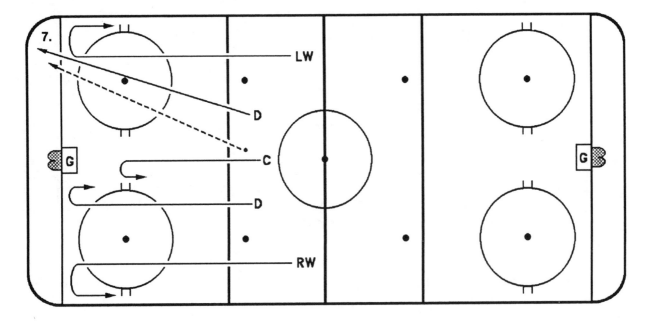

Continued: When the forwards reach the far defense, they pass to them instead of attacking, as in 6, and regroup with that defense pair. This is the first regroup. Meanwhile, the first defense pair has skated back into position for a five-on-two attack by the group that has the puck. When the forwards reach the blue line, they again pass to the defense and regroup. This is the second regroup. The forwards then skate down to attack the goal five-on-two, and the next group starts from the other end.

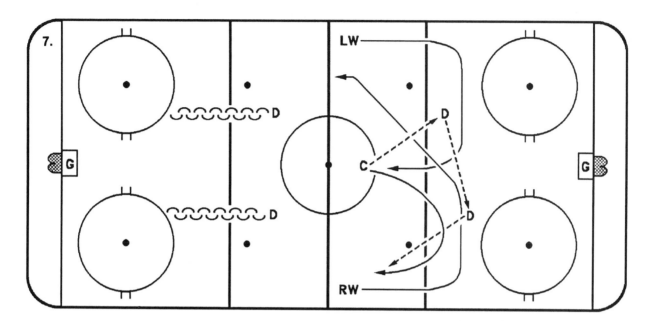

When they have mastered all these drills, set up a scrimmage in which they try to use the neutral zone regroup whenever it is appropriate; that is, when they can't carry or pass the puck across the opponent's blue line. Instead of shooting the puck in, they swing back, regroup, and attack again.

To make sure the neutral zone regroup is done correctly, watch for the following points:

• When players swing, they should skate for open ice. Make sure they fill all three lanes.
• Players should think about what they are doing, be under control, and try to get into position to receive a pass.
• Although the players may swing out of their lanes, the lanes still have to be filled. This means they have to be ready to alternate (e.g., if the center moves over to the wing, that winger should move into the center, and so on).
• During the regroup, players should also cover different depths in the neutral zone, as pointed out earlier (near the defense, mid-ice, past mid-ice). This adds a dimension to the regroup systems and requires each player to read and react quickly to what his linemates are doing.

PLAY FROM THE NEUTRAL ZONE INTO THE OFFENSIVE ZONE

Basic three-on-two plays, those plays made by the offensive team into the offensive zone, are usually made from the neutral zone just as the play approaches the opposition's blue line. The play then continues until there is a scoring opportunity.

The basic concept in offensive team play is that one forward should be driving for the net at all times to create an opening or to draw a defenseman with him. A forward other than the puck carrier and the driving man should trail the play. This is sometimes referred to as the one-two-three principle.

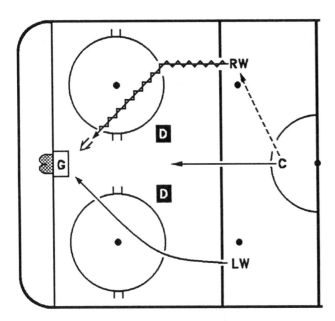

OFFENSIVE ZONE DRILLS
1. Offside Winger to the Net
The center passes to the winger, who cuts around the defenseman and shoots. The offside winger cuts to the far post for a rebound. The center trails the play in the high slot area.

2. Center Trails
The center passes to the winger. The center trails the play slightly to the side of the puck carrier. The winger goes wide to take the defenseman over. The winger passes the puck back to the center, who either shoots or passes to the other winger, who shoots.

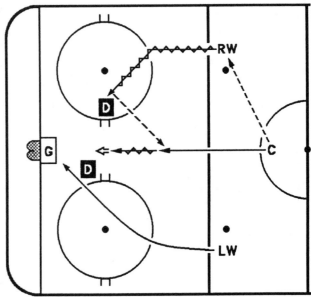

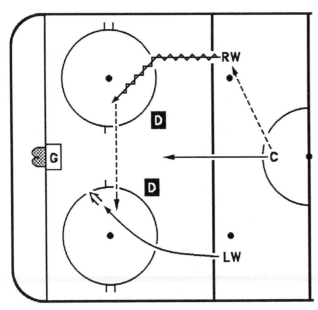

3. Winger to Winger
The center passes to the winger. The winger cuts behind the defenseman and passes across to the opposite winger. The opposite winger shoots. This play works well if the opposition defensemen are well out toward the blue line.

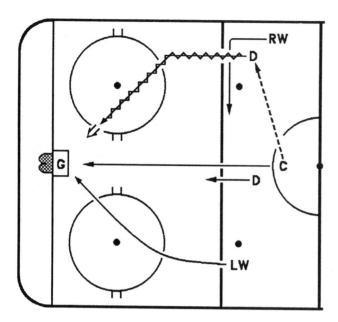

4. Winger Cuts Across

The winger, ahead of the play, skates parallel to the blue line. The defenseman on the winger's side moves quickly up the boards. The center passes to the defenseman. The defenseman cuts in and shoots or drops the puck back to the trailing center, who shoots. The left winger goes to the net for a rebound.

5. Behind the Net

The center passes to the winger, and the winger cuts wide and goes behind the net. The center trails the play and moves to the slot area. The winger passes to the center, who then shoots.

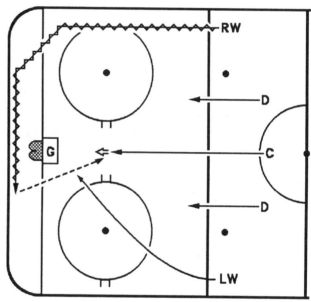

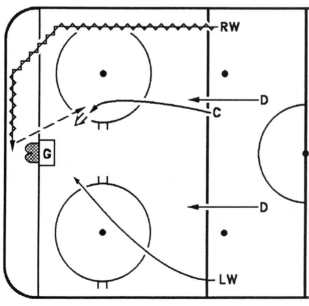

6. Pass Back on Same Side

The winger drives hard behind the net and passes the puck back on the same side. The trailing forward tries to shoot quickly, as the goalie tends to move from the post because he believes the winger is continuing behind the net with the puck.

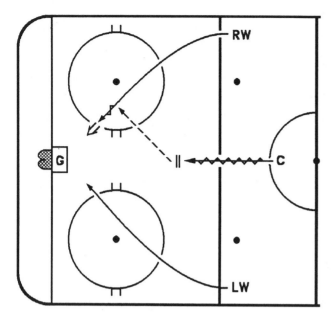

7. Center Stops

The center is slightly ahead of the winger, who cuts wide and goes to the net. The center trails the play and moves to the slot area. The winger passes to the center, who then shoots.

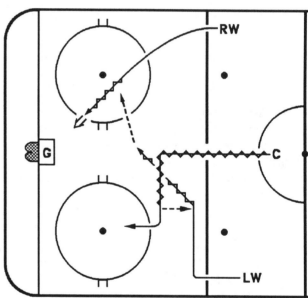

8. Cross-and-Drop Pass

The center is ahead of the wingers when crossing the blue line. The center cuts across to either wing. The winger on that side cuts behind the center. The center drops the puck back to the winger. The winger passes to the offside winger, who is cutting for the net. The offside winger shoots.

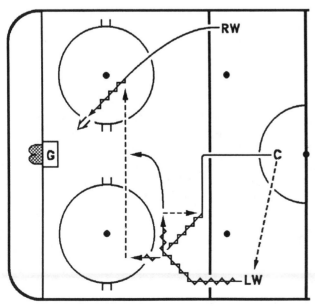

9. Cross and Pass

The winger cuts across over the blue line. The winger takes a pass from the center and cuts toward the middle of the ice in front of the defenseman. The center cuts behind the winger and is in a position to go wide with a return pass. The offside winger may cut wide or cut toward the center of the ice.

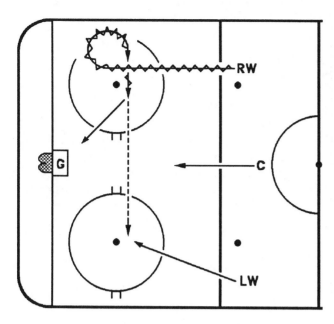

10. Delay
The forward skates hard into the offensive zone and then does a tight turn (delay) and passes off or then drives again for the net.

11. Offensive Triangle
The winger moves into the offensive corner for the puck. The center trails the winger on the boards. The offside winger moves for the slot area.

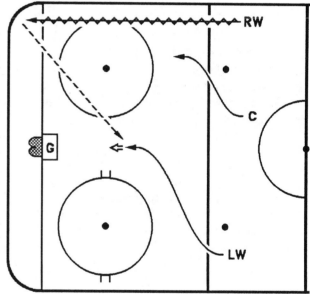

12. Offensive Triangle Variation
In this variation of 6, the winger may pass to the offside winger or to the center. If the center receives the pass, he can shoot or pass to the offside winger who is moving to the net.

The winger and center on the puck side may alternate positions.

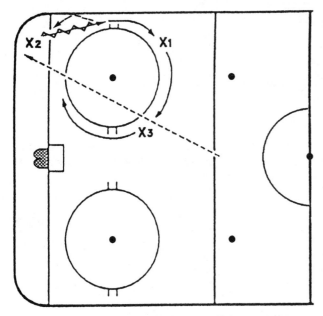

13. Cycling

A forward, X2, carries the puck from the corner and makes a board pass back into the corner as he skates out of the corner. X3 picks up the puck and can repeat the same backboard pass. This offensive play can be used with two or three players.

DRILLS FOR SHOOTING THE PUCK IN
1. Off the End Boards

This play is used when the wingers are covered and a play cannot be made or if one offensive player is breaking quickly and can beat the defenseman to the puck. It is imperative to gain control of the puck after it has been shot into the offensive end.

The center or winger shoots the puck off the end boards. The center and the winger on the puck side go for the rebound off the boards. The offside winger trails the play and moves into the high slot area.

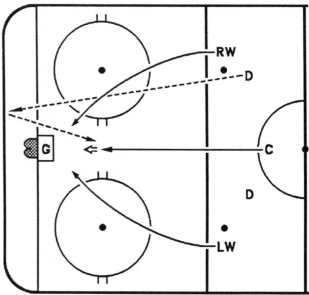

2. Puck Shot in the Corner

The center or winger shoots the puck into the corner at such an angle that the puck will come out in front of the net. The center goes for the slot area. The offside winger cuts to the front of the net.

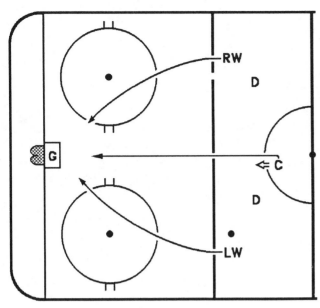

3. Puck Shot at the Net
The center or winger shoots the puck at the goaltender, using preferably a bounce shot, to allow the forwards time to move in. The center moves straight in. The wingers cut in for the goalposts looking for a rebound.

4. Rim the Boards
The forward gets over the offensive blue line near the boards and shoots the puck around the rim of the boards to the far corner. The forward on the far side moves directly to the corner to pick up the puck. The puck should be shot hard and about one foot off the ice to prevent the opposition goaltender from stopping it behind the net.

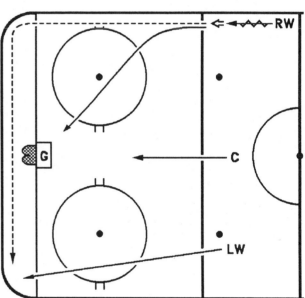

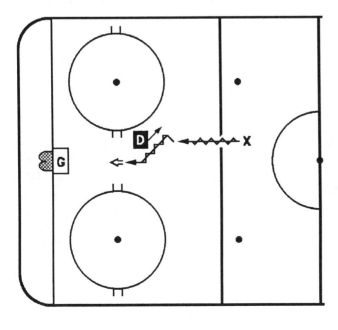

OTHER OFFENSIVE PLAYS
1. One-on-One
The offensive player should attempt to pull the defenseman away from the slot area. Having done this, the offensive player will try to move into the slot area using a shift on the defenseman. He should use the defenseman as a screen and shoot if the defenseman does not move from the slot area.

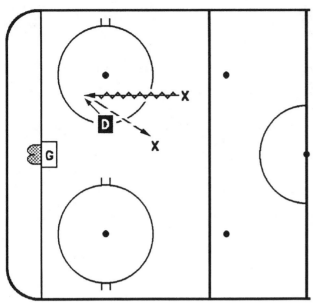

2. Two-on-One Trailer

The offensive player with the puck attempts to draw the defenseman over and away from the slot area. The player with the puck drops the puck back to the other, trailing, offensive player.

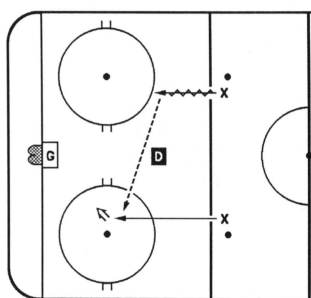

3. Behind the Defenseman

The offensive player with the puck cuts wide. The other offensive player cuts behind the defenseman and receives the pass.

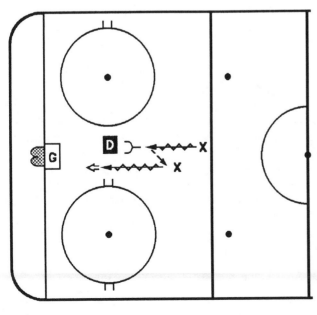

4. Drop Pass

The offensive player with the puck moves directly at the defenseman. The player with the puck drops a pass to the other trailing forward. After dropping the pass, the offensive player takes out (picks) the defenseman long enough for the other forward to skate to the goal.

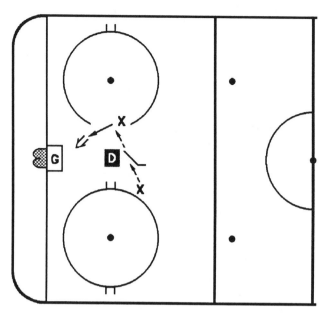

5. Through the Stick
The forwards are abreast with the defenseman between. The forward with the puck passes over the defenseman's stick or between his stick and skates to the other forward.

6. Two-on-One Crossing
The forward with the puck cuts across in front of the defenseman, with the other forward cutting behind him. The pass is usually across, or a drop pass may be used.

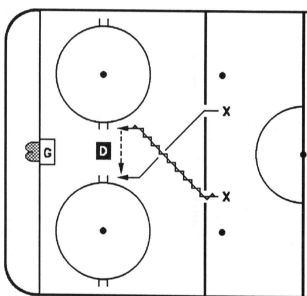

7. Pass Back
Players attempt to isolate one defenseman, making a two-on-one situation. The offensive player with the puck moves wide and draws one defenseman over. The offensive player passes the puck back to the other forward and moves to the net for a rebound.

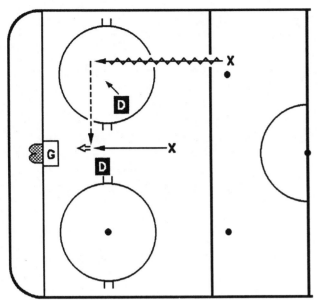

8. Two-on-One to the Net

The offensive player with the puck moves wide and draws the defenseman over. The other forward slips through the defense and receives a pass.

9. Drop Pass

The offensive player with the puck skates directly at the defenseman and then drop passes the puck to the other forward. After the drop pass, the offensive player moves into the defenseman to act as a screen. The forward receiving the drop pass either shoots or goes around the defenseman.

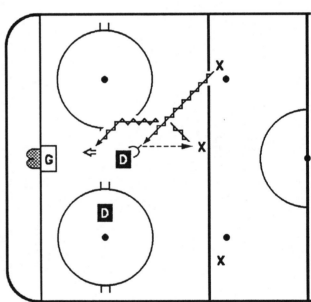

10. Cross-and-Drop Pass

The forwards cross in front of one defenseman, and the pass is dropped with the man receiving the pass cutting to the inside or outside.

DRILLS FOR OFFENSIVE PLAY

1. One-Two-Three Principle—One Player

The player receives a cross-ice pass, drives around the pylon, and takes a shot on goal. After shooting, the player stays at that end on the same side of the rink. Players alternate sides.

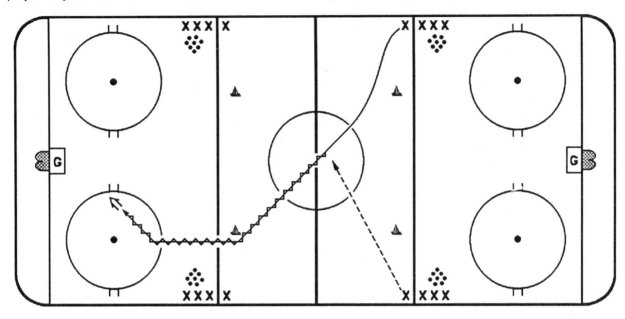

2. One-Two-Three Principle—Two Players

In this variation on 1, two players leave at the same time from the same side. The first player takes a cross-ice pass, drives around the pylon, and takes a shot on goal. The second player drives for the net. Players alternate sides.

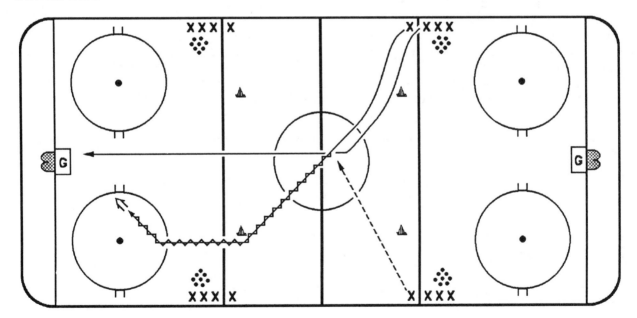

3. One-Two-Three Principle—Three Players

In this variation on 1, the players leave at the same time. The third player cuts around the opposite pylon and trails the play. The second man drives for the net. The puck carrier passes to the trailer.

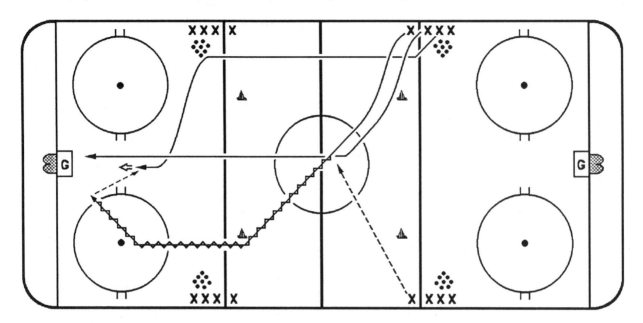

4. One-on-One (not shown)

Drills 1 and 2 on page 39, in chapter 8, "Stickhandling and Puck Control," can be used to drill players on the one-on-one situation.

5. One-on-One from Both Directions

The defenseman skates behind the net, turns up ice, and passes to a forward coming off the boards. Another defenseman stands on the blue line and begins skating backward for a one-on-one. The defenseman passing the puck follows the play up to the far blue line and stops. The drill is repeated from the other end with the defenseman who passed the puck from the one end acting as the defensive man coming in the opposite direction. The defensemen, after passing and working defensively, return to the end of the ice they started at. The forwards take the pass and then work offensively and stay at the opposite end on the opposite side of the boards.

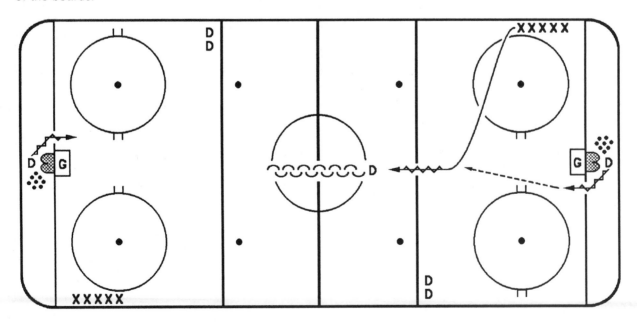

The objective of the forwards is always to drive for the net, to occupy the slot, and to be in a position either to score or to screen the opposition goaltender.

6. Two-on-One Drill

Players work on two-on-one drills in both directions. The defensemen stay on the same side of the ice. The forwards work in both directions. Defensemen work both sides by changing sides halfway through the drill.

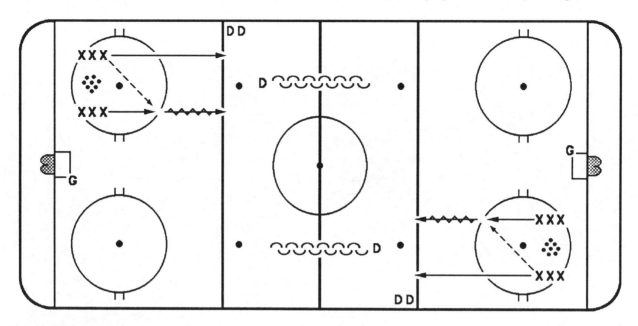

7. Two-on-One Variation

This drill uses the full ice surface. The forwards work from the corners with rink-wide passes. The defensemen work the same end, and the forwards work in both directions. The forwards working in the opposite direction do not start until a play has been completed on the net.

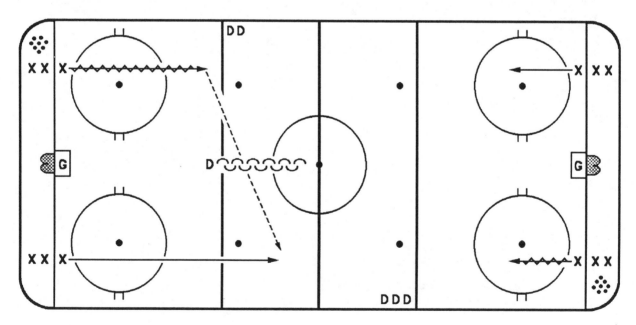

8. Defensemen Behind the Net

In this variation on 7, defensemen at both ends pass the puck to the forward by circling the net. The drill works in both directions.

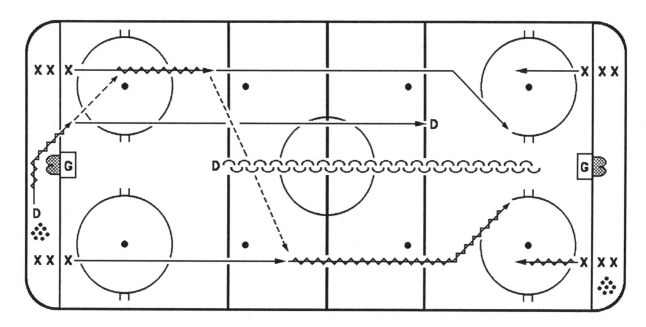

9. One Way

In this two-on-one drill the forwards start from the two corners. The defenseman starts the play by circling the net and passing to either forward. Another defenseman is standing at the blue line and takes the two-on-one.

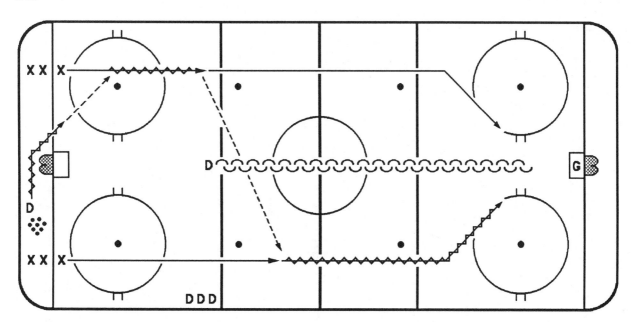

10. Half-Ice in One Direction

This two-on-one drill simulates a three-on-two situation in which a center and one winger are working on one defenseman. The other winger and defenseman are eliminated, but the play is made on only one side of the ice as if it were a three-on-two.

The center stays on the same side of the ice as the winger. The first center goes with the right winger. The next center goes with the left winger. The center starts with the puck.

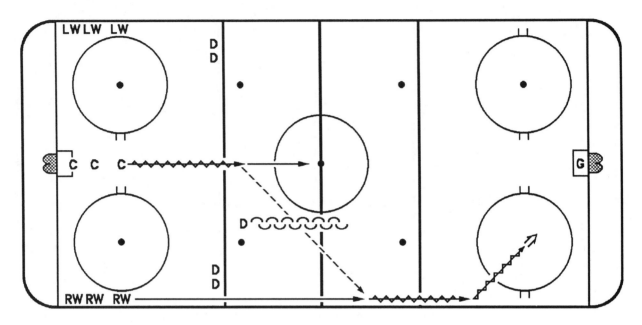

11. Half-Ice in Both Directions

In this variation on 10, also a two-on-one drill, players switch sides halfway through the drill. The centers start with the puck.

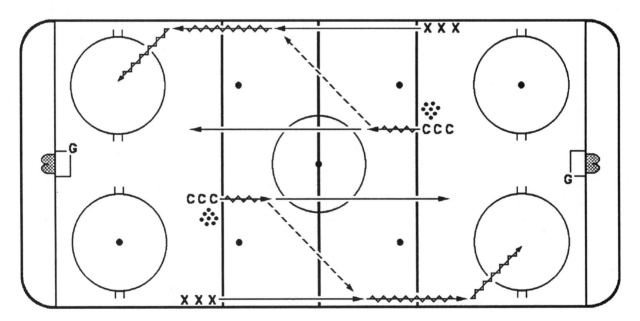

12. Two-on-One Swing Drill

Two forwards skate over the far blue line and receive a pass from a defenseman in that end. D1 starts at the same end as the forwards, skates around the center circle, turns backward, and defends against the attacking forwards. Once D2 has made the pass to one of the swinging forwards, the first two forwards and D2 start doing the drill the same way but coming from the opposite direction. Players return to the lines they came from.

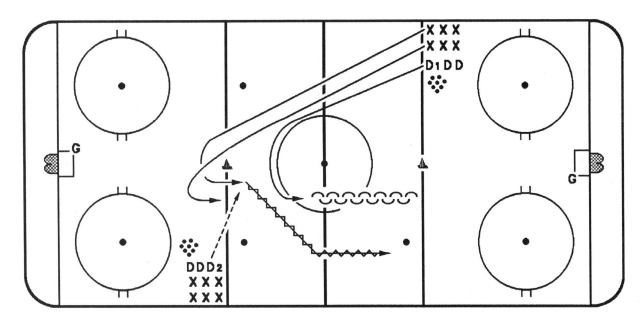

13. Three-on-Two in One Direction

The defenseman behind the net starts the passing for the three-on-two. The defense pairs take turns passing the puck up and working defensively.

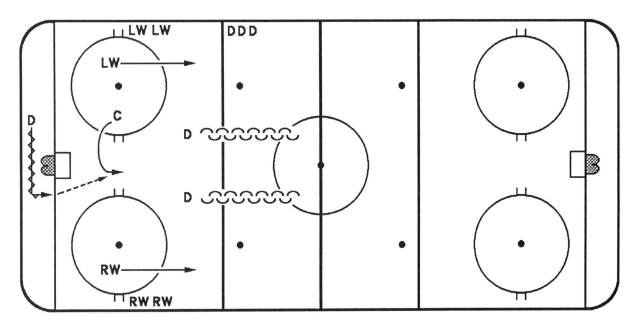

14. Three-on-Two in Both Directions

There must be a minimum of three forward lines and four defensemen for this drill. If six defensemen are available, have one at each end to start the play. Two forward lines must be at the end at which the drill starts. The forward lines stay at the opposite end after completing the rush and return in the opposite direction when their turn comes again.

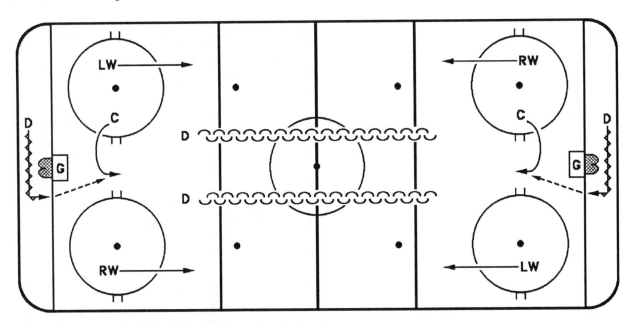

15. Three-on-Two in Both Directions with One Line in Succession

In this variation of 14, the forward line, after making a play in one direction, immediately moves back in the other direction against another defense pair.

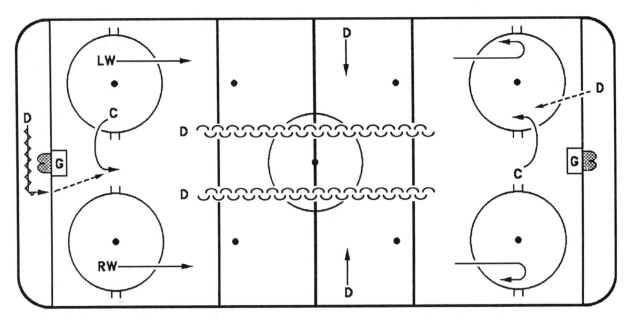

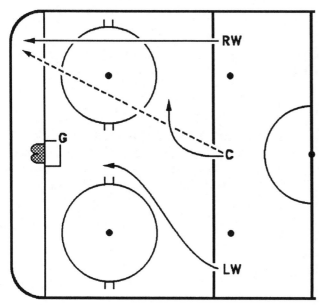

16. Offensive Triangle Drill

The forwards line up on the blue line and the puck is shot into the corner. The forwards work the various options of the offensive triangle. They shoot the puck into both corners.

17. Offensive Triangle Drill Against Defensemen

The defenseman on the side the puck is shot into goes to the corner for the puck. The other defenseman goes for the front of the net.

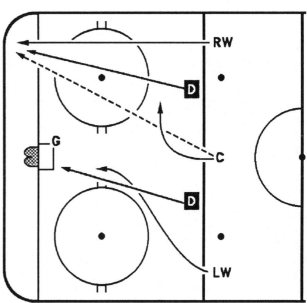

18. Pass Back Drill

The first forward with the puck goes behind the net and passes the puck back on the same side to the trailing forward.

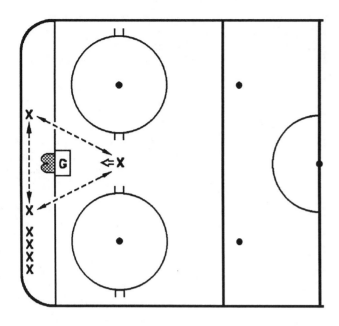

19. Offensive Triangle Around the Net
Three forwards pass the puck quickly around in the triangle, and the forward in the slot takes a shot on goal. Rotate the players in and out.

20. Five-on-Five
Have players execute 13 when moving out of their own end.

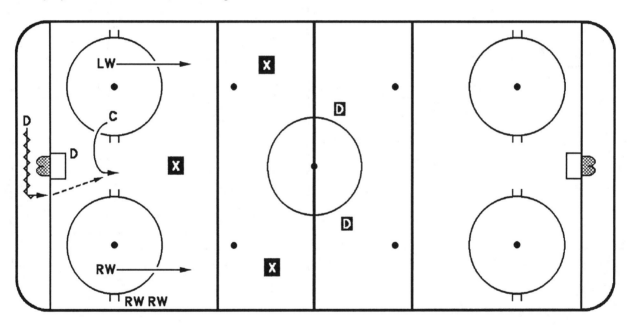

11. DEFENSIVE TEAM PLAY

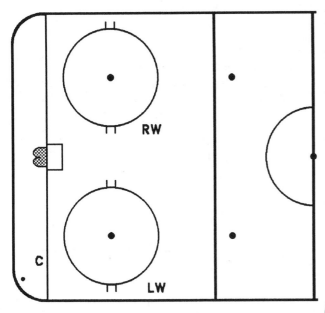

Defensive play is initiated in the opposition's end of the rink by a forechecking pattern. It continues through the neutral zone and becomes extremely important in the defensive zone. The object of defensive play is to gain possession of the puck from the opposition and therefore prevent a score and initiate the offense.

FORECHECKING PUCK IN THE CORNER SYSTEMS

1. One Man In (One-Two-Two)

In this system, only one forechecker moves in, and the other two forwards pick up the opposition's wingers. The forechecker can be either the winger or center, depending on which man is in first.

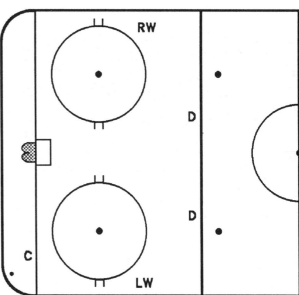

2. Center In (One-Two-Two)

This system is similar to 1 except the center is always the first man in. Wingers pull up on the boards, covering the opposition's wingers.

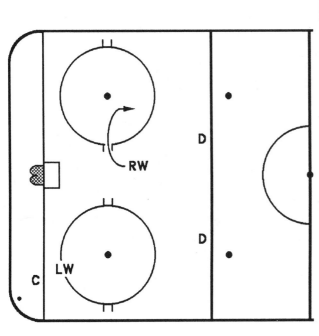

3. Two Men In (Two-One-Two)

The first forechecker takes the man out of the play, with the second picking up the puck. The third offensive man stations himself in the high slot. If the opposition gains possession of the puck, the winger in front of the net skates back with the opposition's winger.

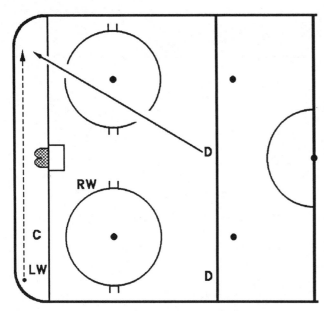

4. Three Men In

This is an all-out pressing type of forechecking system that could be used when a team is behind in a game by one or more goals. If the puck moves to the far-side corner, the offside defenseman moves in.

5. One-Two-Two or One-Four

In this type of forechecking, one forward forechecks, while the other two forwards pick up the wings and pull back as the opposition breaks out. The defense also pulls back. This is used to protect a lead or to forecheck a superior team in a defensive manner.

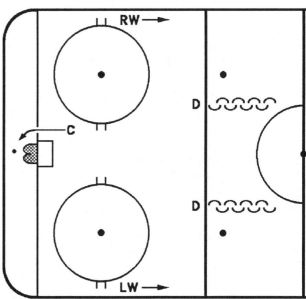

6. Two-One-Two

The wingers forecheck and the center plays high in the slot area in this system. If a winger is slow in moving in, the center switches positions with the winger. If the defenseman pinches in on the puck side, the center takes the defense position.

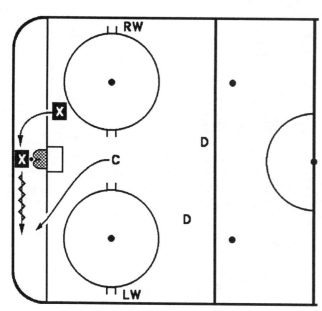

FORECHECKING PUCK BEHIND THE NET
1. Moving Puck Carrier
One man cuts off the puck carrier. The fore-checker cuts across the front of the net to ride the man out. The wingers pick up the opposition wingers on the boards.

2. Two Men Cut Off the Puck Carrier
This is the same as 1 except the winger on the puck side moves in to help cut off the puck carrier. The defenseman on the puck side moves in to take the opposition wingers.

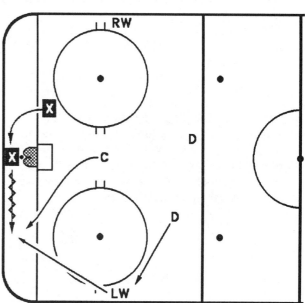

3. Puck Carrier Stops Behind the Net
The forechecker who stops in front of the net is the first man in, usually the center or the winger. The other two forecheckers cover the opposition wingers on the boards. When the puck carrier moves, the center moves with him. The wingers stay with the wings.

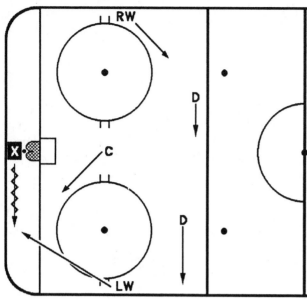

4. Two Men Cut Off the Puck Carrier Variation

In this variation of 2, when the puck carrier moves, the center moves with the man and the winger moves in. The defenseman on the puck carrier's side moves in to take the forward to the boards.

5. Puck Carrier Is Chased Behind the Net

This system sacrifices a forechecker in order to inhibit the opposition from setting up a breakout pattern. The winger on the puck carrier's side moves in to check him. The defenseman on the puck side moves in to cover the winger.

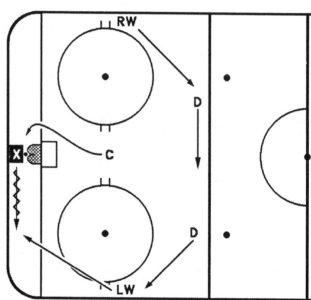

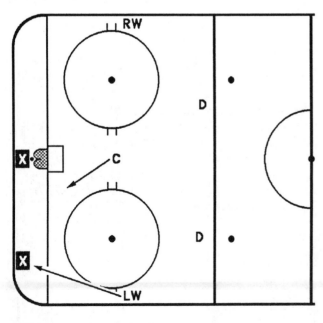

FORCHECKING DEFENSEMAN IN THE CORNER

The following systems address the situation in which the puck carrier stops behind your net and the opposition defenseman moves to the corner.

1. Forechecker in Front of the Net

The wingers pull back with the wingers on the boards. The winger on the defenseman's side moves in if the pass comes to the defenseman.

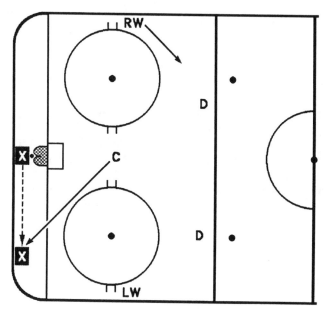

2. Forechecker in Front of the Net Variation

This is another way to defend the net if the forechecker stops in front of the net. The wingers stay on the wingers. The center follows the pass to the defenseman.

3. Puck Side-to-Side Rotation

The puck moves from one side to the other side. The first man in chases the puck to the net and then swings out to the slot. The second man in moves across to the far side. The man in the slot moves to the corner where the puck has moved.

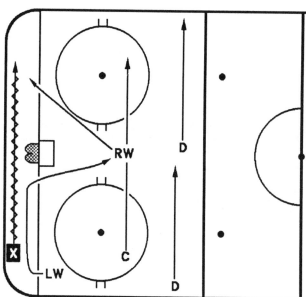

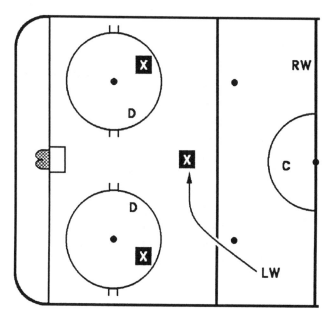

CHECKING SYSTEM FROM THE NEUTRAL ZONE INTO THE DEFENSIVE END
1. Wingers Uncovered

The defenseman must back in but attempt to give as little ice as possible. The first trailing forward picks up the slot area. The other trailing forwards pick up the wingers on the boards.

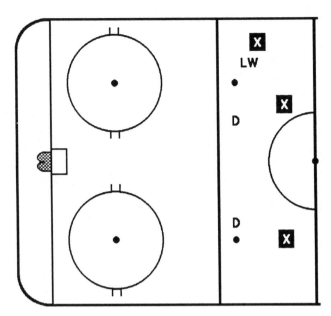

2. Three-on-Two with One Winger Covered

With one winger covered, the two defensemen attempt to make a three-on-three situation, with the winger covering one man, keeping to the inside. The defensemen keep a short distance between themselves and the offensive men. The next trailing forward picks up the slot area.

3. Three-on-Two with Both Wingers Covered

Both defensemen can stand up over the blue line and force the offensive man to make a play before the blue line. If the puck is shot into the defensive zone, the wingers should be the first to pick it up.

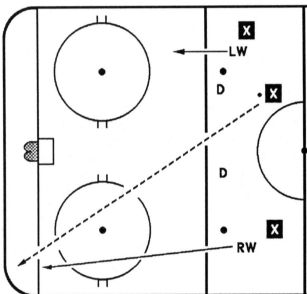

SYSTEMS IN THE DEFENSIVE ZONE

The defensive forwards should stay with the offensive forwards until a play has been made on net. The trailing forward picks up the opposition's next player into the zone, who could be an opposition defenseman. When the play settles into the corner or back to the opposition defenseman at the blue line, the defensive system should go into effect. The systems described are shown with the opposition with the puck in the corner.

1. Wingers on the Points, Center Low

The two wingers are responsible for the opposition defensemen, and the center plays low. The two defensemen cover the opposition forwards.

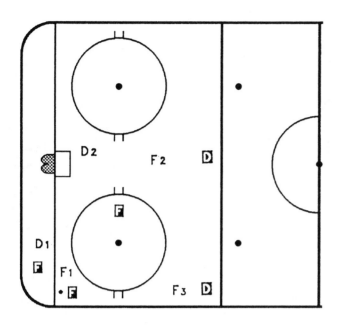

2. Man-on-Man, One-Two-Three

The first forward back, F1, goes to the puck. The second forward back, F2, goes to the slot. The third forward back, F3, goes to the puck side, high boards. D1, D2, and F1 play three-on-three low. F1 and F2 cover the opposition defenseman.

3. Zone

The offside winger covers the high slot and the offside point. The closest winger or center covers the corner, with the other forward covering the near side point. One defenseman covers the corner, with the other defenseman covering the front of the net.

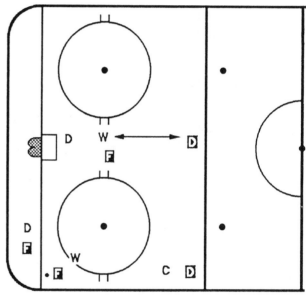

4. Wingers on Wingers, Center on the Points

One defenseman goes to the corner on the puck. The other defenseman stays in front of the net. If the puck is moved quickly to the offside point and the point man moves in, the defenseman in front of the net moves out.

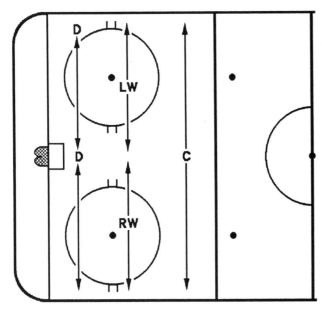

5. Sliding Zone

The center man covers the blue line area. The wingers cover from the board area to the slot. The defensemen cover from the front of the net to the corner.

6. Combination System

The center or the winger is on the puck in the corner. The forward (not in the corner) covers the net side point. The offside winger covers the slot area first and the far side point if the puck comes across to this man. The defensemen cover the front of the net or the corner if the puck is on the other side. A defenseman and a forward are always on the puck in the corners.

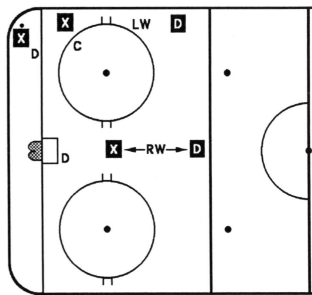

DEFENSIVE TEAM PLAY DRILLS

In addition to the drills that follow, all forechecking drills discussed in chapter 9, "Checking," can be used here.

1. One-on-Five Drill

The puck is shot into the offensive zone, and one forechecker attempts to break up the breakout play. Both ends of the rink can be used for this drill.

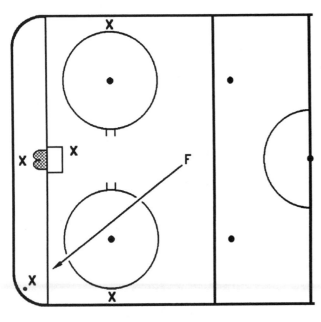

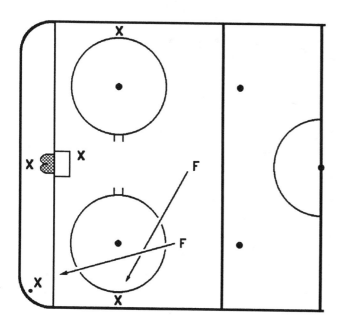

2. Two-on-Five, Three-on-Five, Five-on-Five

In this variation on 1, two forecheckers attempt to break up play, then three forwards and two defensemen. The drill can be executed at both ends of the rink.

3. Without Opposition

Work a defensive system against no opposition. The coach can describe the situation, and the players react by positioning themselves quickly, e.g., puck is in the left corner, the puck moves behind the net, or the puck moves to the far corner. Also drill players on reacting to hand or stick signals by coach. The drill can be run at both ends of the rink as well as in neutral zone if you have three nets.

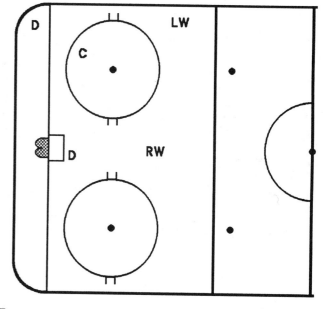

4. Opposition Defensive Team Without Sticks

The offensive team moves the puck around while the defensive team plays without sticks, concentrating on positional play. Both ends of the ice can be used for this drill.

5. Five-on-Five Drill (not shown)

This drill is the same drill as 4 except defensive players have sticks. The drill is worked in the defensive zone, with the offensive team being given the puck in the corner or at the point and worked from that point. The play ends when a goal is scored, the goalie or players hold the puck, or the puck is moved out of the defensive end over the blue line. The drill can be worked at both ends of the rink.

12. PENALTY KILLING

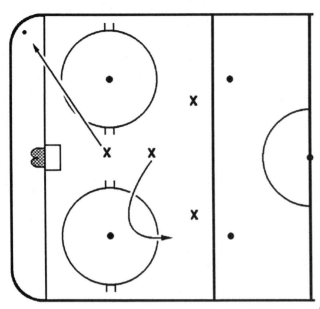

There are a number of penalty killing systems used in hockey.

FORECHECKING PATTERNS IN THE OFFENSIVE ZONE
One Man Short
1. Stacked Formation ("I")
The first forechecker moves to the puck side. The second forechecker swings to the opposite side and picks up the winger on that side.

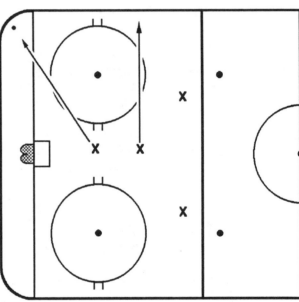

2. Stacked Formation Variation
In this variation of 1, both of the forecheckers move to the same side to attempt to break up the play.

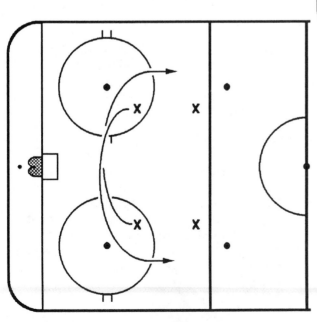

3. Forecheckers Crisscross
The first forechecker swings across to one side. The second forechecker swings to the opposite side.

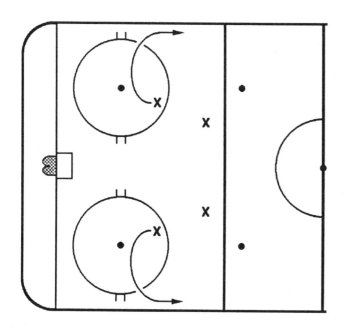

4. Forecheckers Pick Up the Lanes
Both forecheckers pick up the lanes on each side of the ice.

5. Forecheckers Pick Up the Lanes at the Blue Line
In this variation of 4, the forecheckers do not go further than just inside the offensive blue line.

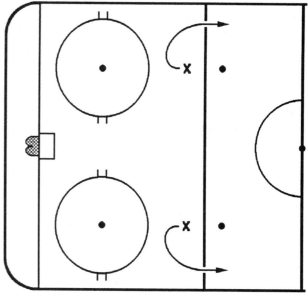

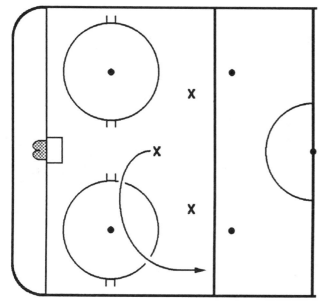

Two Men Short
6. Forechecker Swings
The forechecker moves in and swings with the puck carrier and then picks up the lane.

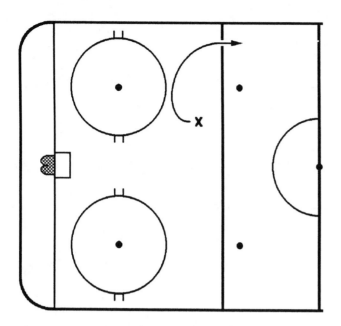

7. No Forecheck
In this variation of 6, the forechecker moves in no further than the blue line and then picks up either lane.

BACKCHECKING PATTERNS IN THE NEUTRAL ZONE
One Man Short
1. Forwards in Lanes
With the lanes covered, the defensemen stand up at the blue line.

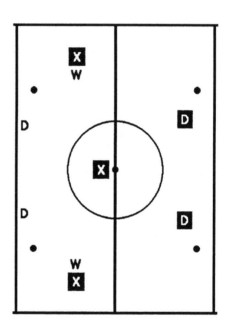

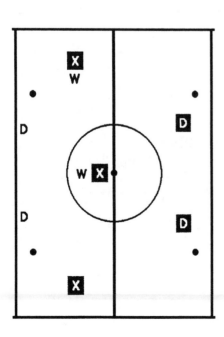

2. One Forward in Lane
In this pattern, one lane is covered, and the other forechecker is in the mid-ice area. The offside defenseman moves over. The forechecker in the mid-ice area moves on the puck carrier.

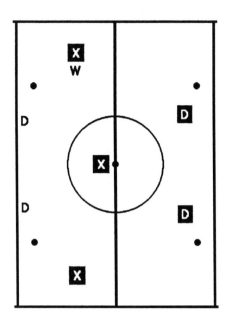

Two Men Short
3. Cover the Lane

The forechecker picks up either lane.

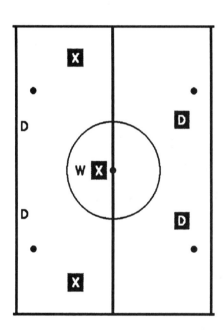

4. Cover the Center Area

The forechecker picks up the center area.

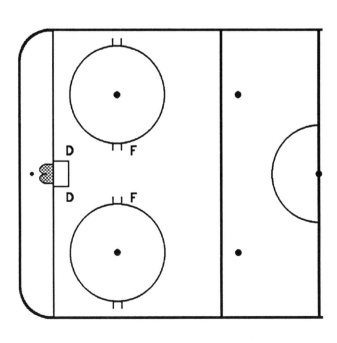

DEFENSIVE ZONE SYSTEMS
One Man Short
1. Standard Box

In the standard box formation, two wingers and two defensemen force the play to the outside. The four defenders move to the outside of the box for the puck only if they have a 90 percent chance of gaining possession.

The puck is behind the net or in the center area.

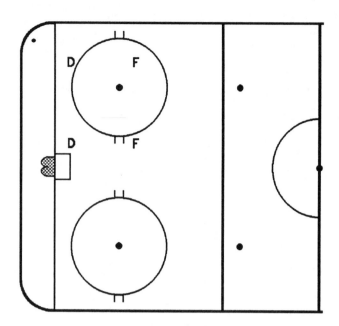

2. Standard Box Variation
In this variation of 1, the puck is in the corner or at the point.

3. Collapsible Box
This pattern is the same as 1 except the box moves to the net area. The box moves out when the puck moves to the corner or back to the point.

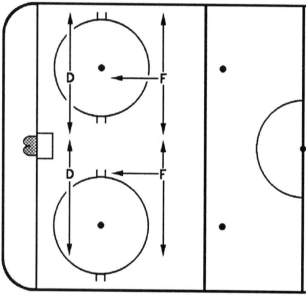

4. Sagging Box
This pattern is the same as 1 except the offside winger to the puck side moves back into the slot area. This man moves out again if the puck is passed to the defenseman on his side.

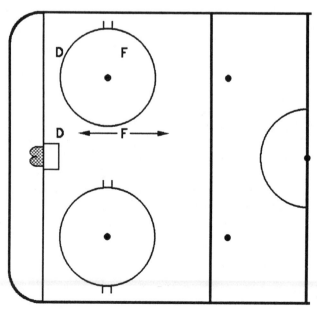

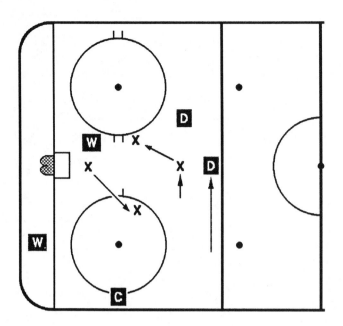

5. The Diamond (Rotating Box)

In this box pattern variation, when the opposition is on the power play, the defenseman moves to the middle of the blue line. The penalty killing forward moves to the middle of the ice with the defenseman. The defenseman on the same side moves out, and the offside defenseman moves to the front of the net. The offside penalty killing forward drops off to form the diamond.

Two Men Short
6. Standard Triangle

The forward at the top of the triangle moves from side to side covering the high slot area and the points.

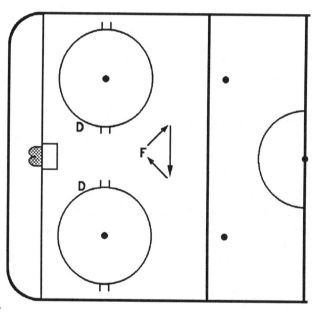

7. Rotating Triangle

This pattern is the same as 6 except the defenseman moves out on the point man if the forward is trapped on the offside. The forward then moves back as a defenseman, and the other defenseman moves to the offside. The defenseman who moves out becomes the top man in the triangle.

8. Sliding Triangle

In this triangle pattern there are one defenseman and two forwards. One defenseman stands in front of the net, moving only from one side of the crease to the other depending upon the side the puck is on. The other two forwards move in and out, eliminating the top man's getting trapped, which is the weakness of the normal triangle formation.

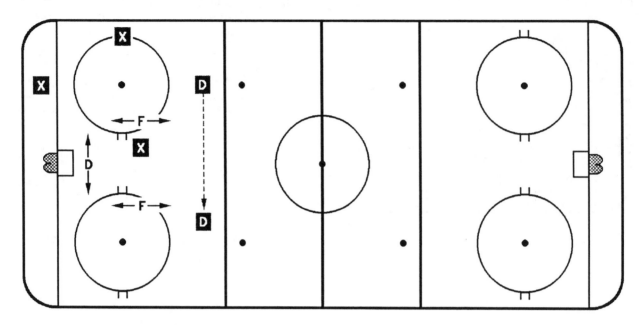

DRILLS FOR PENALTY KILLING

Use the full ice surface to drill players on penalty killing. The puck may be shot into the offensive end by the coach with the offensive team attempting to start the play from there. Time limits for each offensive and defensive unit may be used.

1. No Opposition

Players work the box and triangle patterns without any opposition, reacting to the coach's hand or stick signals.

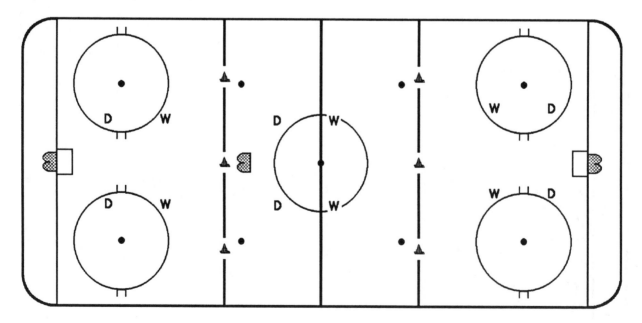

2. With and Without Sticks

Have players work the box and triangle patterns against any offense at each end of the ice, first without sticks and then with sticks.

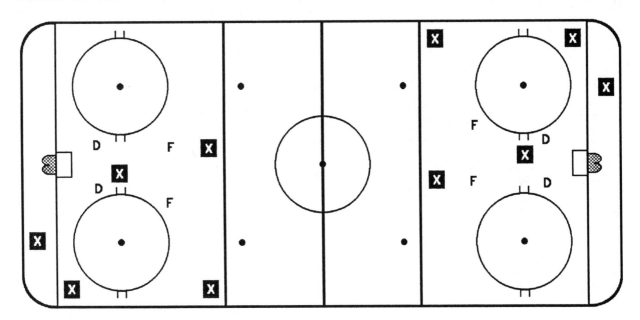

3. Forwards Against Offensive Team

Drill the players on the box and triangle patterns with the forechecking forwards working against the offensive team, bringing the puck out of their own end. This drill can be worked at both ends.

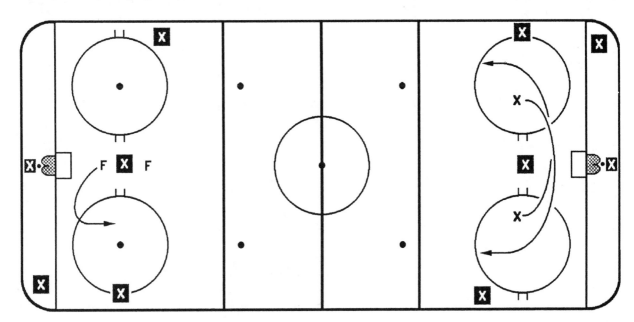

13. POWER PLAY

The objective of the power play is to move the puck into the defensive zone and maintain possession until an excellent scoring opportunity can be set up.

ORGANIZING IN THE DEFENSIVE ZONE

In many instances, the power play is initiated in the defensive zone after the shorthanded team has shot the puck the length of the ice from their defensive zone. There are a number of different methods used to move the puck from the defensive zone of the team with the power play.

DEFENSIVE ZONE DRILLS
1. Behind the Net
The center circles behind the net and takes the puck from the defenseman and moves straight up the center of the ice. The defenseman in front of the net can move to the boards and follow behind the winger to set up a crossing pattern at the far blue line.

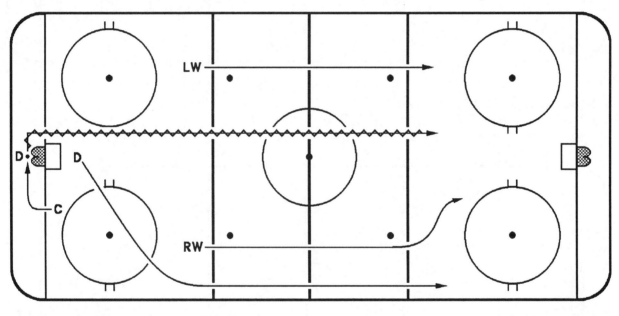

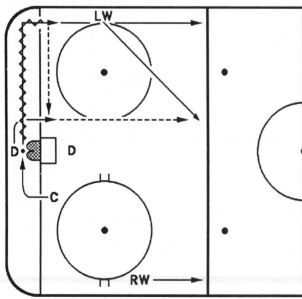

2. Center Behind the Net
The center circles behind the net, takes the puck and moves wide to the corner, and then drops the puck back to the defenseman. The defenseman moves straight up the ice or returns the pass to the center, who has circled back to the center of the ice or to the winger cutting from the boards.

144

3. Defenseman Behind the Net

The defenseman stops behind the net, and his partner moves to the corner. The center makes a tight turn at the goal line on the opposite side to the defenseman in the corner. The defenseman behind the net gives the puck to the center. The other defenseman in the corner goes straight up the ice to form a four-man attack.

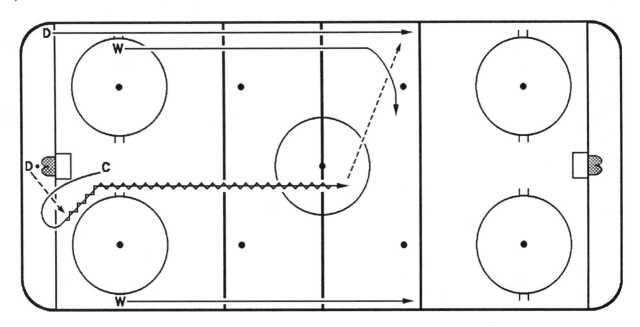

4. Defenseman Behind the Net Variation

The defenseman stops behind the net, and his partner moves to the corner. The center makes a tight turn at the goal line on the opposite side to the defenseman in the corner. The defenseman behind the net gives the puck to the center or the defenseman in the corner. If the puck goes to the defenseman in the corner, he will then take two strides with the puck and pass to the circling center. The defenseman who was in the corner then moves down the boards and becomes the outlet man for the winger cutting across at the blue line.

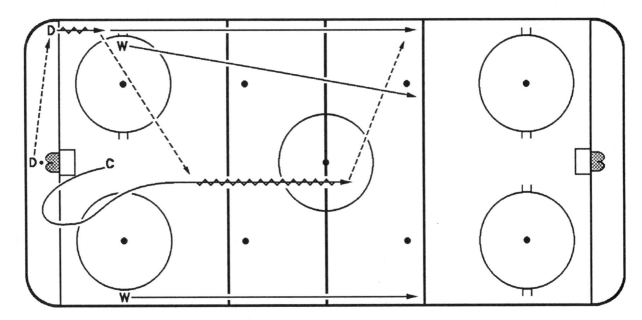

5. Breakout (not shown)

Any standard breakout play can be used in moving the puck from the defensive zone, such as one in which a defenseman is in the corner or one in which a center swings to the corner, such as 21 on page 98.

6. Double Swing with Wingers High at the Blue Line

The defenseman and the center swing to the corner. The wingers are high at the blue line, they cut across, and they are available for a pass from the defenseman or the swing man.

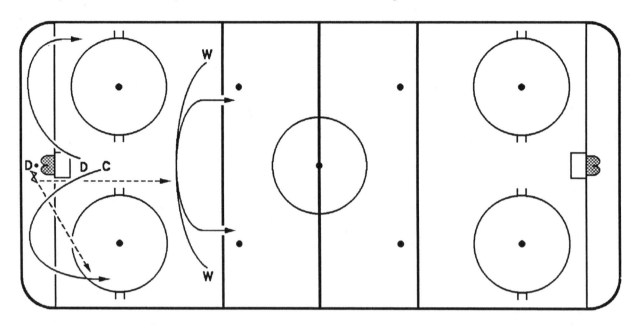

7. Double Swing Variation

In this variation of 6, one winger is at the near blue line, and one winger is at the far blue line. The winger at the near blue line loops in, and the winger at the far blue line cuts across for a pick or a pass as the play moves up the ice.

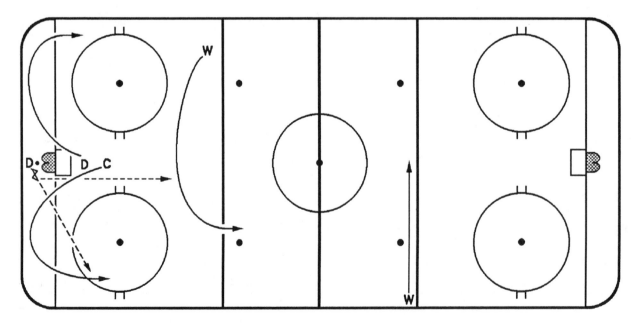

MOVING THROUGH THE NEUTRAL ZONE

In most cases, the team with the power play attempts to have a fourth offensive player involved in the play as the puck is moved across the opposition's blue line.

NEUTRAL ZONE DRILLS
1. Defense up the Boards
The center carries the puck. The winger cuts in, with the defenseman moving down the boards. One defenseman follows the winger up quickly on either side. The winger cuts to the center area to pull his check with him. The center passes the puck to either the defenseman or the winger.

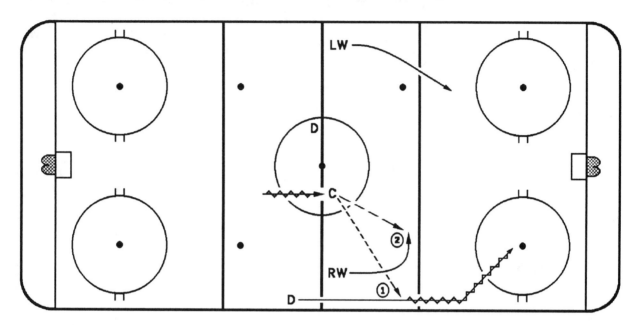

2. Center up the Boards
The defenseman carries the puck, with the center following the winger up the boards. The play for the winger is the same as in 1 except the defenseman passes to the center or the winger cuts across.

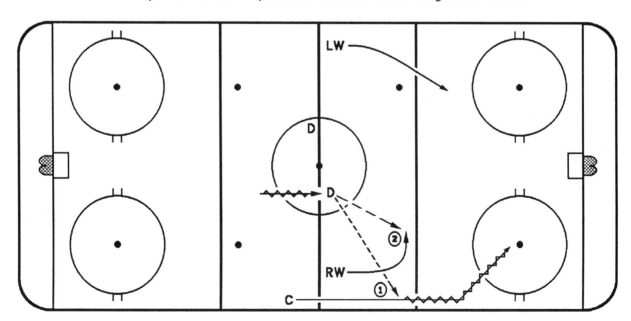

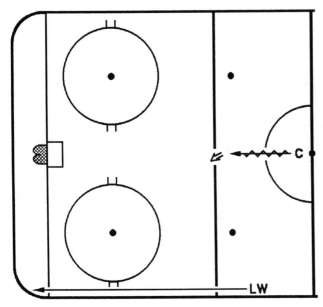

3. Shoot In
The puck carrier shoots the puck into the offensive zone. It is important that the puck is shot into the offensive zone with the wings in full flight. Getting possession of the puck after shooting is extremely important; otherwise, the play is ineffective.

4. Rim the Boards
The puck carrier moves down the ice close to the boards and shoots the puck in to rim the boards. It is picked up by the outside forward. The puck can then be passed quickly back to the defense to set up the power play.

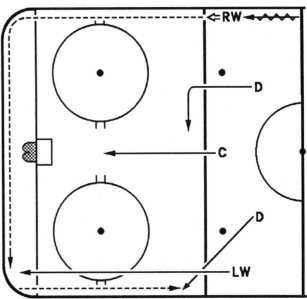

PLAY IN THE OFFENSIVE ZONE

When you're one or two men shorthanded, the object in the offensive zone is for the players to move the puck quickly and for the offensive players to be placed strategically so they can set up in an open area for a scoring opportunity.

DRILLS
1. Wingers in the Corners
The wingers are in the corners, and the center is in the slot area.

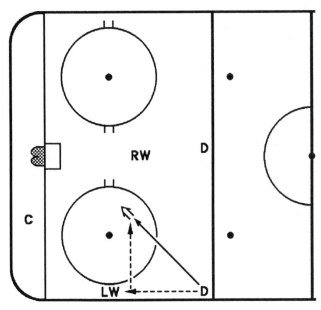

2. Give-and-Go with Defenseman
The defenseman passes to the forward in the corner and then moves to the net for a return pass.

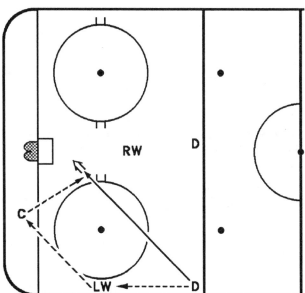

3. Give-and-Go Variation
In this variation of 2, if the defender moves with the defenseman, the forward can pass to another forward in the corner.

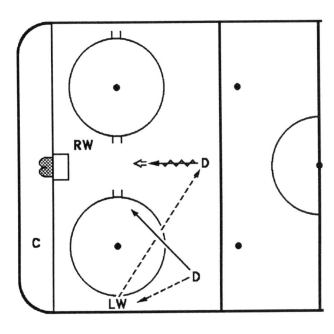

4. Pass to Offside Defenseman
This play is the same as 3 except the forward passes to the offside defenseman.

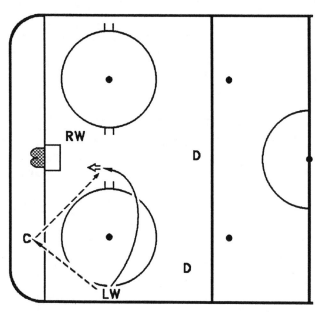

5. Give-and-Go in the Corner
The winger passes to the center and then moves to the net for a return pass on the give-and-go.

6. Two-on-One in the Corner Variation
If the defenseman moves with the winger, the center can pass to the defenseman moving into the high slot.

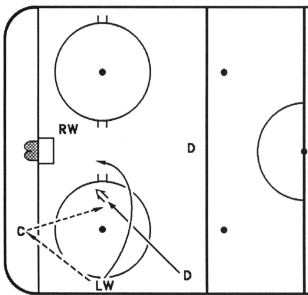

7. Pass to the Far Side Winger
One defenseman passes to the other defenseman, who passes to the far side winger stationed at the offside post. The forward takes the pass and shoots in one motion. The pass can come directly for the offside defenseman.

Note that in any pass it is often an advantage to the offside winger to have the winger playing his off wing, e.g., the right winger is a left shot and the left winger is a right shot.

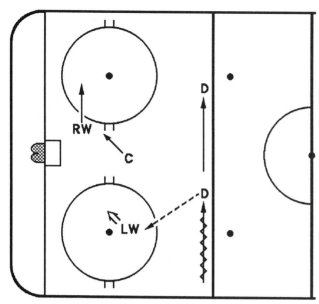

8. Defense to Winger
The defensemen move across the blue line. The one with the puck passes back to the winger. The object here is to shift the defensive box to one side and then pass back.

9. Pass Across
The center moves to the front of the net to tie up the defenseman. The winger coming from the corner passes the puck across to the offside winger, who is standing off the far side goalpost.

If the winger coming to the net is covered, the winger should look for the defenseman moving down into the high slot.

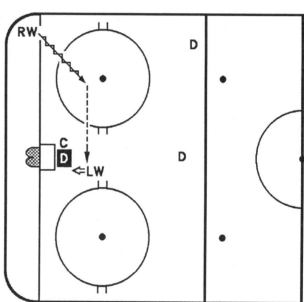

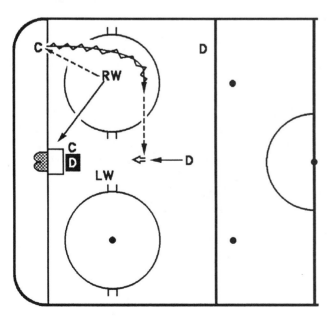

10. Pass to Offside Defenseman
A two-on-one situation is set up in the corner, with the other forward tying up the defenseman in the front of the net. The forward in the corner tries to pass to the offside defenseman moving in from the point.

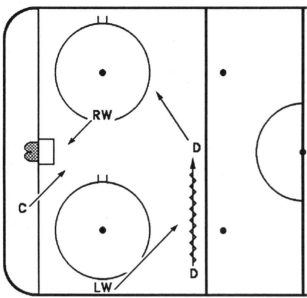

11. Defenseman to Middle

The point man with the puck at the blue line moves across the blue line and stops. The other point man moves in on the far side. The winger on the side of the puck moves out, and the other winger and center move to the front of the net to pick the opposition defenseman.

Note that the defenseman with the puck at the blue line can shoot or pass to the winger or the other point man. If the point man passes to either side, he can wait for a return pass or move through the center and receive a return pass.

12. Walk out with Pick

The center with the puck moves around behind the net and circles in front to pass to the far side winger or shoots. The winger in front of the net picks the opposition defenseman on that side.

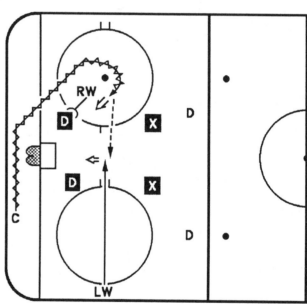

13. High Pick

The center with the puck circles behind the net, continues out near the blue line, and then moves down the middle for a shot. The two wingers pick the opposition defensemen in front of the net. The near side defenseman picks the near opposition forward at the top of the box.

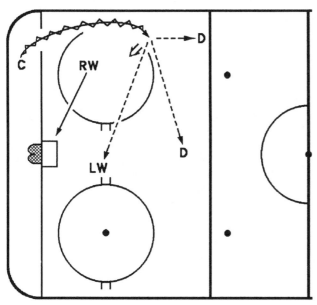

14. Combined System

From a two-on-one situation in the corner, the forward looks for the following possibilities in sequence:

- pass to the give-and-go man
- move out from corner for a possible shot
- pass to the offside winger
- pass the offside point man
- pass to the near side point man

15. Around the Outside

The puck is passed quickly around the outside from the center, left winger, defenseman, defenseman, and right winger and then quickly across to the left winger, who is moving in for a direct shot.

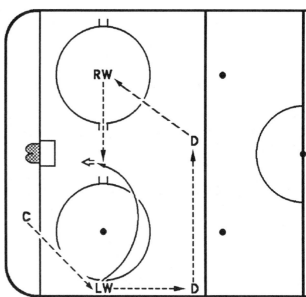

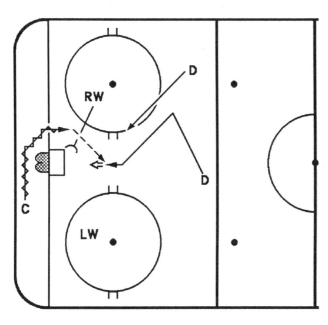

16. Behind the Net

The center moves from behind the net. The right winger picks for the defenseman, the right defenseman moves through the slot, and the left defenseman moves over, takes a pass from the center, and shoots.

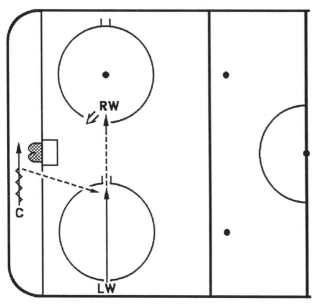

17. Pass Back

The center goes behind the net and passes back on the same side to the winger moving in. The winger either shoots or passes the puck across to the offside forward.

18. Defense Moves to the Boards

The defenseman takes a pass from the other defenseman in the middle of the ice. The defenseman receiving the pass then skates toward the boards and passes the puck back to the offside defenseman, who has moved to the middle of the ice. The defenseman shoots, and the other forwards go to the front of the net.

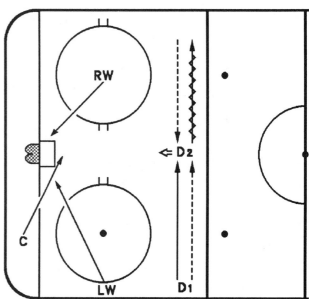

19. Two Men Short

The puck is passed from defenseman to defenseman, and the center picks off the top man in the defensive triangle.

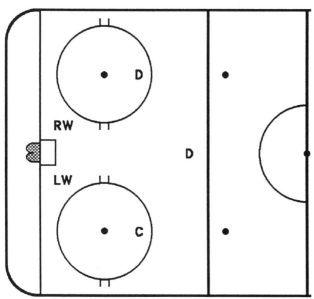

20. Defenseman to Middle with Two Men Short

The defenseman moves to the middle part of the ice, the offside defenseman and another forward form an umbrella (or outlets), and the other two forwards go to the front of the net.

DRILLS FOR THE POWER PLAY
1. No Opposition

Work breakout patterns and neutral zone plays with no opposition. The drill can be worked at both ends, with the groups not passing the red line. Plays worked between the red line and offensive blue line can work between the defensive blue line and center red line.

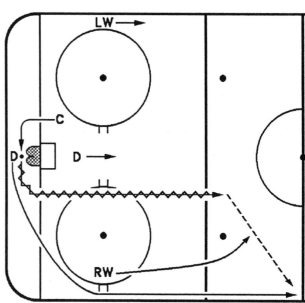

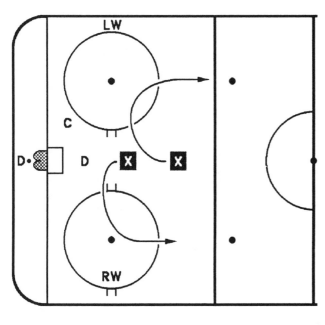

2. Two Forecheckers

In this variation of 1, two forecheckers attempt to break up the play.

3. No Opposition

Drill players on offensive patterns against no opposition. Three areas of the ice can be used.

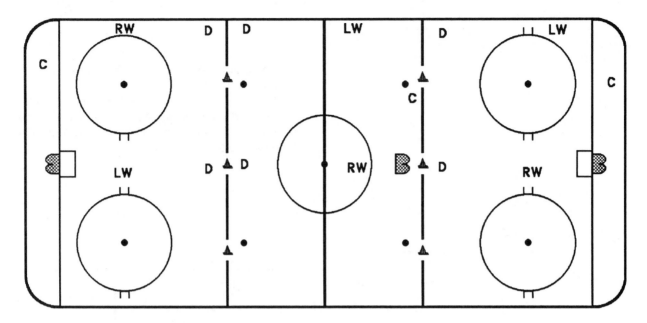

4. Defenders Without Sticks (not shown)

Drill players on offensive patterns against defenders without sticks. Both ends of the rink or three areas can be used.

5. Defenders with Sticks (not shown)

Drill players on offensive patterns against defenders with sticks.

6. Full-Ice Power Play Drill

Players work against a team while they are one and two men short. The puck can be shot into the defensive end and worked out against the penalty killing team. Time limits for each offensive unit can be used.

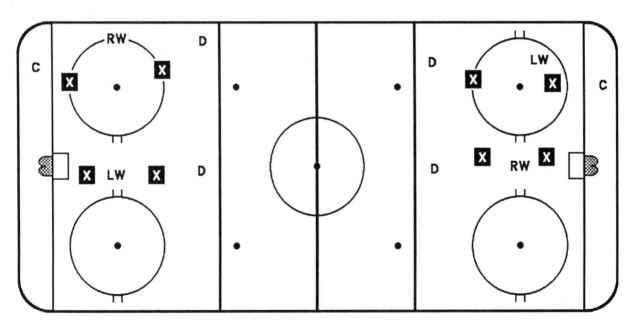

7. Five-on-Three (not shown)

An important teaching progression is to have players work the power play five-on-three. This allows the power play unit to have success. Then add a fourth man, first without sticks and then with. Once the power play is working well, you can allow the penalty killers to be more aggressive. Try to use all of your players.

14. FACE-OFF ALIGNMENTS

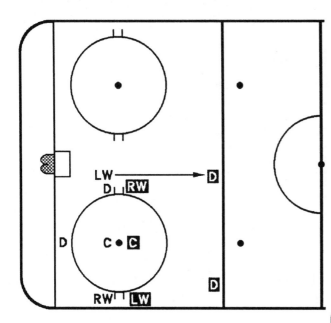

Note that all face-offs are reversed for the opposite side of the ice.

DEFENSIVE ZONE FACE-OFFS
1. Full Strength
Assignments:

(LW) Takes right defenseman
(RW) Takes left winger
(C) Takes draw and center
(LD) Takes right winger
(RD) Takes puck drawn back or center moving to net

2. Full Strength
Assignments:

(LW) Takes right defenseman
(RW) Takes left winger and then left defenseman
(C) Takes center
(LD) Takes right winger
(RD) Takes puck drawn back or center

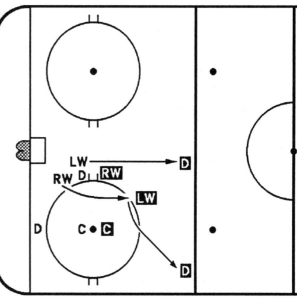

3. Full Strength
Assignments:

(LW) Takes right winger
(RW) Takes left defenseman
(C) Takes left wing then right defenseman
(LD) Takes center
(RD) Takes puck drawn back or center moving to net

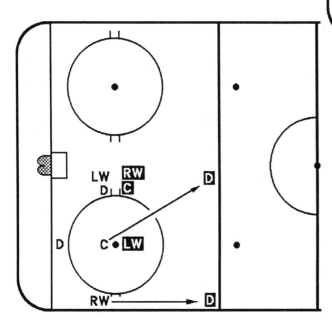

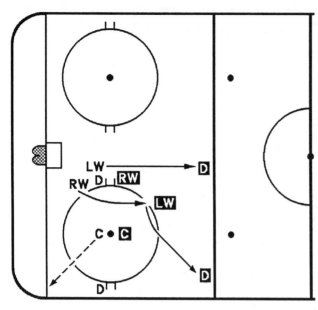

4. Full Strength
Assignments:

(LW) Takes right defenseman
(RW) Takes left winger then near side point
(C) Takes draw and center
(LD) Takes right winger or goes to net
(RD) Takes puck drawn back or moves to net

5. One Man Short
Assignments:

(W) Takes right defenseman
(C) Takes center and left defense
(LD) Takes right winger
(RD) Takes puck drawn back or center moving to net

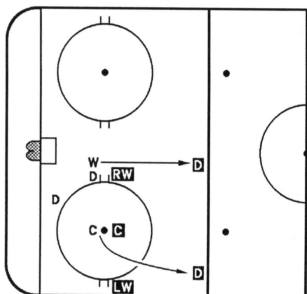

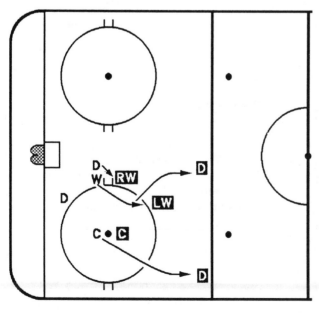

6. One Man Short
Assignments:

(W) Takes left winger and then left defense
(C) Takes center
(LD) Takes right winger
(RD) Takes puck drawn back or center moving to net

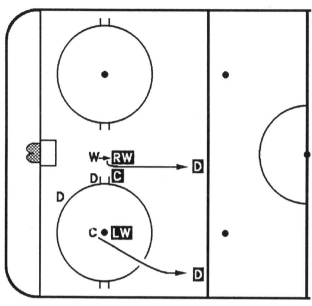

7. One Man Short
Assignments:

(W) Takes right winger then right defenseman
(C) Takes left winger then left defenseman
(LD) Takes center
(RD) Takes draw and left winger moving to net

8. Two Men Short
Assignments:

(C) Takes center then left winger
(LD) Takes right winger
(RD) Takes puck drawn back or center moving to net

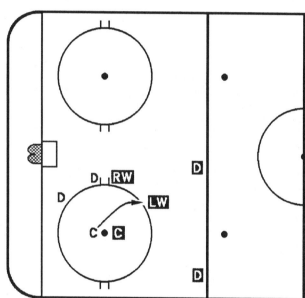

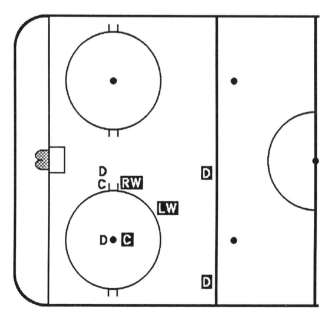

9. Two Men Short
Assignments:

(C) Takes left winger
(LD) Takes right winger
(RD) Takes center

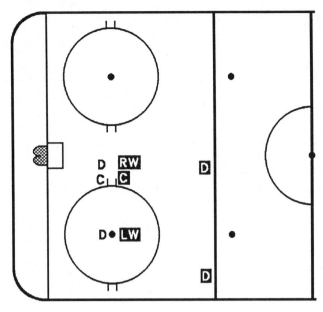

10. Two Men Short
Assignments:

(C) Takes center
(LD) Takes right winger
(RD) Takes left winger

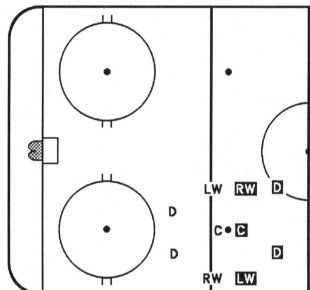

NEUTRAL ZONE FACE-OFFS OUTSIDE OWN BLUE LINE
1. Full Strength
Assignments:

(C) Pushes puck straight forward or to either wing
(LW) Takes right winger or goes for puck
(RW) Takes left winger or goes for puck

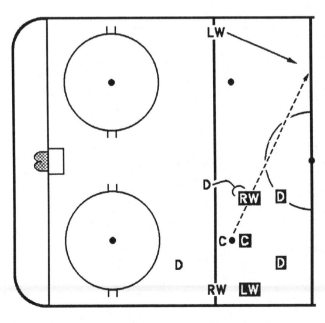

2. Full Strength
Assignments:

(C) Pushes puck forward to the left side
(LW) Goes for the puck
(LD) Moves to cut off right winger
(RW) Covers left winger
(RD) Backs up play

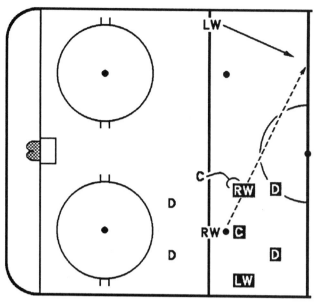

3. Full Strength
Assignments:

(LW) Goes for puck
(C) Cuts off right winger
(RW) Shoots puck to the left side
(LD) Backs up play
(RD) Covers left winger

4. One Man Short
Assignments:

(W) Takes right winger
(C) Takes center
(LD) Backs up the play
(RD) Takes left winger

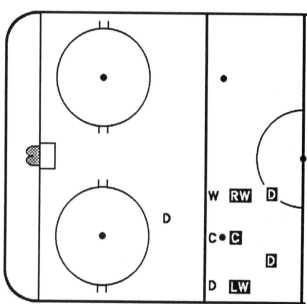

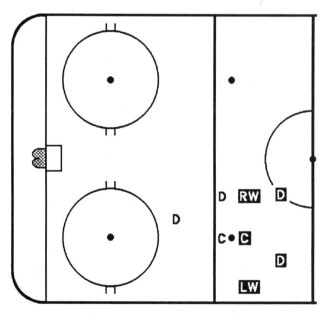

5. Two Men Short
Assignments:

(LD) Takes right winger
(C) Takes center
(RD) Backs up play and watches left winger

The player taking the face-off needs good peripheral vision to watch the puck in the referee's hand and the opponent's stick at the same time. Quick reaction time is essential.

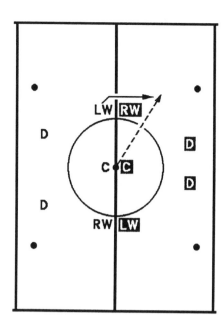

NEUTRAL ZONE FACE-OFFS AT CENTER ICE

1. Full Strength

Assignments:

(C) Shoots puck forward to left or right winger
(LD) Backs up play
(RD) Backs up play
(LW) Goes for puck
(RW) Goes for forwards

2. Full Strength

Assignments:

(C) Draws puck back to left defenseman and gets in position to receive puck from right defenseman
(LD) Receives puck and passes to right defenseman
(RD) Passes puck to center
(LW) Covers right winger
(RW) Covers left winger

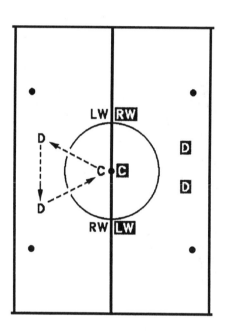

3. Full Strength

Assignments:

(LW) Takes right winger
(C) Shoots puck to right winger
(RD) Cuts off left winger
(RW) Goes for the puck
(LD) Backs up the play

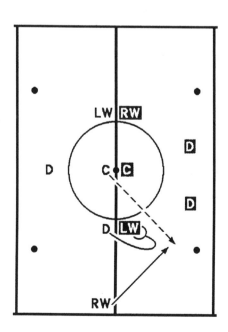

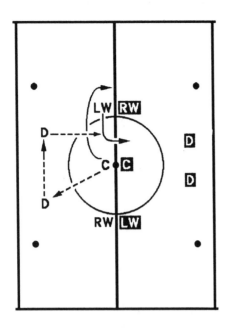

4. Full Strength
Assignments:

(C) Draws puck back to right defenseman and crosses with center
(RD) Passes to left defenseman
(LW) Crosses with center
(LD) Passes puck to crossing left winger

5. One Man Short
Assignments:

(W) Takes right winger
(C) Takes center
(RD) Takes left winger
(LD) Backs up the play

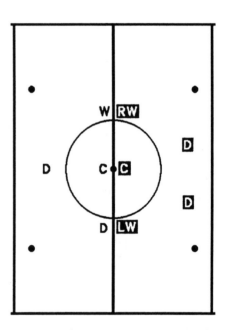

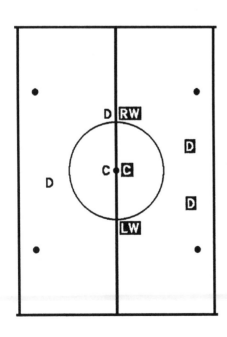

6. Two Men Short
Assignments:

(LD) Takes right winger
(C) Takes center
(RD) Backs up the play and watches left winger or lines up opposite the left winger

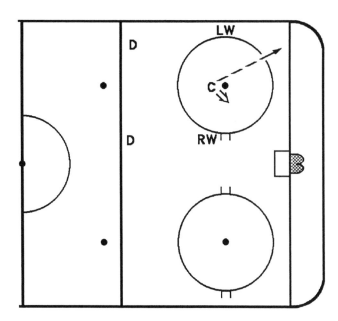

OFFENSIVE ZONE FACE-OFFS
1. Full Strength
Assignments:

(C) Shoots for net or draws to the left side
(LW) Goes for the puck in the corner
(RW) Goes for the net

2. Full Strength
Assignments:

(C) Draws the puck back to the left winger
(RW) Prevents opposition from reaching left winger and then goes for the net
(LW) Takes the draw from center and shoots for the net

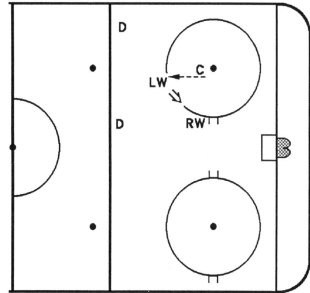

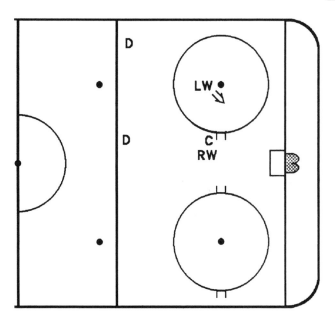

3. Full Strength
Assignments:

(LW) Shoots for the net
(C) Goes for the net
(RW) Goes for the net

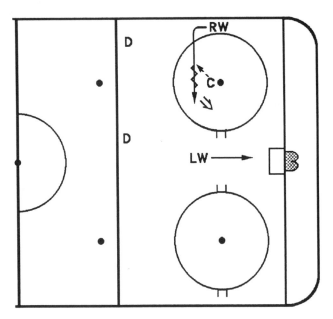

4. Full Strength

Wingers with right-hand shot switch to the left side. Right winger moves across circle and shoots. Left winger blocks defensive player.

5. Full Strength

Assignments:

(C) Draws the puck back to the left defenseman
(LW) Goes for the net
(RW) Goes for the net
(LD) Shoots
(RD) Backs up the play

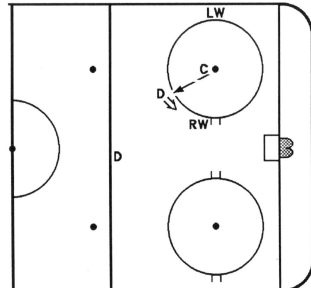

6. One Man Short

Assignments:

(C) Takes center
(W) Takes left winger or goes for the net
(LD) Backs up the play
(RD) Backs up the play

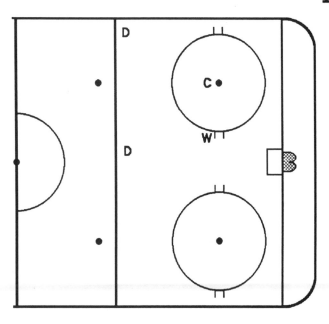

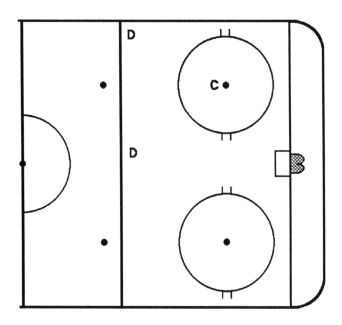

7. Two Men Short
Assignments:

(C) Takes face-off
(LD) Backs up the play and is in position to receive draw
(RD) Backs up the play and watches for a quick break

DRILLS
1. One Versus One (not shown)
Working in groups of three, one player drops the puck, and the other two face off. They rotate. Have them use all face-off spots on the rink.

2. Team Face-Off Drills (not shown)
Drill players on face-offs using various positions and concentrating on defensive and offensive aspects. Have them practice drills for play when one man short or two men short.

15. GOALTENDING

Most hockey experts believe that the goaltender is the most important player on a hockey team. An excellent goaltender can make the difference on any team and be instrumental in improving the team's chances for success.

QUALITIES OF A GOOD GOALTENDER

SKATING ABILITY
Many think that the goaltender should be the best skater on the team. He is required to complete many quick skating movements. All good goaltenders master the fundamentals of skating, such as starting and stopping, skating backward and forward, moving side to side, dropping to the knees and returning to a standing position, dropping on the side and back and returning to a standing position, pivoting, and making quick turns.

REACTION TIME
The goaltender must be able to react quickly to the movement of the puck and to move the whole body, catching glove, stick glove, or leg to stop the puck, which can be improved through constant practice.

PLAYING ANGLES
As the goaltending position is studied further, it becomes increasingly apparent that in certain situations the puck shot is faster than the body can react to stop the puck. Positioning the body at the optimal angle to reduce the openings in the net is one of the key objectives for successful goaltending. It is important that the goaltender plays the angles evenly and does not over cover or under cover the short or far side. Experienced goaltenders stop many shots by body position alone.

GOALTENDING STANCES

STAND-UP
The feet are apart so that the inside of the pads are barely touching. The stick is held in front of the skates with blade flat and at a 90-degree angle to the ice. The stick glove hand holds the stick slightly up the shaft from the wide part of the blade. The upper body leans forward with knees bent. The catching glove is held at the side at a point even with the top of the pad and slightly to the side.

CROUCH
The crouch differs from the stand-up style in that the upper body is bent well forward at the waist. The legs are further apart and the knees are in a half squat position. The stick is held on the thin shaft next to the wide part of the stick, and the catching glove is only slightly to the side of and halfway down the pad.

BUTTERFLY OR "V" STYLE
The legs are well apart, and the feet are outside the width of the shoulders. The catching glove is usually only slightly below the waist and out from the pad. The stick is held in front of the opening between the pads and usually out from the pads and tilting slightly backward.

GOALTENDING SKILLS

Covering the angles evenly and cutting down the target area are essential in all situations. It is also extremely important that the goaltender know through continued drill how his teammates will react.

MOVING SIDE TO SIDE
The skate is pushed sideways off the near skate and the far skate is slid sideways to the far post all in one movement. The stick is pushed to the outside of the goalpost to prevent a pass from the corner. The body faces forward and the head turns slightly to the side.

MOVING IN AND OUT
The skates turn outward slightly to glide forward. The skates turn inward slightly to move backward. This move cuts down the angle of the shooter. The goaltender moves outside the crease while the puck is outside the blue line and moves back in as the puck carrier approaches the goal area.

SKATE SAVE

The skate save is executed by rotating the leg outward and turning the foot to 90 degrees or better to the angle of the puck. The skate blade is kept on the ice and the leg continues to move sideways to deflect the puck to the corner.

FULL SPLITS SKATE SAVE

The legs split apart and the skate save leg rotates outward and fully extends with the foot turned to 90 degrees. The other leg moves outward and slightly backward with the knee slightly bent. The catching hand is held upward. The stick is held between the legs. The full splits save is only used as a last resort to stop a puck shot low to the far side.

HALF SPLITS SKATE SAVE

The skate save leg rotates outward and fully extends with the foot rotated to a 90-degree angle to the puck. The other leg bends and the pad is put flat on the ice. The goaltender can return to a standing position faster with the half splits than with the full splits. The half splits save is used instead of a full splits save whenever possible, as the goaltender is in a better position to recover.

DOUBLE LEG SAVE

The goaltender keeps both pads together and shoots both legs out to the side with one pad on top of the other. The glove hand is held high above the pads, and the stick arm is extended above the head along the ice. This move is used when the goaltender has to make a fast move from the far post with the shooter at the far side of the net with the puck.

From the butterfly position, the goaltender extends his legs outward with the inside surface of the pads being on the ice. The blade of the stick is flat on the ice, and the catching hand is held high. This move is used for low shots and screened shots.

GLOVE SAVE

The glove should be open and in a ready position, to the side of the body. The player should try to catch all pucks to the glove side and release immediately to the corner or to a teammate. He should not let the puck hit the boards if possible. The glove hand is brought to the body if face-off is desired. Shots at the midsection should be controlled by the glove hand. Only the pucks on the glove side should be caught. The stick, pads, and skates are used only for low shots, and the goalie should not try to catch every shot on the net.

FREEZING THE PUCK WITH THE GLOVE

To freeze the puck with the glove, the goalie puts the blade of the stick in front to protect the hand. The body is put directly behind the puck.

STICK GLOVE

Shots to the stick glove can be either deflected to the corner or (preferably) covered and controlled by the catching glove. To deflect shots, the stick glove should angle only slightly to the corner and down. Pucks shot to the midsection of the body should be blocked by the stick glove and controlled by the catching glove.

BLOCK PASS FROM CORNER

The blade of the stick is kept outside the goalpost to prevent the pass from the corner to the front of the net. The goalie should be in a position facing forward, ready to save the shot if the pass is completed to the offensive man in front of the net.

BEHIND THE NET

The goalie must be able to skate quickly from the net and stop the puck behind the net. The stick is held in one hand and the puck is left approximately six inches from the boards so that a teammate can easily take possession. If the goalie is rushed by the attacking players, the puck should be shot back to the corner it came from. Once the puck is stopped, he should return quickly to the net. Until he has gained confidence, he should stop only shots from outside the blue line behind the net.

PASSING THE PUCK

The goaltender should attempt to clear all shots to a teammate. To pass the puck on the forehand side, he should use two hands on the stick and one hand for the backhand.

GOALTENDER POKE CHECK

The poke check can be used when the offensive player cuts across from the side of the net or moves straight in close to the goaltender. When the offensive man cuts across in front of the net, the goaltender should make the poke check with the bottom of the blade as the puck carrier draws even to the net. When the player comes straight, the goalie waits until he reaches to within extended stick length. This move is not advisable unless the puck carrier has his head down and is in close.

To poke check, the goalie pushes the stick forward and holds the stick at the end of the handle. He hits the puck with the bottom of the blade. The stick arm should be fully extended. The front knee is on the ice and the back leg is extended. The goaltender must make sure that the puck carrier is in range before he makes the push with the stick.

BOUNCE SHOT SAVE

Pucks shot at the stick should be steered to a teammate or to the corner by angling the blade to an angle greater than 90 degrees. The blade of the stick should not rest against the skates but should be held in front. Pucks hitting the skates should be steered to the corner. The pads should be bent forward slightly to allow shots to project downward instead of outward. Shots to the body should be controlled by both gloves. Shots to the stick glove should be deflected downward or to the corner or, if possible, controlled by the glove hand. Shots to the glove side should be caught cleanly and quickly thrown to the side or back to a teammate. If time permits, in a glove save the puck should be dropped to the stick and passed forward or to the side to a teammate.

CLEARING THE PUCK

The goaltender must be quick to clear any pucks in front of the net to a teammate or to the corner. Either the forehand or backhand pass with one hand on the stick is the quickest method. If time permits, a two-hand forehand pass can be executed.

SCREEN SHOTS

The goalie keeps low and moves to try and get a view of the puck. He moves out of the net to cut down the angles. The defenseman can help the goaltender by moving the players from in front of the net.

BREAKAWAY

On a breakaway, the goaltender should stay well out as the player crosses the blue line. He should move back into the crease only as the player moves in closer. He should stay out if the player has his head down.

TWO-ON-ONE, THREE-ON-ONE, THREE-ON-TWO

In a two-on-one, the goaltender should play the puck carrier and leave the open man to the defenseman. If the puck carrier moves right to the net, the defenseman must then move to prevent the puck carrier from cutting across in front of the net. The goaltender must play the puck, being aware that the other offensive player may have moved to the slot area. The goaltender must play the puck at all times, in all other three-on-one and three-on-two situations.

ON-ICE DRILLS FOR GOALTENDERS

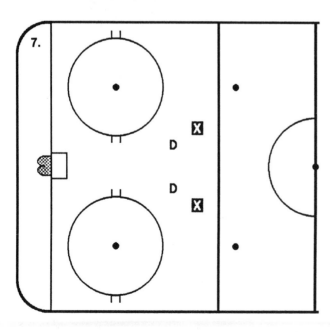

1. Skating (not shown)
Players perform all drills in chapter 5, "Skating."

2. Shooting (not shown)
Players perform all drills in chapter 7, "Shooting."

3. Knees and Up (not shown)
In this agility drill, goalie goes down on both knees and quickly jumps up to his feet.

4. Side to Side (not shown)
In this agility drill, goalie moves from post to post as quickly as possible.

5. In and Out, Side to Side (not shown)
In this agility drill, goalie moves in and out and side to side in his crease.

6. Saves (not shown)
The goalie practices the following movements on both knees: skate saves, full splits, half splits, double leg slides, and butterfly pad saves.

7. Movement Drill
Players pass the puck around and the goalie moves with the puck.

The goaltender must be able to react quickly to the movement of the puck. Positioning is also important: experienced goaltenders stop many shots by body position alone.

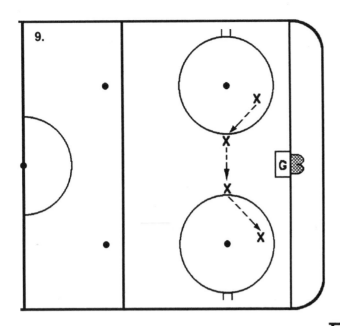

8. Pick Up Pucks (not shown)

In this agility drill, goalie, without stick, picks up the puck from a pile on one side, places it in the middle of the crease, moves to the opposite side, and repeats.

9. Movement Drill Variation

Players pass the puck across in a semicircle in front of the net. Goalie moves with the puck.

10. Puck to Corner (not shown)

Players throw or shoot puck at goalie, who steers puck toward corner.

11. Bounce Shots (not shown)

Players throw or shoot bounce shots at goalie.

12. Pass (not shown)

Players shoot on goalie, alternately passing the puck to a breaking forward and to both sides.

13. Behind the Net (not shown)

Players shoot pucks around the boards, and goalie stops them behind the net.

14. Clear (not shown)

Players pass pucks from the corner, and goalie stops the pucks and clears.

15. Angle Drill

Players are stationed at various positions with pucks. Players shoot on command, and goalie covers angle of shooter.

16. Over the Pads (not shown)

Goalie lies on his side. The coach kneels by his side and drops the puck in front of the pads. A player skates in and tries to shoot the puck over the pads.

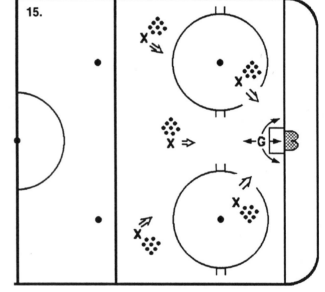

17. Tight Turn (not shown)

Goalie skates around net with a tight turn.

18. Backward Turn (not shown)

Goalie skates around the net with a tight turn and turns backward.

19. Agility

Goalie jumps over stick, stops, jumps backward, and stops.

20. In and Out (not shown)

Goalie makes a poke check at puck.

21. Jump (not shown)

Goalie jumps over stick waved two feet off the ice.

22. Screen (not shown)

Goalie rebounds and screens shots from in close.

23. Agility

Goalie does a front roll and then stops a shot.

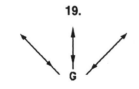

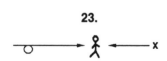

24. Shots from Coach (not shown)
Goalie lies on his side parallel to front of net or on his stomach perpendicular to front of net. Coach has pucks in a semicircle in front. On command, goalie gets to his feet as quickly as possible and stops shot by coach. This is repeated.

25. Agility (not shown)
Goalie moves on coach's signal all ways.

26. Agility (not shown)
Goalie goes across ice with short side steps.

27. Agility (not shown)
Goalie moves across ice with leg-crossing side steps.

28. Angle Drill (not shown)
Coach moves to various positions, and goalie moves with him to cover angle for shot from that position. Coach advises goalie if angle is correct.

29. Off the Backboards (not shown)
Players shoot pucks off the backboards so that they end up in front of the net, and goalie clears the pucks either to the corner or to a player.

OFF-ICE GOALTENDING DRILLS
Off-ice training for goalies should emphasize flexibility, agility, speed, and strength training. Head and leg movements similar to those used in a game may also be simulated in off-ice training. Remind players to do all exercises slowly.

Flexibility
1. Alternate Toe Touch

2. Double-Leg Toe Touch

3. Hurdler's Stretch
Goalie touches forehead to alternate knees and then forehead to knees held together.

4. Backward Bend
In a kneeling position, goalie grasps the ankles and bends backward.

5. "V" Sit

6. Bent-Knee Sit-Ups

7. Crouch and Jump
Goalie crouches and jumps as high as possible with arms stretched.

Agility
1. Jump
Goalie jumps back and forth with two feet at once, holding the arms in goaltending position.

2. Jump
Goalie jumps back and forth going from one to two feet.

3. Jump
Goalie jumps sideways from one foot to the other.

4. Butterfly Position and Up

5. Forward, Backward, and Sideways Running

6. Front Roll to Fast Stop
From initial stance, goalie performs front roll quick start and fast stop and then moves sideways and sits down on chair.

7. Front Roll and Fast Stop Variation
From initial stance, goalie performs front roll quick start and fast stop and then moves sideways and sits down on chair. Coach hits tennis ball at goalie after front roll and fast stop.

8. Dive to Crouch
Goalie dives forward and then comes back to a crouched position.

9. Kip Up
Goalie does a front kip up and then a back kip up.

10. Front Roll to Half-Splits Position

11. Cartwheel

12. Trampoline Work
Goalie does jumps, spins, forward and backward somersaults, and jumps with knees up.

Specific Catching Drills
1. Catch Tennis Balls
Standing five feet from the wall with a tennis ball in each hand, goalie throws the balls alternately and together against the wall and catches them on the rebound.

2. Throw Tennis Balls
Working in a pair, two goalies throw two tennis balls back and forth.

3. Juggle
Goalie juggles two tennis balls.

4. Hit the Tennis Ball
Goalie hits the tennis ball at the glove side and stick side.

5. Medicine Ball
Working in a pair, two goalies throw a medicine ball or volleyball back and forth.

6. Butterfly Catch
Two goalies face each other in a butterfly position. A tennis ball is dropped between them, and the two players attempt to catch the ball.

7. Racket
The goalie stands in front of a piece of plywood the size of a net with both stick and catching glove. The instructor stands 15 feet away and hits tennis balls with a racket high and low, trying to hit the plywood.

8. High and Low
The goalie stands in front of a piece of plywood the size of a net with both stick and catching glove. A screening player stands in front of goalie. The instructor stands 15 feet away and hits tennis balls with a racket high and low, trying to hit the plywood.

16. PLAY OF THE DEFENSEMEN

The play of defensemen is an important topic when discussing the requirements for a successful team in today's style of hockey. Defensemen have to be as skilled as anyone on the team. Their traditional defensive role is still important, but their offensive involvement is of increasing value. The good defenseman is expected to

• work the defense
• be big and strong to move people away from the front of the net
• be quick and agile in moving the puck to initiate the play in the defensive zone

In order to control the middle of the ice you need to have your most skilled players on the defense and at center. If you don't have defensemen who can handle the puck well you may have to think about converting a forward. This is the type of player teams are looking for. Few teams win without them.

Prepare defensemen for this style of play by

• knowing the skills required for being a successful defenseman
• using drills appropriate for teaching the specific skills
• being able to evaluate the learning efforts of the player and offering feedback

TECHNICAL SKILLS REQUIRED FOR PLAYING DEFENSE

Some say that you only need to teach the technical skills to the young players, but this is not so. All age groups can benefit from technical improvement. Contrary to the way many coaches feel, even the 16 to 20 age group can make great progress if taught properly.

SKATING
In hockey, defensemen have to perform all the skating skills—not just tight turns and quick starts, but backward skating, pivoting, and all the other skating skills. The skating skills that are particularly important for defensemen are

• backward crossovers, so that skaters can accelerate while skating backward in order to keep in front of the puck carrier
• turning—especially from backward to forward, as it means moving laterally to stop someone from going wide around defensemen
• backward stop and start
• tight turn and moving forward with quick acceleration
• quick start

PASSING
If the defenseman can't pass the puck, none of the basic ideas for breakouts are going to work. Good passing is essential for getting organized in your own end and for performing the regrouping plays in the neutral zone. All passing skills should be constantly reviewed, with players using both the backhand and the forehand. Some of the more important skills include

• a sweep and snap pass while skating backward and forward
• a sweep and snap pass coming out of a tight turn
• "one touch" passing
• a clearing flip pass

CHECKING
The defensemen are expected to be good checkers, but often they are not taught the details of performing the various checks. The basic checking skills used by the defensemen are

• poke check
• shoulder check
• hip check. In the past there have been some real masters of this check, but it is seldom practiced today. Interestingly, there are some coaches who feel that the hip check shouldn't be used at all, especially along the boards, because if the defenseman misses, the opponent is home free. They would rather have

the defenseman turn outside and face the man than go in with the rear and risk missing him. The hip check, if executed properly, is really effective in the neutral zone.

- controlling the man along the boards
- controlling the man in front of the net
- a diving poke check. If a defenseman gets caught in a one-on-none and has been beaten, this check can be used in a last effort.

PUCKHANDLING

- skating backward with the puck and then passing it, which often occurs in the neutral zone
- making a pivot and then accelerating forward
- stickhandling through tight turns

SHOOTING

- quick releasing the puck
- slap and snap shots, especially with low follow-throughs for a low shot
- wrist shot
- one-timing the shots

INDIVIDUAL TACTICAL SKILLS

There are players who have reasonable technical skills but lack the ability to fully utilize them in games. Helping players use their skills effectively in a game requires constant work. Do not assume that a defenseman will know how to defend against a one-on-one unless it is practiced. The tactical skills that a defenseman should have are discussed below.

DEFENSIVE ZONE
Defensive Skills

- making a diving poke check in a one-on-none when a defenseman is beaten and is the last man
- making a poke check with head up, stick in one hand, and elbow bent when in range on a one-on-one, while keeping the head up and continuing to take the man
- defending on a two-on-one. The last defender should imagine a line running the length of the ice between the goalposts and play the opponents there. Also, he might think of the situation as a two-on-two in which the goalie has the outside shots and the defenseman has the middle. When the puck gets within 15 feet of the net, the defenseman should go for the puck carrier because the goalie can then move out to play the shooter. It is preferable that the defenseman use the marking on the ice as reference points when out to challenge the puck carrier.
- (most coaches would advocate) staying on your own side and not crossing until there is a threat of scoring on a two-on-two
- playing half-ice on a three-on-two
- closing the gap, and with winger covered, moving toward the middle of the ice on a three-on-two (with one backchecker)
- standing up over the blue line in a three-on-two (with two backcheckers)
- going into the corner to control the opponent
- covering the front of the net
- avoiding and fighting off screens
- intercepting passes and blocking shots, making sure that the blocker is close to the shooter before going down whether with a slide, one knee, or two knees

Offensive Skills

Emphasize the importance of moving the puck quickly, particularly in the defensive zone. In almost all instances this will mean the player makes the pass while moving. Besides getting more power behind the passes, movement also means a greater threat to a forechecker or a defenseman, who will often pull back when a puck carrier is moving toward him.

- retrieving the puck off the end boards at high speed
- feigning moves to get the forechecker off the defenseman as he retrieves the puck off the boards
- being able to pass quickly and accurately coming out of sharp turns
- knowing how to support the play as the last man
- knowing when to pass cross-ice in the defensive zone (a very dangerous play!)

NEUTRAL ZONE
Defensive Skills
- knowing how to look for the opponent who may have cut behind
- knowing how much room to give on attacking situations, e.g., on a two-on-one or a three-on-two with one backchecker, the defender should start from the far blue line and maintain fast backward skating to be able to react to any situation
- knowing how to read the attack
- being able to force the attacker to play to the defenseman's strength

Offensive Skills
- puckhandling skills to set up the regrouping plays: passing laterally to the other defenseman and making a pass to a curling forward
- moving up to support the forwards in carrying the puck over the opponent's blue line, the "second wave"

OFFENSIVE ZONE
Defensive Skills
- reading when to hold the blue line and when to retreat
- knowing when and how to "pinch"
- knowing how to play the offensive man one-on-one on the blue line
- knowing how to provide support for the other defenseman
- being able to identify and cover the quick counterattack

Offensive Skills
- skating well enough to carry the puck in
- puckhandling and shooting well enough to move in as a scoring threat
- knowing when and where to shoot from the blue line. It is preferable to make most of the shots from mid-ice. When a shot has to be made from the boards, it should be kept low and on the goal so it can be deflected.
- one-timing the shot from the blue line
- making passes to open up the middle for the slot man

DEVELOPING THE SKILLS

Drills are the means for achieving the desired skills. Being able to show one or two new drills every practice is not as important as using drills that work. Use enough drills to keep things from getting monotonous, but concentrate on ones that emphasize the fundamentals.

The key to using drills properly is knowing what you want to achieve. If there is a particular problem or skill that you feel should be dealt with, then this should be the basis for selecting your drill. If the drill can also be made to simulate game conditions, that will eliminate the further problem of transferring what has been learned to a game situation. When a drill is done with game intensity, it will also add spirit and enthusiasm to your practice that is similar to what is expected during a game.

Besides setting up drills that are skill- and game-specific, note what kind of learning is taking place. The mark of a good coach is knowing the details of what is required and comparing it with what is actually being demonstrated by the players. Evaluating the outcome and offering constructive feedback is essential in the proper use of drills.

How much time should be spent on defensemen-related drills? Certainly there should be a component in every practice, and many of the drills for the forwards could involve the defensemen. If the time is available, consider having a special practice once a week just for the defensemen.

Start all practices with the simplest drill, to build up players' success rates and confidence. Gradually add to the complexity and get closer to game conditions.

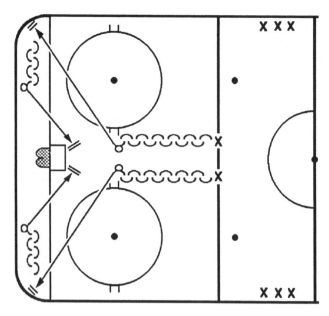

DEFENSEMEN DRILLS
1. Backward Turning, Both Sides

When the offensive team brings the puck into the defensive zone, the defensemen usually have to play their man by pivoting to the inside or outside.

Players skate backward from the blue line and, at an ice marking or signal, turn to the outside, skate forward into the corner, and stop. They then skate backward a few strides, turn in an opposite direction to their first turn, and skate to the net and stop. Have them switch sides after each time through.

2. Agility

During the game, the defensemen must be able to move quickly in a confined area, e.g., playing the box against a power play.

Players skate forward from the goal line to the blue line, do stepovers halfway across the blue line, skate backward to the middle of the circle, turn to the outside and skate deep into the corner, and make a sharp turn and return to the front of the net.

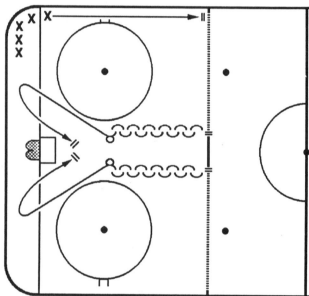

3. Cross-Ice Crossovers

Defensemen are expected to be able to skate backward, accelerating and moving side to side.

Players move as a wave across the ice, making three to four crossovers each way.

Variation: Players execute the same exercise but change direction in response to a signal and do it going lengthwise.

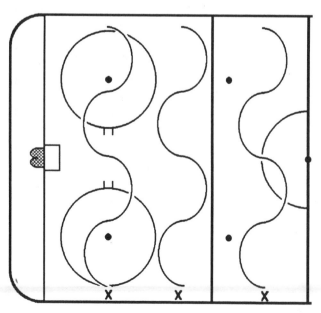

4. One-on-One Cross-Ice

Defensemen must be able to stay face-to-face with an opponent while backing up.

Players are paired off. Attacking players skate forward using three to four crossovers. The defenders skate backward, attempting to stay in front.

Variation: Attackers use a puck, but the defenders do not aggressively attempt to check it away.

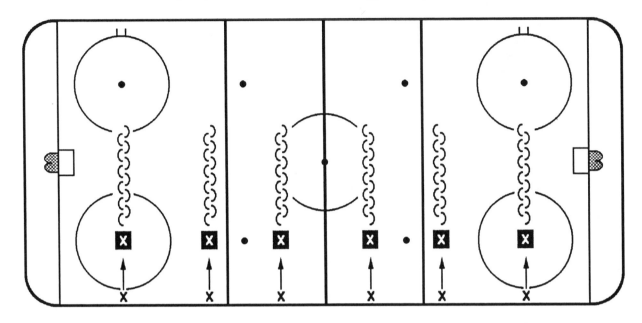

5. Zigzag

Defensemen always have the need for fast backward skating speed plus the ability to quickly transfer to sharp lateral movement to stay with an opponent.

Players skate backward to each of the lines and then cross-step along the length of each line.

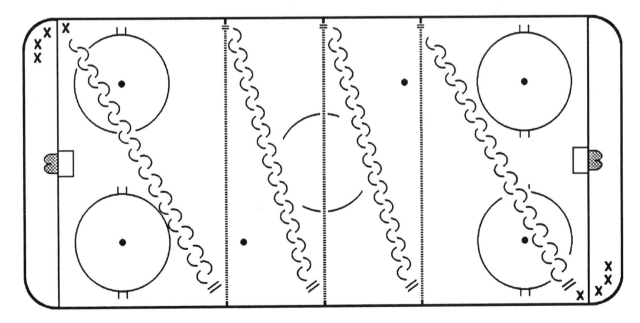

6. Quick Turn

Defensemen must be able to quickly retrieve a puck off the end boards under strong forechecking pressure, make a sharp turn, and move the puck up ice.

Each player dumps the puck in the corner and retrieves it by making a sharp turn and quickly accelerating out with the puck. It is important to pick the puck up using maneuvers that throw off the forechecker, e.g., a head fake or a wave movement of the stick in the opposite direction. Add forecheckers to the drill later.

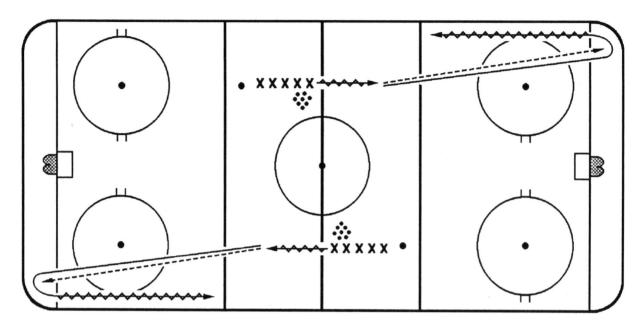

PASSING DRILLS
1. Shuttle Drill

There are a number of occasions during a game when a defenseman has to make passes while skating backward or forward and be able to convert these passes from receptions that vary from a puck sliding along the ice to a puck knocked down by a glove.

One player moves forward, the other moves backward across the ice. The puck is passed back and forth using different skills, e.g., flipping the puck and batting it down with a glove or one touching a return pass.

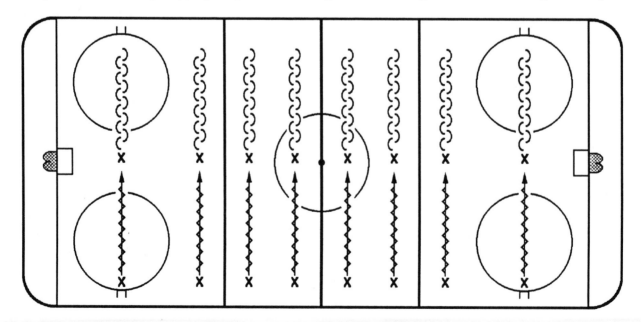

2. Backward Passing

Skating backward with the puck is very important in today's game. Good neutral zone play is difficult if the defensemen can't skate backward with the puck to help spread the forecheckers and give the regrouping forwards time to find open passing lanes.

The front player in each line (the one with the puck) skates to mid-ice and passes the puck to his partner. Both skate backward to the goal, passing the puck between them.

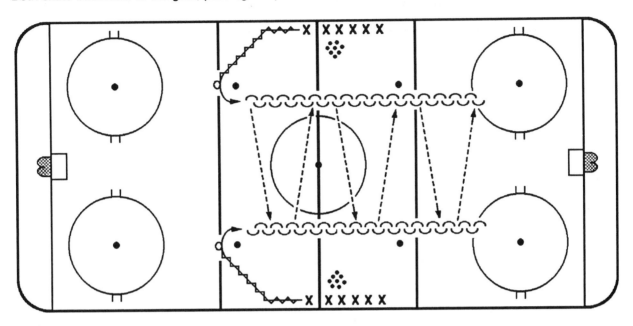

3. Defenseman-to-Defenseman Passing

In neutral zone regrouping, it is often necessary for one defenseman to pass to the other before moving the puck to a curling forward.

The forward starts out with the puck and passes to the defenseman on his side. The defenseman skates backward with the puck and passes it to his defense partner, who then gives the forward a pass as he curls around center circle.

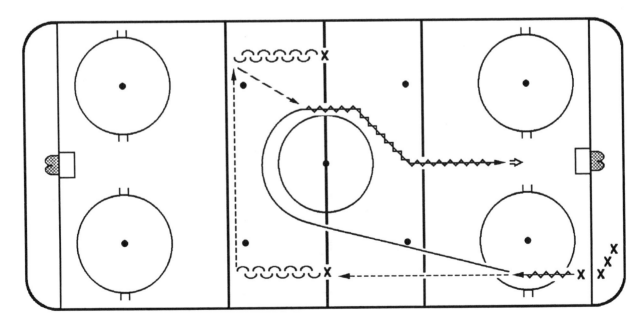

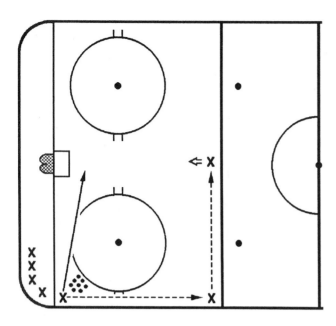

SHOOTING DRILL
Defenseman-to-Defenseman Shooting

Point men often have to make quick decisions on a pass out or when clearing a shot from a corner. To add to the complexity, the puck often arrives in a manner that is difficult to receive.

The player in the corner passes to the defenseman in different ways: off the boards, off the glass, bouncing, and so on. He then goes to the net for deflections. The defenseman learns to play a variety of pass outs. He relays a pass to his defense partner as quickly as possible. He should look toward his partner before passing and not get in the habit of passing blindly. Slow passes likely will have to be returned to a corner man, in which case give-and-go from the corner man can be made.

CHECKING DRILLS

1. Hip Check (not shown)

Defensemen have to have many ways of checking. Sometimes hip checking an opponent is the most effective way. There is a tendency to ignore teaching this type of check, which, if done correctly, can be very effective in taking a man completely out of the play.

The drill begins with the defenseman practicing along the boards. The defenseman goes into the boards with his hip and checks the man. When some success has been attained, the players move out to open ice.

2. Diving Poke Check (not shown)

Sometimes the defenseman is the last man back and is beaten by the puck carrier. A diving poke check is often the only recourse available. Have players experience the different ways of sliding along the ice. Have them slide along the ice trying to touch the puck and the stick of the puck carrier first.

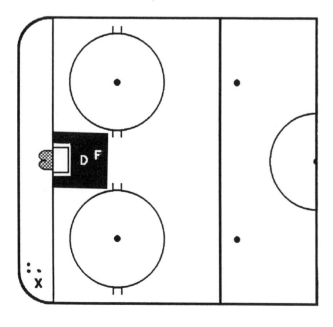

3. Controlling Man in Front of the Net

It is necessary for defensemen to control the area in front of the net. Knowing how to tie up a man is an important part of this play.

The player in the corner has three pucks and passes them out to the forward in the low slot. The forward must move around the low slot area to try to get open for a pass for a shot on goal. The defenseman practices controlling in a legal manner by angling, blocking, pushing, or using his stick.

4. One-on-One

Defensemen should be aware that they can sometimes get beaten on a one-on-one. However, they shouldn't become so obsessed that they are caught leaving the blue line before they have to. The defenseman can keep the puck in if he moves in quickly and challenges the puck carrier before full speed is attained.

   The player starts from a corner with the puck. The defenseman should close the gap with the puck carrier by getting within a stick's length before too much speed is built up. The defenseman starts at the blue line and moves at an angle, two strides inside the blue line, to pick up the player coming from the corner. The defenseman now skates backward to play the one-on-one.

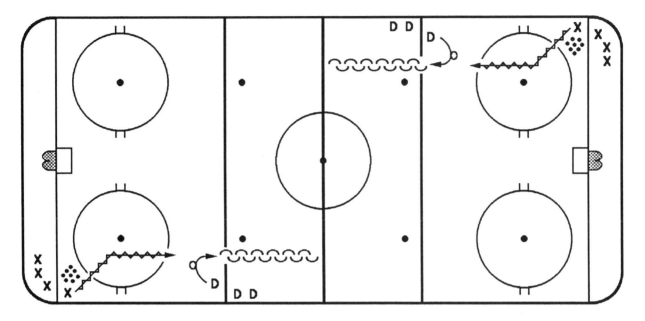

5. One-on-One Swing

Have defensemen execute this drill to improve their backward skating speed.

   The player starts the play without a puck and swings around a pylon at the far blue line. He receives a pass from the corner and stickhandles down the ice in a one-on-one. When the original player who started the drill leaves, a player from the inside line leaves and swings around center circle, pivots, and plays the one-on-one. Defensemen rotate lines each time they come back.

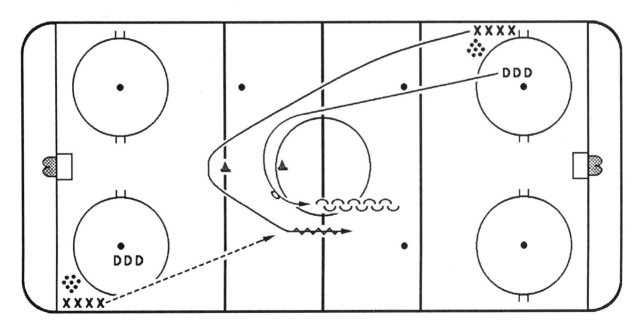

6. One-on-One Swing

This drill forces the defenseman to stretch his backward skating speed to its maximum level. The player starts from the corner without the puck and receives a pass from the defenseman, who swings around the pylon at the blue line. The puck carrier goes for the far net with game intensity. The defenseman skates around the pylon, pivots, and plays the man one-on-one so that it will require all-out backward skating.

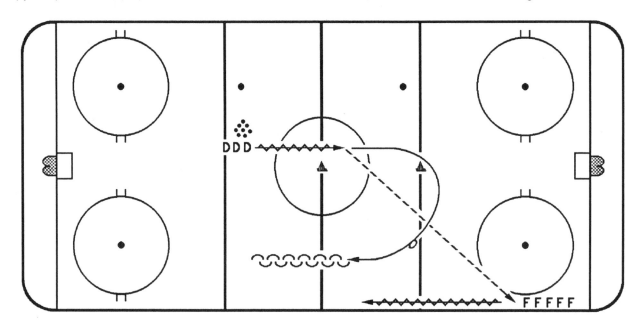

BLOCKING SHOTS

Defensemen sometimes go down to block shots in the high slot, and if they miss, they give the puck carrier an open road to the net.

Set up a drill in the low slot where you want a block to occur, and if necessary, build up the blocker's confidence by using tennis balls. Have the players practice different styles: the slide and one- and two-knee blocks. Experiment with each one to determine its blocking value and effectiveness in preventing the shooter from avoiding the block.

TEAM PLAY SITUATIONS

Defensemen should be starting all the team drills. The more they do this, the more they will have a chance to practice their passing skills. I'm not a believer in the two-on-nones or three-on-nones. Maybe they are good for a warm-up drill, but not for working on something that you are going to use in a game. Besides, a three-on-none is not a gamelike situation. The defensemen should be in drills at all times. They should start the play and be in it all the way because that is what happens in a game.

Too often the defenseman on a two-on-one or three-on-one becomes overanxious and moves out of the mid-ice zone, giving the attacker the inside shot. Preferably, the defenseman should stay in the middle and go no farther than the imaginary line between the posts on either side. When the puck gets back to within 10 to 15 feet of the goal, the defenseman has to play the puck carrier.

TEAM PLAY DRILLS
1. Two-on-One

The defenseman starts the play for two forwards with a breakout pass. The defenseman then skates hard for the far blue line and prepares to defend against a two-on-one on the return rush.

The forwards execute a two-on-one rush. Upon completion of the two-on-one play, the defenseman defending the two-on-one play picks up a puck and starts a rush the other way.

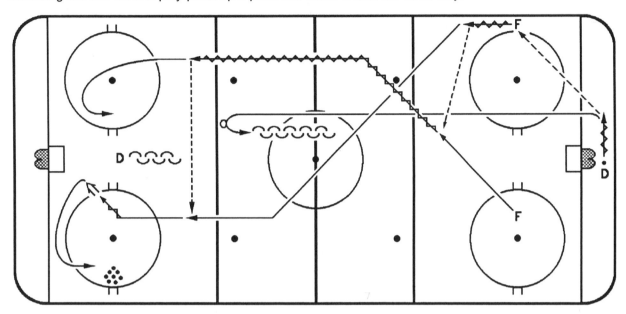

2. Backchecking Drill

In this drill, the coach tries to get the defense to stand up at the blue line. The drill starts with a defenseman-to-defenseman pass, a pass to a forward, and a five-on-four breakout. The two backcheckers pick up the lanes, allow the defensemen to stand up at the blue line, and concentrate on the puck carrier. When the initial rush is completed, the flow is maintained with a five-on-two going the opposite way. This is repeated two or three times.

Variation: Use just one backchecker or one forechecker in the offensive zone and one backchecker in the neutral and defensive zone. Have backcheckers vary their activity by filling lanes, covering a winger, or checking the puck carrier so the defensemen can practice reading and reacting to different situations.

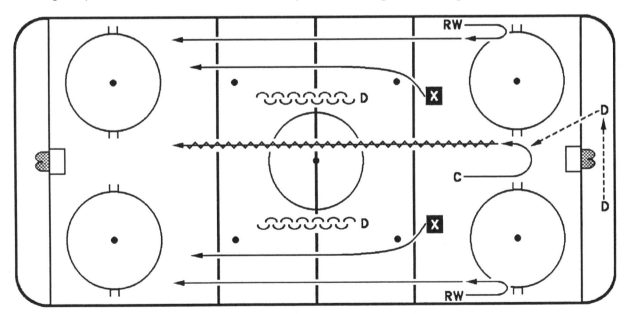

These backchecking drills should be part of almost every practice. The flow and the variations also make it possible to build up the intensity and simulate game conditions.

17. PLAY OF THE FORWARDS

SPECIFIC ABILITIES OF FORWARDS

A winger needs the ability to

• cut in after taking a pass
• make a quick, hard, accurate shot coming off the wings
• speedskate well
• take and give a pass
• pick up a check

A center needs to

• have good hockey sense
• pass well on forehand and backhand
• stickhandle well
• skate well and quickly and crossover while accelerating
• shoot quickly
• check well
• have better-than-average endurance
• be a good face-off man

POSITIONAL PLAY

DEFENSIVE END
Wingers should station themselves near the boards with the stick in a position to receive and give a pass quickly. The center should be circling with his stick on the ice in a position ready for a pass. The puck should be passed to the head man as quickly as possible.

NEUTRAL ZONE
Wingers should be skating down by the boards looking for an opening to put on a quick acceleration. The stick should be on or near the ice in position for receiving a pass.

OFFENSIVE ZONE
The winger should be in the corner if the puck is on his side. He should have his head up, take the man first, and then go for the puck.

   If the winger receives a pass, he should be able to cut in without losing stride and shoot or drop the puck in the slot. The far side winger should position himself in the slot area squared off to the net, ready to shoot.

   The center should make the play, if possible, just as the winger hits the offensive blue line. The center should trail the play or go on the forecheck if the puck has been shot in.

   Chapter 10, "Offensive Team Play," describes the offensive play of the forwards.

FACE-OFF TECHNIQUES

The man taking the face-off should make sure that all players are in position before taking the face-off.

   The player taking the face-off should be able to watch the puck in the referee's hand and the opponent's stick at the same time by using peripheral vision. Quick reaction time is essential in this skill.

   Players taking the face-off should have many methods of winning:

BACKHAND
This is the most common method. The player draws the puck at an angle or, in some instances, directly back on the backhand side.

FOREHAND

The player anticipates the dropping of the puck. He rotates his body by a quarter turn. He comes in front of, behind, or under an opponent's stick.

ANTICIPATE THE DROPPING OF THE PUCK

The player anticipates the dropping of the puck. As soon as the puck leaves the official's hand, he hits the blade of the opponent's stick and then draws the puck back.

HOLD AND DRAW

The player holds the opponent's stick with the blade of his own stick until the puck has made contact with the ice. Then he draws the puck back.

LIFT AND DRAW

If the opponent is attempting to slash the blade of the stick and is not going for the puck, the player taking the face-off lifts the blade of the stick and then goes for the puck.

SHOOT

The puck is shot directly from the face-off.

SKATE THROUGH AND SHOOT

The face-off man pushes the opponent's stick upward, skates through the face-off dot, and kicks the puck to the stick.

DRILLS FOR FORWARDS

All shooting, passing, stickhandling, and checking drills mentioned in chapters 2, 3, 4, and 5 are excellent for forwards. Special emphasis should be placed on the forward's taking a pass in full stride and shooting quickly.

All one-on-one, two-on-one, two-on-two, three-on-one, and three-on-two drills in which the winger or wingers are covered should be emphasized. Individual face-off practice and team skill are also essential. Offensive zone drills in chapter 10, "Offensive Team Play," are also excellent drills for forwards.

18. SCOUTING, GAME PREPARATION, AND BENCH MANAGEMENT

The saying "Failure to prepare is preparing to fail" is a coaching truism. Careful planning and preparation for games give the athletes and coaches a sense that they are ready for the contest. A well-prepared team knows what to expect from the other team, and this gives the players a feeling of confidence.

Game preparation can be divided into five areas: scouting the opposition, practice utilization for the opposition, pregame meeting, bench management during the game, and between-period adjustments.

SCOUTING

Scouting the opposition should be done as close to the game date as possible. Trends, new personnel, changes in tactics, and so on, are reasons why the latest game of the opposition team should be viewed. Usually one or two members of the staff and the team should scout the game. The scouting report on pages 189–90 can be used to critique and analyze the opposition.

GAME PREPARATION

PREGAME MEETING
It is useful to have a meeting to discuss the opposition's strengths and weaknesses. Such topics as playing style, power play, penalty killing, breakouts, forward lines, defense pairings, goaltending style, outstanding players, and so on, can be discussed during this meeting. The scouting report can be used to discuss the opposition, and if short video segments are available on power play, breakouts, penalty killing, and so on, they can be used at this time.

The pregame meeting should be no longer than 20 to 30 minutes. This should be more than enough time to highlight the opposition. Each player should be aware of such details as arrival time at the arena, the proper time to be in the dressing room, and game and warm-up times.

PREGAME PRACTICE
The practice prior to the next game may also be used to prepare a team for the opposition. Practicing against the opposition's style of forechecking, penalty killing, power play, and breakouts is a way to prepare your team against certain systems.

A pregame meeting may occur before the practice or could be conducted on game day. Skate sharpening and preparation of sticks and equipment should be done after the last practice and before the game, as the players' focus should be totally on the game when they arrive at the arena.

ARRIVAL AT THE ARENA
Coaches and players need information about such details as the size of the ice surface, shape of the corners, height of the glass around the rink (for pucks shot above the board level), type of ice (fast or slow, especially near the end of a period), lighting, and size and location of the entry gates to the bench.

Home Games
Most coaches have a set time at which the players must be in the dressing room. In most situations, players should be there a minimum of 45 minutes before the scheduled warm-up. If dressing room stretching exercises are part of the routine, the players should be prepared for this one hour before the warm-up. A good working relationship with the arena personnel is important in gaining their cooperation in flooding the ice and cleaning the dressing rooms, and so on.

Away Games
That the players have thorough knowledge of all details such as location of arena, parking, entrance doors, and so on, is important for the smooth preparation for a game. The location and size of dressing rooms and information on the availability of a blackboard and chalk or rink diagram board is important information for the coach to know.

OPPOSITION SCOUTING

| Score | Team Scouted | vs. | Opposition | Score |

| Scouted by | Date | Place |

| **Forward Lines** | **Order of Lines** | **Defensive Pairs** |

Order of Lines columns: 1st   2nd   3rd

Own End with Puck	
How puck is brought out How they set up center circles Pass up the middle Defensemen carry	
Opposition End with Puck	
Shoot or carry puck across the blue line Position of center (net or slot) Good shooters Special plays	
Power Play	
How puck is brought out Center come behind net Center pick up or leave for defenseman How they bring puck in over the blue line Special plays Shoot or carry across blue line Special plays in opposition end Position of center in relation to box	

Penalty Killing Force play, how Pick up wings Defense up at the center for rush (at blue line or back in) Any forechecking pattern Box tight or loose Do they cover slot well Special face-off plays Two men short	
Own End (Defensively) Who covers points Wingers up, center back; or reverse Defense rough in front Weaknesses Face-off plays	
Opposition End (Checking) Who forechecks Position of center Do defensemen hang in at blue line Weaknesses	
Goaltending Rebounds Clearing puck Glove hand Stick hand Half splits Skate save Long shots Bounce shots Conditioning Other comments	
General Comments Roughness How they start the game Face-offs (unusual) and best man Comments on lines Players to watch Unusual plays Other	

BENCH MANAGEMENT

Bench management is very important. The coach has to adjust to the opposition as well as handle the team in an efficient manner during a game. Details such as the location of the gates on the players' bench and the movement of players going on and coming off the ice are very important. In most cases an assistant trainer or other administrative personnel can open the gates. Some coaches prefer the defensemen to sit at the end of the bench, closer to their own end of the rink, with the forwards at the other end. Players usually come in through the gates and go out over the boards (younger age groups should use the door at all times). Another useful idea is to have the players sit together in lines and defense pairs and move toward the middle of the bench. They are then ready to go over the boards when their names are called. This also allows the coach to be aware of those players who have not been on the ice recently or who have been sitting on the bench for some time, as they will be on the middle of the bench. Some players may be on the bench by design of the coach, or they just may have missed shifts due to penalty killing or power play situations.

It is important for a coach to plan before the game. He needs to plan which players he is going to use in certain situations such as power play and penalty killing, how many lines he is going to use, which players will play more when the team is behind or ahead in the game, and which players can be switched in event of injuries. The coach must also decide if he wants to match lines or cover certain players with a defensive-type player.

Having done all this, the coach must be ready to make quick decisions on playing personnel throughout the game and must have a feel for which players are playing well on a certain night.

It is important that your players know who is going on the ice next. There are different systems for calling players, such as by line or defense pairs, but in most cases the individual name of each player should be called for each line or defense pair up for the next shift. Little problems such as players with the same first or last name should be solved in advance by using nicknames. A good idea is to tell the players to turn and ask the coach if no names were called or if the players did not hear the names. The players should also be aware that they are responsible for replacing a player on the ice when he comes to the bench for a change. Therefore, they must be aware of which player on the ice is playing which position. In penalty killing and power play situations the coach may want to designate which position a replacement is filling on the ice. It is also the responsibility of the player on the bench to make sure that player on the ice is actually coming to the bench. Changing "on the fly" is something which should be practiced. Most changes should be made while your team is in possession of the puck and the play is in the neutral or offensive zone. Some coaches time the on-ice shifts using a stopwatch, with the alternate goalie or assistant coach doing the timing. This allows the players to get into a routine of quick changes. They will also be aware that the coach knows the length of each player's shifts.

If a delayed penalty is indicated and an extra man can be put on the ice when the goaltender comes to the bench, the coach should have a system for the player that replaces the goalie. Usually the coach designates one specific player or a specific position, such as the center of the next line up, to take the place of the goaltender.

The coach should be very aware of the momentum of the game. If his team is being outplayed badly, slowing the pace of the game may be a good strategy. Coaches have been known to change the lines and defense pairs more frequently than usual, change goalies, or even call a time-out if this type of strategy is warranted in an attempt to change the momentum of the game.

The coach should also be in total control of the bench and, along with an assistant coach, should not allow negative comments about fellow teammates or yelling at the referee. The coach should be under control behind the bench, but that does not preclude showing emotion or displeasure with a bad call by the referee. It is important that the coach keep control, as emotions can allow him to get carried away and cause him to be unready for the next quick decision. Emotions, when used wisely, can sometimes be a motivational factor for the players.

On most teams the head coach makes the line changes and personnel adjustments, while the assistant coach gives individual feedback to the players. It is important that the head and assistant coaches are coordinated and that each has a definite role behind the bench. A very important job of the coaches is to have the right players out at the right time and give feedback to the players during the game.

BETWEEN PERIODS OF THE GAME

A good practice for coaches is to meet with the assistant coaches before going into the dressing room between periods. At this time, they could discuss the period statistics, such as shots on goal and where they were taken, plus/minus, weaknesses of the team, strengths of the other teams, players playing well and players playing poorly, and general strategy. After this has been done the head coach can go into the dressing room to discuss strategy and possible changes. Depending on the situation and how the team is performing, the coach can be positive or negative. If the team is playing well, very little need be said. If the team is playing poorly, strategy changes, adjustments in style, personnel changes, and so on, can be discussed. If the coach feels that the team is underachieving, it may be a situation in which the coach can be negative or can use anger to motivate. If the coach has been negative, it may be wise to use some positive motivation just before the team returns to the ice to start the next period.

POSTGAME REVIEW

After the game is over, it is usual practice for a coach to enter the dressing room and make some general comments and congratulate the team on a win or make comments on a loss. The coach should let the players have a few minutes to cool down before making any comments. The coach could then review the schedule for the next practice or game. Some situations such as a big loss or poor play may require a team meeting. Some coaches have a team meeting after each game, when the players are dressed and showered. It may also be necessary to meet individually with any players who are having problems or who may have caused a problem during the game.

In many situations, the head coach meets with the assistant coaches to discuss the games, analyze the statistics, and in some cases view the video of the game if this is available. If there are two or three assistant coaches, and if a video of the game is available, the job of breaking down and analyzing is done by the assistant coaches before the next practice or game. In some cases, the head coach may ask for certain video replays, such as defensive breakdowns or power plays. In most cases the assistant coaches and the head coach will meet to discuss and view the video of the game. This can help the coaches to plan the next practice and work on apparent weaknesses.

A good coach is well organized and will have his team as prepared as possible at all times. Remember, success comes more easily to those who are prepared.

The coach should be in total control of the bench. He must be ready to make quick decisions on personnel throughout the game and have a feel for which players are playing well.

19. STATISTICS

Statistics are a very important tool for the coach to use to assess what is happening during a game and to analyze what happened after the game is over. Over a longer period of time, statistics can show trends which will help the coach assess the strengths and weaknesses of individual players and of the team as a whole.

Although statistics may not be as meaningful with young hockey players, with older players and at higher levels of competition, statistics are important in the analysis of the total game or period by period. Strategy can be devised or altered depending on what is happening during the game. After viewing the statistics, a coach may have notice tendencies in individuals or in the team as a whole that can be countered by a simple change in strategy.

Statistics point out individual and team errors that provide feedback to the coach. The coach in turn can then provide feedback to his players. In many cases the coach may have already spotted some or all of these errors, but statistics serve to reinforce or change an idea a coach may have from observation. It is important for the coach in most cases to correct errors and use positive reinforcement. Although negative reinforcement can occasionally be used at the higher levels, it is very important that statistics be used wisely by the coach and that the coach does not become negative to the players by continually emphasizing what they are doing wrong. In most cases statistics can be used in a positive way to emphasize what a player is doing right.

After a thorough review of a game, the coach can also use the statistics to help plan his practices by emphasizing the weak areas of individual and team play. The practices may also be based on game strategy for the upcoming opponent, with the statistics of a previous game against the team as a basis for this planning.

Statistics can also be used as a motivational tool. Over a period of time, statistics can measure improvement and provide goals for both the team and the player. A large battery of statistics, rather than just goals and assists, will point out the importance of all aspects of the game and the value of different types of players on the team.

With younger players, analyzing game statistics may not have the same value, as their learning the basic fundamentals and having fun should be the most important aspects of the game. Emphasizing wins and losses, goals, and assists may mean that few if any statistics are used. Skill testing may be far more useful than spending time on complex statistics. Performance expectations have to be altered with the young hockey player with the major emphasis being skill improvement.

Statistics, however, do not tell the whole story of a game, and it is important that a coach be able to quickly detect team and individual errors that are happening during a game. Statistics may confirm or change an opinion a coach may have reached through observation. It is the combination of an analytical eye and thorough game analysis that makes the complete coach.

The chart on pages 196–98 exemplifies the types of statistics that can be taken, the purpose of the statistics, and how to use them.

The forms on pages 199 and 200 are examples of a statistics sheet and a compilation of statistics for a team.

In conclusion, statistics are an important part of game analysis. They should be used positively to correct individual and team errors as well as to plan and change strategies before and during a game. If compiled properly and accurately, they can be an important aspect in the success of a team and the development of individual players.

USING THE VIDEO FOR EVALUATION AND GAME ANALYSIS

The video is a common evaluation instrument used by today's hockey coach. Video is used extensively in game analysis for games played, prescouting, and training camp evaluation.

Scoring chances, defensive breakdowns, and team and individual errors can be analyzed. Segments of the video can be shown to the team the next day or even between periods if the video viewing equipment is available. The video assists the coaches in giving a thorough evaluation of the game played. When prescouting a team, a short video presentation can help prepare a team for the upcoming opponent. The opposition's breakouts, power play, penalty killing, forechecking, and so on, can be highlighted in this presentation.

The video can also be used by the coach to assist with individual instruction for players. The player's viewing himself on video with the coach showing and correcting errors can assist in the teaching process.

It is also important to show the player some good aspects of his game, to use the video as a positive teaching tool.

In training camp it is useful to video scrimmage games for replay, especially if you are undecided on the selection of some players. Similar to a team game analysis, the video can isolate segments of specific players' play.

The video has many uses for hockey coaches. The expense of the video machines, cameras, and television set for viewing must be considered by a team before making a decision to use the video as a coaching tool. It should also be taken into consideration that the video can be overused in coaching. Long video viewing sessions on a regular basis will sometimes make players negative to its use. Highlighting clips of games that show both the positive and negative aspects of the previous game may be a more significant method for use. It is not necessary to have the players watch the video of every game, but it is a tool that the coaches can use extensively for analysis.

The video, like any coaching tool, is only as good or bad as the people using it. Use it wisely.

STATISTIC	PURPOSE OF STATISTIC	YOUR TEAM	OPPOSITION
Shots attempted	To determine the number and location of shots taken by your own team and the opposition. These shots may or may not hit the net.	**INDIVIDUAL** Not attempting enough shots. Too many bad angles or outside shots **TEAM** Not shooting enough Too many outside shots	**INDIVIDUAL** One player taking too many shots and not being checked closely enough Player getting no or few shots Reinforces good checking job **TEAM** Too many shots from slot area and/or points Team getting very few shots
Shots on net Team opponents' totals Location of shots (team and opposition) Location of goals scored (team and opposition)	To determine the accuracy of the shooting To determine the location of the shooter when the shots are on the net	**INDIVIDUAL** Not shooting enough on net Shooting from too far out **TEAM** Very few shots on net Too many shots from bad angles or from the outside Not shooting from the slot area	**INDIVIDUAL** One player getting too many shots on net Player getting very few shots on net Positive reinforcement on checking **TEAM** Too many shots on net from the slot Too many shots on net from the point or one side of the ice (e.g., right wingers or left defenseman getting too many shots)
Scoring chances	To determine how many direct scoring chances an individual or team is getting Scoring chances are only counted when a shot is taken in from the high slot area and in toward the net.	**INDIVIDUAL** No chances means a player is not moving to the slot area for a scoring chance or a player is not being passed to in the scoring area. **TEAM** No chances means the opposition is clearing the slot and checking well or the team generally is not moving to the slot area.	**INDIVIDUAL** One player may be getting free in the slot area. **TEAM** Many good scoring chances means that the slot area is not being covered well.

STATISTIC	PURPOSE OF STATISTIC	YOUR TEAM	OPPOSITION
Shooting percentages	To determine the percentages of shots taken on goal and goals scored	INDIVIDUAL To determine which players are the most proficient in the scoring area TEAM To determine if the team's shooting accuracy is adequate	INDIVIDUAL To determine players who must be watched more carefully, as the scoring percentage is high TEAM Teams that shoot high percentages must be checked more closely.
Scoring statistics Goals	To determine the top goal scorers	To determine the top goal scorers and get them on the ice at times when goals are needed (e.g., power play, behind one or two goals, pull the goalie, key face-off in opposition zone) Period-by-period breakdown may show a trend.	Check the top scorers more closely. Get checkers out against the top scorers. Period-by-period breakdown may show defensive weakness at certain times in the game.
Scoring statistics Assists	To determine the best play makers	Should show best play makers and good or poor line combinations	Top play makers may be the key to a line and should be checked closely.
First goal Tying goals Winning goals	To determine players who tend to get key goals	To determine which players tend to score key goals To know what players to use in critical situations in a game	To determine which players tend to score key goals in games To be able to defend against these players in critical game situations
Penalties: minor major unsportsmanlike misconduct match/gross misconducts	To determine which players are penalized, what type of penalties they get, and which players are seldom penalized	To determine which players tend to get more penalties than others To determine when not to play players who have a high tendency to be penalized	To determine which players tend to get more penalities than others To try to draw a penalty from the highly penalized players
Plus/minus (full strength)	To determine the players who are on the ice when a goal is scored for or against while playing full strength	A trend will develop if a certain defense pair or line is on for an unusual number of goals for or against. The coach may want to split up a weak defense pair or not play them in critical situations.	Detects strengths/weaknesses of defense pairs or forward lines that are high or low in this category Close checking may be required against a high plus line. A stronger line may be sent out against a high minus line.

STATISTIC	PURPOSE OF STATISTIC	YOUR TEAM	OPPOSITION
Plus/minus (power play and penalty killing)	To determine the players who are on the ice when a power play goal is scored for or against	A trend will develop to identify best power play and penalty killing players and/or units.	To determine strong or weak penalty killing units of each opposition Match your strength against strength and weakness against weakness.
Power play success percentage	To determine the overall success of your power play Thirty percent or better is considered quite good.	To determine the efficiency of your power play in general and against certain teams	To determine the strength and scoring percentage of the opposition's power play
Penalty killing percentage	To determine the efficiency of penalty killing Eighty percent or better is considered quite good.	To determine the efficiency of your penalty killing teams	To determine the efficiency of the opposition's penalty killing teams
Giveaways	To determine the number of poor passes in your zone that are intercepted	To correct errors in thinking and/or execution in your zone To determine which players have poor passing skills and which players react well or poorly under pressure in your zone	To determine which players are poor passers or panic under pressure in their defensive zone To know when and who to pressure in the opposition zone
Body checks or takeouts (hits)	To determine the number of body contacts made by the individual and team	To determine which players are on or are not taking the man out and finishing the check To determine the need for more checking drills and correction of errors in skill	To determine if the opposition is a physical team or not If a team is not taking the body, more liberties can be taken in the corners, etc.
Face-offs	To determine the number of face-offs won, lost, or tied in the defensive, neutral, or offensive zones	If done poorly, work on face-off techniques should be increased in practice. Be able to put the best face-off men out in critical situations. Be able to match against opposition face-off men. Be aware of a poor matchup of face-off men as the game progresses. Be aware of the efficiency of face-off men in each zone.	To determine the strong and weak face-off men To be able to match against strength and weakness
Length of shifts	To determine the average length of shifts for each player	To determine if shifts are too long or too short Note if fatigue seems to be a factor.	To determine if the opposition has a marked tendency toward longer or shorter shifts This will aid in line matching as well.

STATS SHEET

Date: _____

Opposition: _____

☐ 1st period
☐ 2nd period
☐ 3rd period

Shots on net _____
Giveaways _____
Hits _____

Plus

Minus

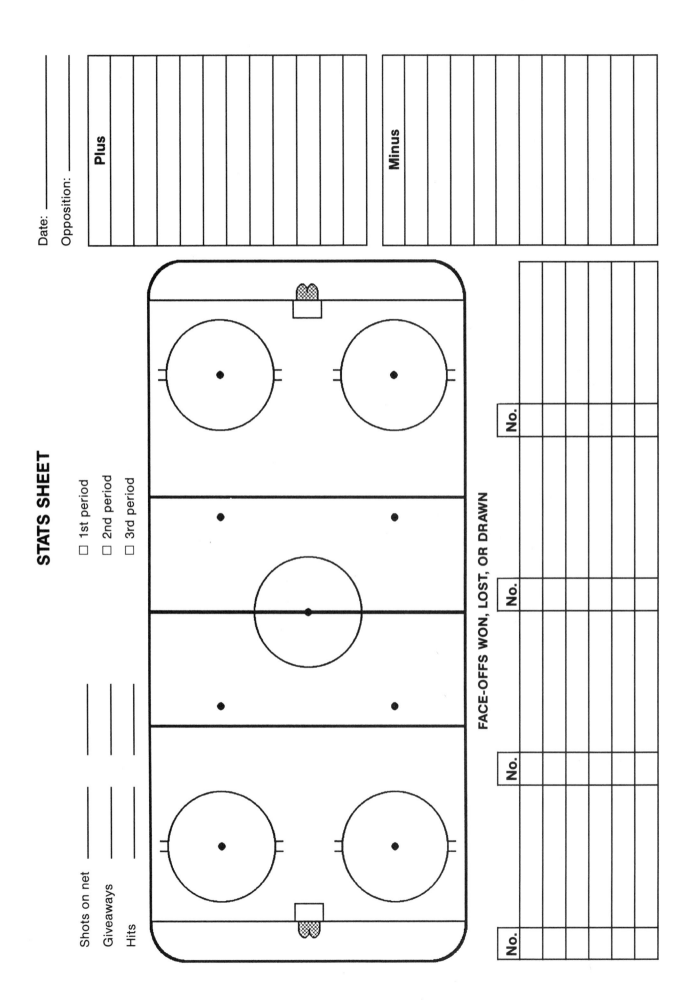

FACE-OFFS WON, LOST, OR DRAWN

No.						No.					

No.						No.					

GAME SUMMARY

No.	Name	Games Played	Hits	Shots	Goals	Assists	Points	Minor Penalties	Major Penalties	Misconduct & GM Penalties	Goals Against, Evenhanded	Goals For, Evenhanded	Plus/Minus	Power Play, Goals For	Penalty Killing, Goals Against	Shorthanded, Goals For	Bad Pass Giveaways	Face-Offs W	Face-Offs L	Face-Offs %

20. CONDITIONING

Conditioning for ice hockey should be a year-round program to enable the player to reach his full potential. The physiological factors of strength, power, speed, agility, flexibility, reaction time, and cardiovascular and muscular endurance should be tested for and improved as they relate to ice hockey.

THE TWELVE-MONTH PLAN

To develop a conditioning program for hockey, the year should be divided into the following main periods:

- preparation period, general and specific (off-season)
- precompetition period
- competition period (competitive season)
- taper
- playoffs
- transition period (postseason)

APRIL	MAY	JUNE	JULY	AUG.	SEPT.	OCT.	NOV.	DEC.	JAN.	FEB.	MAR.
Tran-sition	Preparation				Precompetition		Competition			Ta-per	Play-Offs
	General		Specific								

PREPARATION PERIOD (16 WEEKS)
The preparation period of training is extremely important for the player. During this period the athlete must attempt to raise his total conditioning level as high as possible. In most cases the total conditioning level is not improved by any great percentage during the season, and in some components of total fitness only a maintenance level is achieved during the competitive season.

The first step in the preparation period should be to perform a fitness assessment profile to measure the athletes' strength, power, flexibility, muscular endurance, agility, fat percentage, and cardiovascular endurance (aerobic and anaerobic).

After the fitness assessment profile has been performed, the athletes should go into an intensive training program. The preparation period is divided into two periods, general (eight weeks) and specific (eight weeks). The general period is devoted to building a solid base of strength and aerobic fitness along with flexibility. The specific period includes anaerobic work along with more sports-specific training. Strength and aerobic work also continue along with flexibility.

PRECOMPETITION (TWO TO THREE WEEKS)
The precompetition period usually extends from two to three weeks. It is a time to select players for the team and to have a number of exhibition and scrimmage games. Circuit training for general fitness is one of the best methods for conditioning during this period, as it allows a large number of players to work out at the same time.

COMPETITION PERIOD
During the competitive season it is important to improve, or at least maintain, the conditioning level achieved in the preparation period. The competitive season should consist of an anaerobic and aerobic cardiorespiratory endurance conditioning program and a daily flexibility program, as well as a strength maintenance program.

As the season progresses it will become necessary to train more intensely for short periods of time to increase the fitness level, which may have dropped due to the playing of a large number of games. To raise the fitness level it is necessary to train intensely for three 10-day microcycles. The microcycles should be performed in early October, in December, and two weeks before the end of the season. The microcycle training should be performed for 10 straight days and should involve circuit training using a number of exercise stations.

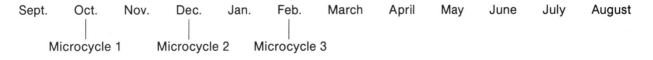

TAPER

One week to the day before the playoffs, intensity remains high, but the volume and length of training is shortened dramatically. More rest days are also included.

PLAYOFFS

Short training periods with rest and strategy included.

TRANSITION PERIOD (4 WEEKS)

The transition period for ice hockey is a time when the hockey player recuperates from the long season, works on general fitness, and perhaps participates in some different sports such as golf, baseball, tennis, or swimming.

During the first week of the transition period the player should have rest and relaxation combined with exercise in an enjoyable sport such as tennis, golf, or swimming with no set exercise pattern. After the long hockey season it is important for the athlete to recuperate and take time out from a regimented exercise routine.

The next three weeks of the transition period should be spent on general fitness, which would include some aerobic work consisting of running, cycling, or swimming distances of a minimum of two miles three times per week. Flexibility exercises should be done daily, and other enjoyable sports should be played to maintain general fitness.

In summary, the transition period is a time for recuperation and maintenance of general fitness. Although it is a time to rest from hockey and relax, it is also a time to get physical exercise, as general fitness should be maintained.

PHYSIOLOGICAL FACTORS IMPORTANT IN ICE HOCKEY

The following factors are important for the total development of the ice hockey player: strength, speed, power, agility, movement time, flexibility, muscular endurance, and cardiovascular endurance.

STRENGTH

Strength is extremely important in shooting, checking, and skating. Strength in the upper body and legs is essential and can be developed by using the principles of progressive resistance and overload. Overload refers to loading the muscle beyond the previous requirement. Progressive resistance refers to a resistance that becomes progressively greater. Strength can be developed through isotonic, isometric, and isokinetic exercising.

Isotonic exercises are those in which muscle tension overcomes the resistance and movement occurs. Examples of isotonic exercises are chin-ups and push-ups. Weight training in which 80 percent of a maximum weight is lifted four to eight times is the best, as the principles of both overload and progressive resistance are put into play. Exercises with resistance, such as shooting or skating, are the best for developing muscle strength in the actual movement.

Isometrics involve exercises where movement does not occur, although the muscles are under tension. Exercises such as pushing against an immovable object like a wall or a rope are examples of isometrics. Although isometrics develop strength, they are only effective if done for approximately 10 seconds with maximum contractions done in stages through a complete range of motion.

Isokinetics refers to training in which the muscle is maximally loaded throughout its full range of motion. Examples of these types of exercises are those found in the Mini Gym, Apollo, and Nautilus systems. Isokinetics now appears to be the best method of strength development, although more research is needed, as there are conflicting opinions—some experts favor free weights over machines.

Devices such as small weights may be placed on the skates, but ankle weights are not effective strength developers because they do not use the principles of progressive resistance and overload.

STRENGTH TRAINING EXERCISES FOR ICE HOCKEY

Coaches should review the following general guidelines for strength training with players and be sure they understand them completely.

- Always have a good warm-up.
- If you're unfamiliar with training, be sure you are properly instructed on technique and that you work with a partner.

- Perform all exercises with a smooth, even rhythm through the full range of joint movement.
- Work out every other day. Eight weeks is a minimum time period for any appreciable gains in strength.
- Do not work the same major muscle groups two stations in a row. For example, exercise legs in one exercise set and arms in the next set.
- Practice breath control by inhaling when lifting and exhaling when lowering.
- Do three sets of each exercise with four to eight repetitions per set. A repetition is one range of movement with the weight.
- Use weights that are 80 to 90 percent of maximum.
- Rest two to three minutes between sets of exercises.
- Progress through the weight training program week by week by adding repetitions until eight repetitions are reached. Then reduce the repetitions to four, add to the weight, and go through the progression again.
- If muscular endurance is desired, the repetitions should be increased and the weight lessened.
- Important: Do not perform maximum lifts during training. The starting weight is a load that you are able to use for the desired repetitions with the last two repetitions being somewhat difficult.

UPPER BODY EXERCISES
1. Military Press
With the feet a shoulders' width apart, the barbell is raised to a bent arm position in front of the chest. The arms are slowly extended overhead.

2. Bent Rowing
The athlete bends from the waist down. His feet are apart, with arms extended downward. Hands are in the middle of the bar, approximately 8 inches apart. The head can be supported on a table with a towel used as a cushion. The bar is pulled up to the chest and then lowered.

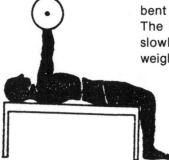

3. Supine Bench Press

The athlete lies on his back on a bench with knees bent at right angles and the feet flat on the floor. The barbell is held flat on the chest. The arms slowly extend upward until fully extended. The weight is then lowered back to the chest.

4. Two-Arm Curl

A reverse grip or a regular grip is used. The athlete starts with the feet astride and arms extended. The bar is raised to the chest and then lowered to the starting position.

5. Tricep Press

The feet are astride and the weight is lowered to the back of the shoulders. The grip is a shoulders' width apart, and the elbows are bent. The arms are extended with the weight thrust above the head. The weight is lowered back behind the shoulders.

6. Lateral Raise

While the athlete is lying on a bench grasping 10-pound dumbbells, the arms are downward and outward. The arms are extended and raised until the dumbbells touch above the head.

7. Wrist Roll

The feet are astride and a 20- to 30-pound weight is placed between the feet. The rope is slowly wound up until the weight is raised to the handle. Then, the weight is slowly lowered to the ground.

8. Forearm Twist

A 20-pound weight is rotated left and right, with the elbow bent at right angles.

TRUNK EXERCISES
1. Bent-Knee Sit-Ups
The athlete lies on his back with hands clasped around the back of the head and the knees bent. The upper body is raised until the elbows touch the knees.

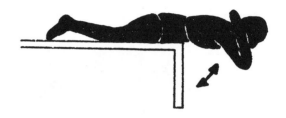

2. Trunk Extension and Flexion
The athlete lies on his stomach on a table with trunk extended. The upper body is raised and lowered.

LEG EXERCISES
1. Half Squat
A bench is placed behind the knees as a safety precaution. The weight is placed on the shoulders with the feet apart. The heels are raised approximately 1½ inches. The knees are bent slowly to the half squat position.

2. Leg Thrust
The player starts in a lying position with the knees bent. The knees are slowly extended, with the buttocks kept on the floor. The knees are fully extended and then lowered to starting position. This exercise can also be performed in an upright position using the Universal weight machine.

3. Heel Raise

The athlete raises his toes 2 inches with blocks. The barbell rests on his shoulders. He slowly rises up on the toes, holds, and then returns to the starting position.

Other strength training exercises that can be used are hamstring curls, upright rows, shrugs, lat pull-downs, dips, french curls, cleans, crunches, and reverse leg presses. One workout per week during the season will maintain the strength gained during the off-season.

SPEED

Speed relates to applying a force to a mass, and strength and technique are key factors. The skating technique should be analyzed to determine if the correct mechanics involved in the start and skating stride are being used.

Strength is a key factor in speed. Any exercise that develops strength in the legs, especially the extensor muscles, is advantageous.

OFF-ICE TRAINING FOR SPEED

Weight training exercises for the legs that emphasize the extension action of the legs are best for speed training, although all muscle groups should be exercised. Running distances of 40 to 100 yards at top speed are excellent off-ice drills.

ON-ICE TRAINING FOR SPEED

Skating widths and lengths on the ice at full speed is good speed training. The same is true for any other drills that involve skating from start to full speed.

POWER

Power is a combination of strength and speed, and the development of these two factors will improve power. Power is important in skating, shooting, and checking and is a key factor in ice hockey.

OFF-ICE TRAINING FOR POWER

Weight training for strength will have an effect on power. It is believed that power can be directly developed by lifting a weight close to the maximum at the maximum rate. Exercises such as stair and hill running are also valuable as power developers for the legs.

ON-ICE TRAINING FOR POWER

Drills that involve skating or shooting against resistance, such as pushing or pulling a resisting player up and down the ice or skating from the boards with large elastic bands attached to the waist, are good power development drills.

AGILITY

Agility is the ability to change directions quickly and is a key factor in ice hockey. Strength and reaction time are important contributing factors to agility. Agility can best be improved by practicing a movement pattern correctly at increasingly faster speeds.

OFF-ICE TRAINING FOR AGILITY

Drills that involve quick changes of direction improve agility. Moving back and forth on a coach's hand signals or running around obstacles, such as chairs, are examples of agility drills.

ON-ICE TRAINING FOR AGILITY

Drills that involve skating and stickhandling around, under, and over pylons or other obstacles are good agility drills. All these drills should be done at top speed.

MOVEMENT TIME

Movement time may be defined as the time from the start of receiving a stimulus to the end of the movement. It is essential in most aspects of ice hockey but is especially important for goalies. Movement time involves reaction and response time. Reaction time begins when a player receives a stimulus and ends at the initiation of the response, while response time spans the initiation to the end of the response. Current research supports the fact that reaction time may be little affected by practice, but response time can be directly affected. Preparatory and distracting signals are factors involved in movement time. Movement time can be improved by continual practice of the correct movement pattern. These movement patterns can be practiced on or off the ice using the exact movement patterns specific to the position. Examples of drills include goaltender reaction drills with glove or stick hand or forwards shooting the puck quickly at a certain area of the net.

FLEXIBILITY

Flexibility exercises are important in ice hockey to ensure full range of motion in movement patterns and for the prevention of injuries. Flexibility exercises should be included in all warm-ups for both practices and games. If ice time is limited, these exercises may be performed off the ice.

ON-ICE AND OFF-ICE TRAINING FOR FLEXIBILITY

The PNF or 3S method of flexibility is used now by many hockey teams. The method is based on the research conducted by Larry Holt at Dalhousie University, and the information can be obtained from his book *Scientific Stretching for Sport*. The PNF or 3S method of flexibility training involves a series of isometric contractions (muscle is under tension but does not move) of the muscle to be stretched, followed by concentric contractions (muscle moves and shortens) of the opposite muscle group, together with light pressure from a partner.

The basic steps for this method are as follows. Repeat a total of three to four times.

1. Stretch the muscle to end point without pain.
2. Partner holds the limb(s) in a stretched position while isometric contraction for six seconds is performed.
3. Stretch the muscle further with light pressure from your partner.

The following flexibility exercises should be done daily. A partner is required for all but one of the exercises.

1. Hamstring Stretch

The athlete lies with one leg straight on the floor and the other straightened and raised as high as possible. The partner holds the leg on the floor and exerts pressure against the raised leg with his shoulder. The athlete attempts to lower the leg with an isometric contraction while the partner exerts the force in the opposite direction. The leg is extended further with light pressure from the partner and then the isometric contraction is repeated. This is repeated with the other leg.

2. Quadriceps Stretch

The athlete lies on his stomach on the floor with one leg flexed and raised as high as possible. The partner extends pressure with one hand under the knee of the raised leg and the other hand on the back. The athlete attempts to pull the knee downward with pressure exerted by the partner in the opposite direction. The leg is then raised to a higher position with light pressure from the partner, and another isometric contraction is repeated. This is repeated with the other leg.

3. Groin Stretch

The athlete sits with the legs as far apart as possible. The partner holds the legs at the ankles. The athlete then performs an isometric contraction against the pressure of the partner. The legs are then moved further apart with light pressure from the partner, and another isometric contraction is performed.

4. Trunk Stretch

The athlete sits on the floor with the legs straight and the trunk flexed forward as far as possible. The partner exerts downward pressure on the shoulders. The athlete attempts to raise the trunk with an isometric contraction. He then flexes further forward with light pressure from the partner. The isometric contraction is repeated.

5. Shoulder Extension

The athlete is in a sitting position with back and legs straight. The arms are extended to the side at shoulder height and moved backward as far as possible. The partner grasps the wrists and exerts pressure backward as the athlete exerts force forward with the arms to execute the isometric contraction. The arms are moved further backward with pressure from the partner. The isometric contraction is repeated.

Flexibility Slow Stretch

This group of exercises is to be done daily and does not require a partner. Exercises should be done slowly. The athlete should hold the extreme position for six seconds, return to starting position, and repeat.

1. Rotate the Head

The head is rotated side to side, forward and back.

2. Arm Rotation

With arms extended to the side, the athlete rotates both arms forward in large circles, finishing with small circles. Then the arms are rotated backward in a similar manner.

3. Trunk Rotation

With the hands on the hips, the athlete rotates his trunk to the left and then to the right.

4. Floor Touching

With the arms straight and the feet astride, the athlete touches the floor as far back as possible between the legs.

5. Hurdler's Stretch

In a sitting position, the athlete performs a hurdler's stretch by extending one leg forward and the other leg back. He grasps the forward leg with both hands and attempts to bring the forehead to the knee, repeating with the opposite leg forward.

6. Legs Above the Head

The athlete lies back, crosses the legs above the head, and then touches the floor with the feet in front of the head.

7. Leg to Forehead

In a sitting position, the athlete grasps one leg behind the knee with both hands. He brings the leg to the forehead, keeping the leg straight, and repeats with the other leg.

8. Bent-Knee Sit-Ups

The hands are clasped behind the head. The knees are bent with the feet flat on the ground. The sit-up is started with the shoulders flat on the floor. The athlete rises, touching the left elbow to the right knee and vice versa.

9. Chest Raise

The athlete lies on the stomach with hands clasped behind the head. He raises the upper body as far off the floor as possible.

10. Knee to Chest

In a standing position, the athlete raises one knee to the chest and holds. Then he repeats this with the other leg.

MUSCULAR ENDURANCE

Muscular endurance is a muscle's ability to make repeated contractions over a long period of time.

OFF-ICE TRAINING

Muscular endurance can be developed using weight training with a lighter load (50 percent maximum) with higher repetitions (20 or more), up to an athlete's limits. Exercises such as push-ups, dips on the parallel bars, and chin-ups are also excellent upper body exercises that can be used to develop muscular endurance.

ON-ICE TRAINING

Any exercise in which muscle contractions are repeated on the ice (e.g., skating and shooting) develops muscular endurance. Dips can be performed using an open gate at the players' bench and push-ups can be performed during the warm-up.

CARDIOVASCULAR ENDURANCE

Intermittent work is the nature of the game of ice hockey. A time analysis of a game of ice hockey is summarized below.

HOCKEY CARDIOVASCULAR DEMANDS: TIME COMPONENTS IN ICE HOCKEY PLAY

	Boys' Competitive League			Inter-Collegiate
Age Group (years)	10.7 (n = 34)	12.2 (n = 33)	14.4 (n = 23)	21 (= 10)
Game Time (stop time, min.)	30	30	39	60
Total Ice Time (min.) (percentage of game time)	12.7 (42)	12.5 (42)	16.2 (42)	24.50 (41)
Number of Shifts (Number/20 min. period)	8.0 (5.3)	8.5 (5.7)	10.5 (5.4)	17.4 (5.8)
Mean Shift Time (sec.)	102.6	88.5	93.7	85.4 (227 off-ice)
Mean Interwhistle Time (sec.)	40.5	43.7	41.4	39.7
Whistle Stop/Shift (n, time − sec.)	2.5 (−)	2.0 (−)	2.3 (−)	2.3 (27.1)

The game times vary with the age group, but the percentage of time was the same (42 percent). The shift times varied, but average shift time was approximately 1½ minutes with two whistles per shift and mean interwhistle time of 40 seconds. The rest period between whistles is approximately 30 seconds, and the number of shifts for intercollegiate was 17.4. For the intercollegiate hockey players the peak heart rate was 173 +/− 5.4, and resting heart rate between shifts was 120+. Heart rates during a shift at play stoppages were only reduced to 166 beats per minute during this time. Mean heart rates were 90 percent of maximum as shown below.

	Boys' Competitive League			Inter-Collegiate
Age Group (years)	10.7 (n = 19)	12.2 (n = 28)	14.4 (n = 22)	21 (= 10)
Mean On-Ice HR (b/min. − 1)	181 +/− 2.4	187 +/− 2.5	194 +/− 1.8	173 +/− 5.4
Mean Off-Ice HR (b/min. − 1)	136 +/− 2.6	148 +/− 2.9	194 +/− 1.8	120+

Values are means +/− SEM.

THE ENERGY SYSTEMS

Cardiovascular endurance is directly related to the body's ability to supply adenosine triphosphate (ATP), a chemical that when broken down supplies the energy for muscle contraction.

ATP is supplied to the muscles by three methods: storage in the muscles (alactate or ATP-PC system), breakdown of glucose without oxygen (lactic acid system), and the breakdown of carbohydrates and fats in the presence of oxygen (oxygen system). The alactate system and the lactic acid system are without oxygen and are classified as anaerobic. The ATP-PC system resynthesizes ATP from the creatine phosphate stored in the muscle.

$$CP + ADP \leftarrow ATP + Creatine$$

The supply of CP is limited and in all-out work can last from 10 to 15 seconds. This process is very important in ice hockey for supplying energy for the short burst sprint. Equally important is the fact that 50 percent of the creatine phosphate can be restored in approximately 30 seconds, and over 90 percent can be restored in 2 minutes. This is extremely important for ice hockey, as there is usually a stoppage of play every 30 seconds, with two stoppages of play every shift. Training the anaerobic system can increase the levels of ATP and CP stored in the muscle and can also increase the activity of creatine kinase, which facilitates the breakdown of creatine phosphate.

The lactic acid system is also a limited supplier of ATP. The byproduct of this system is the buildup of lactic acid, which causes fatigue when it reaches a high level.

$$Glycogen + Pi \text{ (inorganic phosphate)} + ADP \rightarrow lactate + ATP$$

Training the lactic acid system increases the amount of PFK (phosphofructokinase), an enzyme that speeds up the rate glycogen is broken down. In addition, training allows the muscle to tolerate higher levels of lactate, which eventually causes fatigue.

The oxygen system supplies an unlimited amount of ATP as long as the fuel can be supplied by carbohydrates and fats.

$$Carbohydrates/Fats + O_2 + ADP + Pi \; H_2O + CO_2 + ATP$$

Although ice hockey is considered primarily an anaerobic sport, the aerobic component is important over the two-hour duration of the game. Also, each shift in ice hockey includes various tempos varying from all-out effort to periods of stopping and gliding. It appears that by using the oxygen system at certain periods of the game, the player minimizes the lactic acid system involvement. Training aerobically increases the myoglobin content (store for O_2) and increases the oxidation of fats and carbohydrates. All three energy systems are important for ice hockey and should be trained for maximum cardiovascular endurance.

TRAINING THE ENERGY SYSTEMS

Interval training is the best method for the systematic training of the energy systems. Although the traditional stops and starts in ice hockey are a form of interval training, there should be a definite system and progression for their use.

Interval training uses work interspersed with periods of rest to achieve the desired training improvement. In intermittent work the lactic acid accumulation is lower than when the work is done continuously. The ATP-PC system is used more extensively, and consequently the lactic acid system is not fully depleted. Interval training does the following:

- allows the ATP-PC system to be used over and over
- delays the onset of fatigue by not delving so deeply into the lactic acid system
- allows the system to become more tolerant to lactic acid
- works long enough at sufficient intensity to allow an improvement in the aerobic system

The manipulated variables used in interval training are the following:

- rate and distance
- repetitions and sets
- duration of the relief interval
- type of activity during relief interval
- frequency of training

Terms	Definitions
Work interval	Portion of interval training program involving high intensity work bursts
Repetition	One work interval
Relief interval	Time between work interval (can be working, flexing, or light jogging)
Set	Series of work and relief intervals
Training time	Rate at which work is performed

ON-ICE TRAINING FOR CARDIOVASCULAR ENDURANCE
Training the ATP-PC System

The following drills require that you divide your team into three groups.

1. One Width or Two Widths

Have each group skate one or two widths of the rink or from the goal line to the center line in turn. They work for 5 seconds and rest 20 seconds, doing three to four sets of five repetitions each.

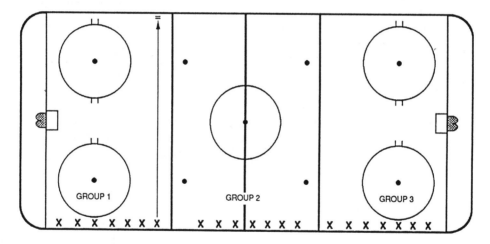

2. Blue Line to Blue Line

Have each group skate blue line to blue line, four times in turn. They work for 12 to 15 seconds and rest 45 seconds, doing two to three sets of four repetitions each.

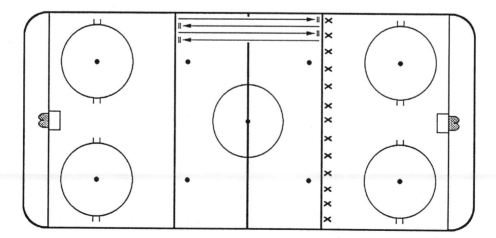

Training the Lactic Acid System

Drills 1 through 10 require the team be divided into three groups.

1. Dot to Dot

Have each group skate from the defensive face-off dot to the one at the far end four times. They work for 30 seconds and rest for 2 minutes, doing two to three sets of four repetitions each. Allow 4 to 5 minutes between sets.

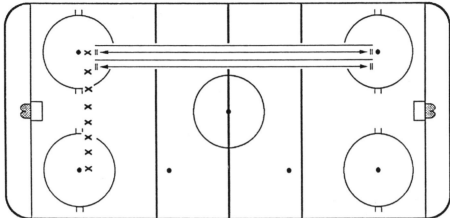

2. Goal Line to Goal Line

Have each group skate from goal line to goal line 4 times. They work for 40 to 45 seconds and rest for 2 minutes, doing two to three sets of four repetitions each. Allow 4 to 5 minutes between sets.

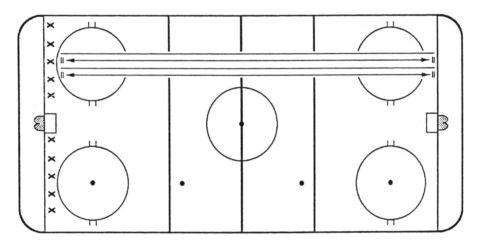

3. Around the Net

Have each group skate around the rink behind the nets for one and one-half laps and then go in the other direction one and one-half laps in turn. They work 40 to 45 seconds and rest for 2 minutes, doing two to three sets of four repetitions each.

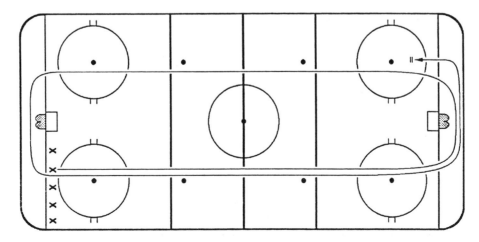

4. Around the Dots

Have each group skate around the defensive zone face-off dots for three laps. They work 40 to 45 seconds and rest for 2 minutes, doing two to three sets of four repetitions each.

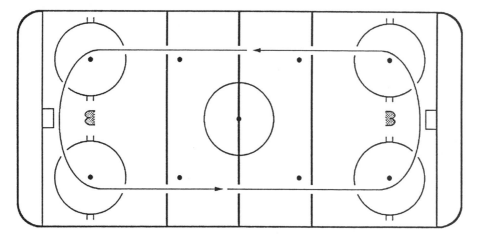

5. Skate the Lines

Have each group skate the different lengths non-stop. They work for 40 to 45 seconds and rest for 2 minutes, doing two to three sets of four repetitions each. Allow 4 to 5 minutes between sets.

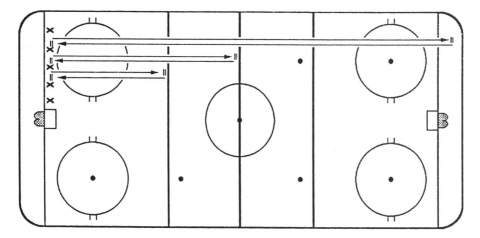

6. Defense, Forwards, Goalies

Defensemen skate forward to the center red line, skate backward back to the blue line, turn, and skate forward to the goal line three times, working on both backward turns. Forwards skate forward across the rink and back three times, touching the boards with their sticks. Goalies skate forward to the red line and drop to both knees with stick and catcher in position, then skate backward to the goal line and do a double leg slide to one side, twice. They work for 30 to 35 seconds and rest for 2 minutes, doing two to three sets of four repetitions each. Allow for 4 to 5 minutes between sets.

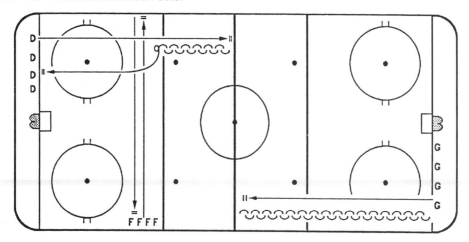

7. Around the Rink

Have each group skate two laps around the rink. They work for 30 to 35 seconds and rest for 2 minutes, doing two to three sets of four repetitions. Allow 4 to 5 minutes between sets.

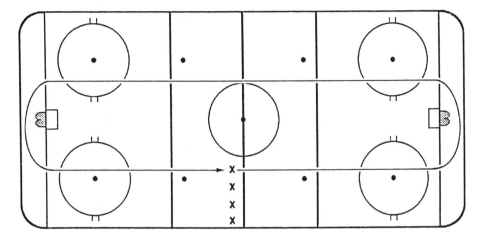

8. Stops and Starts

Have each group do stops and starts using the entire length of the ice, changing direction on the whistle. They work for 30 to 40 seconds and rest for 2 minutes, doing two to three sets of four repetitions each. Allow for 4 to 5 minutes' rest between sets.

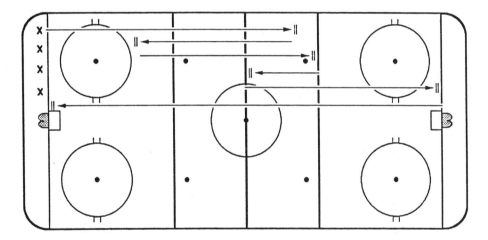

9. Skate the Lines

Have each group skate forward from the goal line to the center red line, back to the near blue line, then to the far blue line, back to the center red line, then to the far goal line, and all the way back. They work for 40 to 50 seconds and rest for 2 minutes, doing two to three sets of four repetitions each. Allow for 4 to 5 minutes between sets.

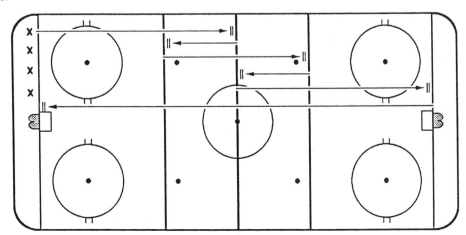

10. Around the Rink

Have each group skate around the rink at 80 to 90 percent maximum speed for 30 to 40 seconds, skate slowly for 30 to 40 seconds, and then repeat. They do two to three sets of five repetitions each. Allow 4 minutes' rest between sets.

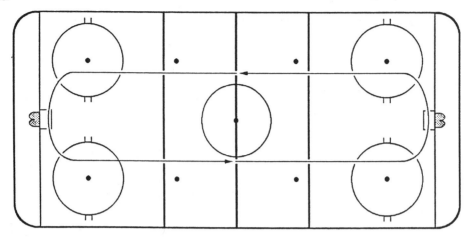

11. Three-on-Three, Four-on-Four

Players scrimmage three-on-three or four-on-four using the full ice. Players change while the puck is in play. When they change lines, the puck is passed back to the goalie. On off-sides, the puck is passed back to the goalie and the offending team must move outside the blue line. They work for 1 minute and rest for 3 minutes. Change on the whistle.

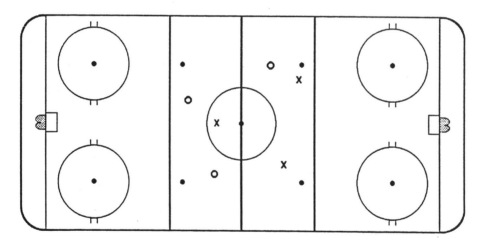

12. Relay Race

Divide the team into four groups and have them run relay races. Each player works for 40 seconds and rests for 2 minutes.

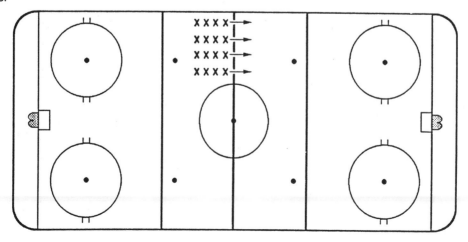

Training the Aerobic System
1. Change Direction
The entire team skates around the rink being sure to go behind each net. They skate for 3 minutes and then change direction and skate the other way for an additional 3 minutes.

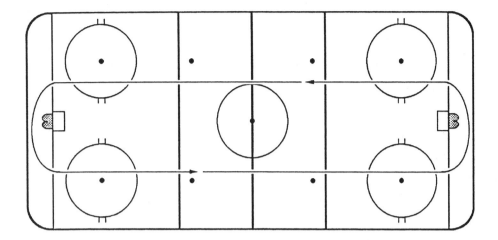

2. Figure Eight
The team repeats 1, but this time skating in a figure eight, crossing at the center ice face-off dot.

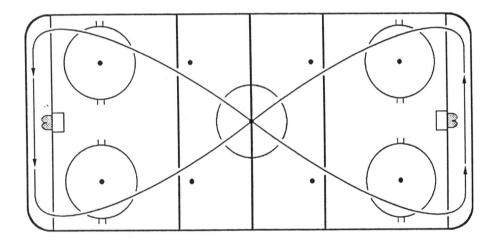

3. The Denver Skate
In this variation on 1, move the nets toward the center with each lap and then back after the first 3 minutes.

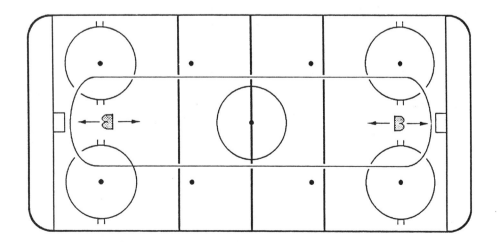

4. Half-Ice Scrimmage

Have the team play two five-on-five scrimmages using half-ice. Each game is 10 minutes in length and players change lines after 5 minutes. They work for 5 minutes and rest for 5 minutes.

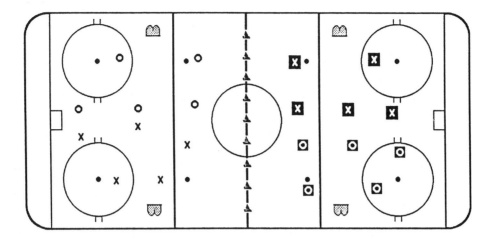

OFF-ICE TRAINING FOR CARDIOVASCULAR ENDURANCE
Anaerobic Training
1. Short Sprints

Players run 60-yard sprints in approximately 10 seconds, resting 30 seconds between repetitions (heart rate 140 beats per minute). Have them rest longer after one set (heart rate down to 120 beats per minute). Five repetitions equals one set. Have players try to build to four sets of five repetitions for a total of 20 repetitions.

2. Longer Sprints

Players run 250-yard sprints in approximately 40 seconds, resting 2 minutes between repetitions. Four repetitions equal one set. Have them try to build to two sets of four repetitions for a total of eight repetitions.

Aerobic Training

Have players run a minimum of 2 miles and attempt to reach 6 miles. Your goal should be for them to run at least 30 minutes per workout.

General Weekly Program (Weeks 1 Through 8)

Monday	Tuesday	Wednesday	Thursday	Friday	Saturday
Strength training Aerobic run of a minimum of two miles	Anaerobic short sprints and long sprints	Strength training Aerobic run of a minimum of two miles	Anaerobic short sprints and long sprints	Strength training Aerobic run of a minimum of two miles	Aerobic run of a minimum of two miles

During weeks 1 through 8 the program is based on strength training and the building of aerobic endurance. It is important for aerobic endurance that the running or skating distance is increased each week and that the goal should be to run 6 miles or skate for 45 minutes at the end of the eight-week session.

Running and/or Skating (Weeks 9 Through 12)

Monday	Tuesday	Wednesday	Thursday	Friday	Saturday
Strength training Anaerobic short sprints and long sprints	Aerobic run of five to six miles	Strength training Anaerobic short sprints and long sprints	Aerobic run of five to six miles	Strength training Anaerobic short sprints and long sprints	Anaerobic short sprints and long sprints

CIRCUIT TRAINING

Circuit training is a general conditioning method in which athletes perform exercises at a number of different exercise stations. Circuit training generally develops muscular strength, muscular and cardiorespiratory endurance, power, and flexibility and allows a number of people to work out at the same time. Circuits can be set up in many different ways and can be done with or without equipment such as weights.

Circuit training for ice hockey can be used in the following ways:

- directly prior to and/or during the training camp period
- throughout the season, two to three times per week, to maintain the fitness level
- two or three times during the season for an intensive 10-day period to raise the fitness level
- during the off seasons as a general conditioning method

It should be noted that the best method of conditioning for the off-season would be specific training for strength (weight training), cardiovascular endurance (running short sprints and long distances), and flexibility. Circuit training is general training but does not develop as high a level of strength as specific weight training. It will have less effect on cardiorespiratory endurance than a sprint and endurance running program.

The following are examples of three different types of circuits for ice hockey. The first two are designed for an exercise area other than the one at the arena, although a room large enough may be included in some arenas. The third circuit can be used at the arena using available space or on the ice if enough ice time is available.

Circuits 1 and 2 are intensive and can be used for three 10-day periods during the season to raise the fitness level or can be used three to five times per week during the off-season to improve the fitness level. Circuit 1 is the most demanding and requires equipment. Circuit 2, although still intensive, requires very little equipment. Circuit 3 can be used on the ice daily during the season as a warm-up general conditioning program or once or twice per week with athletes going through the circuit three times to maintain and improve the fitness level. This circuit requires a minimal amount of equipment.

Each of the three circuits has 10 stations. With a standard hockey team of 20 players, two people work at each circuit for a total of 45 minutes for three complete circuits. An alternative method is for athletes to repeat the same exercise three times before changing to the next station. The exercise would still be 30 seconds with 1 minute's rest before athletes start the exercise once more.

Note that all weights listed for circuit 1 are for junior hockey players aged 16 to 19 years. Younger players should use only circuits 2 and 3.

CIRCUIT 1

This circuit will help maintain and increase strength, power, and muscular and cardiorespiratory endurance. This circuit is strenuous and can best be used three times a season for 10 days to increase the strength levels. It is best performed in a small gymnasium or a room of similar size with bleacher seats or stairs. Two athletes work simultaneously at each station for 30 seconds, with 1 minute allowed for changing stations and rest.

The equipment needed includes two barbells of 65 pounds each, four barbells of 90 pounds each, two barbells of 20 pounds each, two benches, two dumbbells of 15 pounds each, stopwatch, and whistle.

1. Curls
Each athlete grasps a 65-pound barbell using an underhand grip, with hands a shoulders' width apart. With arms extended forward, he raises the bar to the chest by bending arms at the elbows, lowers the bar to the starting position, and repeats.

2. Bench Leap
Each athlete jumps onto the bench with both feet. Then he jumps back down and repeats.

3. Bench Press
Each athlete lies on a bench holding the 90-pound barbell above with hands a shoulders' width apart. He lowers the bar so it touches the chest. He raises the bar back to the starting position and repeats. He should inhale at the start of the movement and exhale at the completion of the movement.

4. Stair Running
Each athlete runs up a flight of stairs one step at a time, runs back down, and repeats.

5. Reverse Wrist Curls

Using a 20-pound barbell in seated position, each athlete rests his forearms along the thighs, which are parallel to the floor. The arms and wrists should be extended past the knees. The bar is held with an overhand grip to raise and lower the wrists as far as possible.

6. Bench Hop

Each athlete jumps over a bench with both feet and repeats.

7. Bent Lateral Raise

With a 15-pound dumbbell in each hand, each athlete bends over at the waist until the upper body is parallel to the floor. The dumbbells are raised laterally until they are level with the upper body and the elbows are slightly bent. He lowers and repeats.

8. Sit-Ups

While lying on his back with knees bent and feet flat on the floor, each athlete clasps his hands behind the head. He starts the sit-up with the shoulders flat on the ground and raises the upper body, touching the left elbow to the right knee, and so on, and repeats.

9. Power, Clean, and Press

With knees bent and back straight, the athlete grasps the 90-pound barbell with an overhand or underhand grip. He extends his legs and lifts the weight to the chest. Then he lifts the weight up to the shoulders by bending the arms. He raises the weight above the head by fully extending the arms. He lowers the weight slowly to the floor and repeats.

10. Stair Bounding

Each athlete runs up the stairs two at a time, runs back down, and repeats.

CIRCUIT 2

The purpose of this circuit is to maintain and develop strength, power, and muscular and cardiorespiratory endurance. This circuit can be used in a preseason training program or during the season in three ten-day cycles. It is best performed in a gymnasium or a large room with a high ceiling. Two athletes work simultaneously at each station for 30 seconds. Allow one minute for rest and changing stations.

Equipment needed includes two long ropes, two chinning bars, two benches, four dumbbells of 15 pounds each, two barbells of 20 pounds each, two wall ladders, stopwatch, and whistle.

1. Rope Climbing

Each athlete climbs the rope to the ceiling using the arms only.

2. Bench Leap

Each athlete jumps onto the bench with both feet. Then he jumps back down and repeats.

3. Chin-Ups

Each athlete performs chin-ups using the underhand grip, completely extending the arms, and without swinging the legs. After raising the chin above the bar, he repeats.

4. Squat Jumps

Starting in a crouched position with both hands on the floor, each athlete jumps in the air, completely extending the legs and arms, and repeats.

5. Push-Ups

With the back straight, each athlete pushes up, completely extending the arms, lowers the chest to the floor, and repeats.

6. Bench Hop

Each athlete jumps over a bench with both feet and repeats.

7. Ladder

Each athlete climbs the wall ladder using arms only and repeats.

8. Sit-Ups

While lying on his back with knees bent and feet flat on the floor, each athlete clasps his hands behind the head. He starts the sit-up with the shoulders flat on the ground and raises the upper body, touching the left elbow to the right knee, and so on, and repeats.

9. Bent Lateral Raise

With a 15-pound dumbbell in each hand, each athlete bends over at the waist until the upper body is parallel to the floor. The dumbbells are raised laterally until they are level with the upper body and the elbows are slightly bent. He lowers and repeats.

10. Reverse Wrist Curls

Using a 20-pound barbell in a seated position, each athlete rests his forearms along the thighs, which are parallel to the floor. The arms and wrists should be extended past the knees. The bar is held with an overhand grip to raise and lower the wrists as far as possible.

CIRCUIT 3

The purpose of this circuit is to increase and maintain muscular strength, cardiorespiratory endurance, power, and flexibility. This circuit requires no equipment and can be done off the ice in the space around the arena or on the ice if enough ice time is available. Note that in this circuit, one person does an exercise for 30 seconds, and then his partner does the exercise for 30 seconds. After both have done it, they move to the next station.

The equipment needed includes one wrist roll, two broom handles each 2 feet long, two ropes, two dumbbells of 15 pounds each, stopwatch, and whistle.

1. Dips

The gate to the benches is opened. The body is raised and lowered using the arms only.

2. Sit-Ups

While lying on his back with knees bent and feet flat on the floor, each athlete clasps his hands behind the head. He starts the sit-up with the shoulders flat on the ground and raises the upper body, touching the left elbow to the right knee, and so on, and repeats.

3. Push-Ups

With the back straight, each athlete pushes up, completely extending the arms, lowers the chest to the floor, and repeats.

4. "V" Sits

Each athlete lies flat on the ground. He raises the back and legs at the same time and touches the feet with the hands, keeping the arms and legs straight, and repeats.

5. Arm Circles

With arms extended to the side, each athlete rotates both arms forward in large circles, finishing with small circles, and then rotates backward in a similar fashion.

6. Leg Flexion

One athlete lies on his stomach, while his partner gives resistance on lower legs. The athlete flexes the legs at the knee and hips, moving slowly through the movement with resistance for 10 seconds, and repeats.

7. Leg Extension

Each athlete lies on his stomach with legs flexed. His partner gives resistance while he extends the legs, moving slowly through the movement with resistance for 10 seconds, and repeats.

8. Groin Exercise

Each athlete lies on his back with legs apart and slightly bent. With his partner standing with legs inside the athlete's knees giving resistance, he presses in for 10 seconds. Then, with his partner's legs on the outside, he presses out for 10 seconds.

9. Wrist Roll

Each athlete rolls the weight up by rolling the handle, which has a rope attached to a 20-pound weight. He lowers the weight in reverse manner and repeats.

10. Hurdler's Stretch

In a sitting position, each athlete extends his right leg forward and left leg back. He grasps the right ankle with both hands and slowly brings the forehead to the knee. This is repeated with the left leg forward and then with both legs together. Each segment of the exercise is done for 10 seconds.

ON-ICE CIRCUIT

In this circuit, players work two to each station with 30 seconds' work followed by 30 seconds' rest, and then the exercise is repeated. Then the players change stations. Allow one minute for rest and changing stations.

(1) Players start at the centerline and skate to the blue line and back to the centerline four times. Each tries to pick up the hockey stick and push back the other player.

(2) Players play keep away inside the face-off circle.

(3) Players practice continuous breakaways from the red line in which one man chases the other man, shoots, and changes each time.

(4) Without sticks, players try to body check the other man out of the face-off circle.

(5) One man skates forward with the puck between the blue lines and passes it to the other man who is skating backward. The man skating backward then skates forward with the puck and passes to his partner, who is skating forward.

(6) Without sticks, players fight for the puck along the boards.

(7) Players practice continuous breakaways from the blue line as pucks are picked up at the side of the net.

(8) Players do stops and starts between the end boards and the top of the face-off circle.

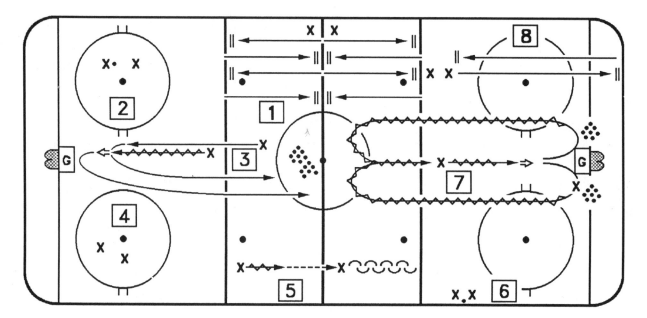

BIBLIOGRAPHY

Bompa, T. *Theory and Methodology of Training*. Dubuque: Kendall/Hunt Publishing Co., 1983.

Bowers, R., and Fox, E. *Sport Physiology*. Dubuque: Wm. C. Brown, 1988.

Canadian Amateur Hockey Association. Coach level manual. Ottawa, 1989.

Canadian Amateur Hockey Association. Intermediate level manual. Ottawa, 1989.

Canadian Amateur Hockey Association. Proceedings of international hockey coaches conference. Ottawa, 1989.

Canadian Amateur Hockey Association. Proceedings of NCCP level V seminar. Ottawa, 1985.

Canadian Amateur Hockey Association. Proceedings of seminar on "Advanced II" level. Ottawa, 1989.

Coaching Association of Canada. "National Coaches Certification Program: Theory, Levels I–III." Ottawa, 1989.

Fleck, S., and Kraemer, W. *Designing Resistance Training Programs*. Champaign, Ill.: Human Kinetics Books, 1987.

Green, H. J. "Glycogen Depletion Patterns During Continuous and Intermittent Ice Skating." *Medicine and Science in Sports and Exercise* 10(3): 183–187, 1978.

Green, H. J., and Houston, M. E. "Effect of a Season of Ice Hockey on Energy Capacities and Associated Functions." *Medicine and Science in Sports and Exercise* 7: 299–303, 1975.

Green, H. "Metabolic Aspects of Intermittent Work with Specific Regard to Ice Hockey." *Canadian Journal of Applied Sport Science* 4(4): 29–33.

Hockey Coaching Journal. 5 vols. Toronto: Hockey Coaching Journal Publishing Co., 1989–1993.

Holt, L. *Science Stretching for Sport*. Ottawa: Coaching Association of Canada.

Kostka, V. *Czechoslovakian Youth Ice Hockey Training System*. Ottawa: Canadian Amateur Hockey Association, 1979.

Lener, Slavomir. *Transition Defense to Offense*. Ottawa: Canadian Amateur Hockey Association.

MacAdam, D., and Reynolds, G. *Hockey Fitness: Year-Round Conditioning on and off the Ice*. Champaign, Ill.: Leisure Press, 1988.

Neilson, Roger. Proceedings of coaches' clinic. Windsor, Ontario, 1993.

Ogrean, D., and L. Vairo. *U.S.A. Hockey Coaches Drill Book*. Colorado Springs, Col.: Hockey U.S.A., 1979.

Perron, J., and N. Chouinard. *Shooting to Win*. Toronto: McGraw-Hill Ryerson, 1991.

Rhodes, T., and P. Twist. *The Physiology of Ice Hockey*. Vancouver: University of British Columbia Press, 1989.

Wenger, H. A. *Fitness: The Key to Hockey Success*. Victoria: British Columbia Amateur Hockey Association, 1988.

Wilmore, J., and D. Costill. *Training for Sport and Activity*. Dubuque: Wm. C. Brown, 1988.

Wilson, G., and Hedberg, A. *Physiology of Ice Hockey: A Report*. Ottawa: Canadian Amateur Hockey Association, 1976.

York University. Proceedings of symposium for elite hockey coaches. Toronto, 1988.